EPQ Toolkit for AQA

A Guide for Students

Cara Flanagan

Jane McGee

Illuminate Publishing

Cara Flanagan is a widely published author of books for A-Level psychology, she also speaks and organises conferences and is senior editor of Psychology Review. She taught for over 15 years and was also a senior examiner.

Cara Flanagan

Dr Jane McGee is a Subject Leader for Psychology at Old Swinford Hospital School. She also works for AQA as an Assistant Principal Examiner for Psychology A-Level and is a Moderator for the Extended Project.

Dr Jane McGee

This book is dedicated to

Lesley, what a friend! *Cara*

My mum Beryl and husband Roger for their encouragement. *Jane*

Updated edition published in 2018 by Illuminate Publishing Ltd, P.O. Box 1160, Cheltenham, Gloucestershire GL50 9RW

Orders: Please visit www.illuminatepublishing.com or email sales@illuminatepublishing.com

British Library Cataloguing in Publication Data

A catalogue record for this book is available from the British Library

ISBN 978-1-911208-61-7

Printed by Cambrian Printers, Aberystwyth

02.19

The publisher's policy is to use papers that are natural, renewable and recyclable products made from wood grown in sustainable forests. The logging and manufacturing processes are expected to conform to the environmental regulations of the country of origin.

Every effort has been made to contact copyright holders of material produced in this book. If notified, the publisher will be pleased to rectify any errors or omissions at the earliest opportunity.

Editor: Geoff Tuttle

Design and layout: Nigel Harriss

CREDITS

©Shutterstock.com: p3, ollirg; p4, chuckstock; p5, PathDoc, stockyimages; p8, Krivosheev Vitaly; p10, iQoncept; p12, Ed Samuel, justasc, Kalmatsuy, bombaert patrik, Thorsten Schmitt; p14, Karramba Production; p15, phipatbig; p22, photka; p23, stockyimages; p24, ra2studio; p26, ollirg; p30, Aquir; p31, Richard M Lee; p32, winui; p33, Renata Sedmakova; p35, HomeStudio; p38, Becky Stares; p40, John T Takai; p42, iurii; p44, mj007; p46, Ivelin Radkov; p47, Ann Baldwin; p49, landmarkmedia; p51, PathDoc; p56, iQoncept; p57, jps; p58, Zhong Chen; p60, ostill; p62, koya979; p63, 360b; p64, vectomart; p69, Mmaxer; p70, Sielan; p71, Amir Kaljikovic; p72, OZaiachin; p74, Alexander Mak, Nixx Photography, Ron Dale; p75, aldegonde, Elzbieta Sekowska; p78, Opra ; p81, SergeyDV; p83, Sashkin; p88, Mariano N. Ruiz; p91, Sarunyu_foto; p92, B Calkins; p94, iQoncept; p99, Maridav; p101, Accord; p107, Morphart Creation, VladislavGudovskiy.

ACKNOWLEDGEMENTS

The authors would like to thank the magnificent team of professionals who have helped make this book a reality. **Rick Jackman**, our publisher at Illuminate, manages to combine enthusiasm, support, encouragement, tolerance and friendship to bring out the best in authors. We thank him.

Nigel Harriss is responsible for the stunning cover and visual presentation throughout the book. A very talented man.

Geoff Tuttle has edited the manuscript meticulously and has been a joy to work with as he does everything superfast and with great professionalism.

We would also like to thank all the others at Illuminate – **Peter Burton**, **Clare Jackman** and **Claire Hart** – for all the extra support we have received and their determined efforts to make sure that everyone knows what a wonderful book this is!

Cara would like to thank her co-author, **Jane McGee**, for providing such a wealth of knowledge about the EPQ as well as a tremendous array of creative ideas. Furthermore, Jane has been extraordinarily patient and positive during the production of quite a major undertaking!

Cara, Jane and the publishing team would also like to thank the students from Old Swinford Hospital school in Stourbridge for the EPQ project work we have used in this book.

Our reviewers

We would like to thank our two reviewers, Helen Brooke and Sarah Fearon, who meticulously read through the manuscript and made invaluable suggestions to ensure that we offered the best support for the EPQ project.

Helen Brooke has enjoyed a long teaching career in both schools and FE colleges, and is currently Head of Psychology at Torquay Girls' Grammar School. Helen has been a Senior Moderator for this qualification for the past five years and is an adviser to new EPQ centres. She has been a keen supporter of the EPQ since its introduction.

Sarah Fearon has taught A-Level History for many years and the EPQ since it started. She is an experienced EPQ moderator and has trained and mentored a substantial number of supervisors and coordinators during that time.

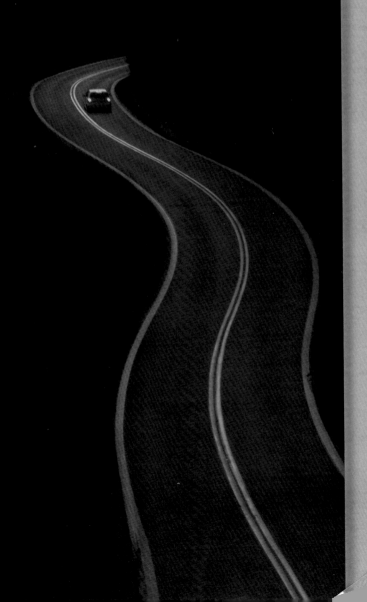

The journey is the reward.

Taoist saying

TABLE OF CONTENTS

Introduction

What is the EPQ?

The Extended Project Qualification (EPQ) can be taken in different ways.

- It can be taken as a stand-alone qualification equivalent to half an A-Level (28 UCAS points).
- It can form part of an Advanced Diploma or the Baccalaureate Qualification.
- It can be taken alongside an A-Level or BTEC programme.

The main value of the EPQ is that is an *independent piece of work* – students must receive some instruction but most of the project is self-guided. This makes it both a challenge to complete and an award worth gaining.

UCAS points
The EPQ tariff

A*	28
A	24
B	20
C	16
D	12
E	8

The benefits of the EPQ

The EPQ will help you to demonstrate, to both Universities and future employers, that you are able to work independently. It will also help you to develop essential skills required for study at a higher level:

- Working with others
- Working to deadlines
- Planning and management of a project
- Decision making and problem solving
- Presentation skills
- Communication skills.

The skills that you develop through the EPQ are excellent preparation for university-level study. Students can refer to the EPQ in their UCAS personal statements and at interview to demonstrate some of the qualities that universities are looking for.

Another benefit of the EPQ is you don't have to revise and prepare for an exam but it will still give you the same UCAS tariff as half an A-Level. It can also help to further your knowledge in one or more of your examination subjects and enrich your performance in that exam.

EXERCISE 0.1 Benefits of the EPQ

For each quality, say how you think the EPQ could enable you to demonstrate these:

What do University admission tutors/ employers look for? List the qualities below.	For each quality state how the EPQ could help demonstrate this.

Supervisor

Centre coordinator

Dr. Jane McGee
who co-authored
this book

External moderator

EPQ at a glance

Individual or group?

The EPQ can take the form of an individual or group project. If you are working as a group you must demonstrate what part you played within the whole project. It is also important that the group members do not produce identical projects or identical PRODUCTION LOGS!

Format?

The EPQ may be based on a variety of forms and contexts – you can produce a written report or a research project or an essay, you can submit a design brief for a product or make something (called an 'artefact'), or you might produce a play or dance performance.

Topic?

The EPQ topic that you select could arise out of one of your study areas. For example, you may wish to explore the political and religious arguments for and against screening for genetic diseases as an extension of your studies in biology.

You can also explore an area of personal interest outside your study areas. For example, investigating how zoos encourage conservation.

However, your topic must not be *directly* related to your studies. You cannot base your project on material that you will be examined on because then you would be getting credit twice. This is known as *dual accreditation*. For example, if you are studying Psychology you might learn about obedience in your classwork. You cannot do a project on obedience research but could take this as a starting point and consider the implications for understanding the behaviour of the Nazis in World War 2. The EPQ may take one aspect of your A-Level course as a starting point and extend this, but it must significantly depart from the specified course of study.

The project must also be your own idea. If you have been given a project to do as part of work experience or as part of a Nuffield Science Course then this is not *your own idea* and therefore cannot be used.

Your supervisor will be asked to confirm that your EPQ topic is not the same as a topic that forms part of any of your studies for other qualifications.

Further guidance on your selection of a topic is given in Chapter 1.

Taught element and independent work

The project consists of these two elements. Your supervisor or someone else at your school/college will organise the taught element, which is likely to include instruction on the skills necessary to complete your project. In total you should spend 30 hours on this part of the project.

The remaining 90 hours of your project time (approximately) should be spent on independent work producing, recording and presenting your EPQ.

Key people

You will have a **supervisor** to oversee and help you through your project. Your supervisor also marks your project.

The **centre coordinator** appointed by your school/college will oversee the whole process.

An **external moderator** from the exam board checks the marks given to your EPQ by your supervisor and may adjust these.

Inital aims	• Student identifies initial idea for a project. • Ideas are discussed with supervisor. • Student completes RECORD OF INITIAL IDEAS.
Formal project proposal	• Student completes PART A: CANDIDATE PROPOSAL. • Supervisor completes PART B: SUPERVISOR'S COMMENTS ON CANDIDATE PROPOSAL.
Approval	• PART C: CENTRE COORDINATOR'S APPROVAL OF CANDIDATE PROPOSAL is filled in by the centre coordinator who either approves the project without recommendations, or may make required recommendations, or requests a resubmission of the form.
Taught element	• In total the project requires 120 hours of guided learning. • About 30 hours should be directly taught for acquiring necessary skills. This taught element is not included in the written record.
Record of progress	• PRODUCTION LOG is completed to reflect the process of completing the project. This includes meetings with your supervisor, your personal planning, reviews of work achieved and reflections on the process.
Presentation	• Verbal PRESENTATION which should include your reflection on the process and which will conclude with Q&A.
Written report	• A project (called the PRODUCT) which consists solely of written work should be approximately 5000 words. A project involving artefacts, performance, etc., requires less writing – a minimum of 1000 words.

Submitting your project

If students are submitting in the November series the deadline is at the beginning of November.
For the May series it is the middle of May.
However, your supervisor may request your EPQ earlier in order to mark the project and have time to post to the moderater by the deadline.
Most students complete their EPQ within a year.

EPQ in more detail

How you will be assessed

Throughout this book we have provided comments from a 'moderator' (the person who will make the final assessment o your work). These comments appear in turquoise boxes.

The EPQ is assessed using four assessment objectives (AOs).

Assessment objective 1 (AO1)	**Manage the project** Identification of the topic to be investigated. Evidence of appropriate aims and objectives. Detailed project plan. Evidence of monitoring the progress of the project, considering the agreed objectives. Completing the work; applying organisational skills and strategies to meet stated objectives.	In **Chapter 1 (Starting out)** we guide you in deciding what topic to choose. In **Chapter 2 (Manage the project)** help is given with your project planning, including ideas for developing your organisational skills. In **Chapter 4 (Develop and realise)** we guide you on how to produce clear aims and objectives in the abstract or introduction to the project. In **Chapter 5 (Review)** the focus will be on how to manage your presentation.	10 marks
Assessment objective 2 (AO2)	**Use resources** Evidence of detailed research from a wide range of relevant resources. Research should demonstrate selection and evaluation. Critical analysis of resources. Clear links between resources and appropriate theories and concepts.	In **Chapter 3 (Use resources)** we explain how to collect primary and secondary data and how to evaluate this data. In **Chapter 4 (Develop and realise)** we look at the conventions for reporting references. In **Chapter 5 (Review)** we describe how your presentation can demonstrate evidence that you have used resources effectively.	10 marks
Assessment objective 3 (AO3)	**Develop and realise** Appropriate data is collected and thoroughly analysed. The project plan is realised to a high standard and consistent with the agreed plan. Any changes to the agreed plan are explained. Information is synthesised from a variety of sources. Findings are communicated fluently in an appropriate format. Findings are presented in a logical and coherent structure that addresses closely the nature of the task.	In **Chapter 4 (Develop and realise)** we look at how you produce your final written report. This is the realisation of your project, where you demonstrate your problem solving, decision making and creative thinking. In **Chapter 5 (Review)** we describe how your presentation can provide evidence that you have achieved what you have set out to do.	20 marks
Assessment objective 4 (AO4)	**Review** Evaluation of the strengths and weaknesses of the completed project in relation to the planning, implementation and outcomes. Evaluation of the candidate's own learning during the project. The review is consistently relevant, well-structured and appropriately presented. In the review candidates clearly communicate their findings and conclusions, based on sound evidence and judgement.	In **Chapter 4 (Develop and realise)** we include issues related to the organisation and structure of your report. In **Chapter 5 (Review)** we describe how to prepare and deliver your verbal presentation. This presentation will include an evaluation of what you have learned.	10 marks

Moderator comment

For AO1 the moderator is looking for evidence in your PRODUCTION LOG that you have *managed* your project. Your project should include clear aims and objectives and your PRESENTATION should also show evidence of planni

Moderator comment

For AO2 the moderator is looking for evidence of well-focused *research*. Evidence can be provided in your PRODUCTION LOG, your PRODUCT and your PRESENTATION.

Moderator comments

For AO3 the moderator is looking for:

- Evidence of autonomy: Ha you worked independently or has your supervisor take too many decisions for you

- Evidence that the project plan and/or title *developed* during the research phase.

- A well-written REPORT, fluent and academic in styl

- Evidence in the PRESENTATION of your EPQ 'journey' and the developments that took place along the way.

Moderator comments

For AO4 the moderator is looking for evidence that a PRESENTATION has taken place. The presentation should demonstrate your ability to *reflect* on what you have learned as a result of completing your EPQ.

How do I work through this book?

It may appear that you can work through each chapter of this book one at a time; however, the chapters actually overlap. For example, managing the project includes using resources and writing the report.

Look at the introductory page for each chapter to get an overview.

Your project will be assessed holistically

The material to be assessed consists of three items:

1. The PRODUCTION LOG.

2. The written REPORT, which may be accompanied by an artefact. Together these are your project PRODUCT.

3. A record of the PRESENTATION to a small audience.

In all that you do you must show evidence of planning, preparation, research and autonomous working.

> You can see that there is not a straightforward relationship between AOs and what you must do to achieve them.

PRODUCTION LOG

This is where you present the record of your journey. Marks for the EPQ are not awarded solely for your final PRODUCT but on how you got there. The final marks given relate to you showing the *process* of producing your project and this is recorded in the PRODUCTION LOG.

This part of your work is assessed as part of AO1 Manage the project. However, your PRODUCTION LOG can also provide evidence of AO2 Use of resources and AO3 Develop and realise, showing to what extent you have achieved what you set out to do. The review parts of your PRODUCTION LOG and your SUMMARY AND REFLECTION can provide evidence of AO4 Review.

Written REPORT

The REPORT is the core of your EPQ – however, the *process* of producing this REPORT (documented in your PRODUCTION LOG) is as important as the end PRODUCT.

This written report is assessed as part of AO2 Use resources and AO3 Develop and realise.

You do not need to state the actual number of words in your REPORT but reports that are obviously too short or too long may be penalised.

Final PRESENTATION

This can take a number of forms including a traditional oral presentation and/or use of other means such as sign language, videos, DVDs, PowerPoint or Prezi; hand-outs and/or prompt cards may be used. Alternatively, you can contribute to a poster session or exhibition, or a witnessed one-to-one 'viva' presentation to the supervisor.

It is important that your PRESENTATION gives details of the EPQ journey rather than just a summary of your project.

This part of your work is assessed as part of AO4 Review. However, the PRESENTATION can also provide evidence of AO1 Manage the project, AO2 Use resources and AO3 Develop and realise showing that you have achieved what you set out to do.

EXERCISE 0.2 EPQ Consolidation Activity

From what you have read so far look at the following statements and decide whether they are true or false

Statement	True	False
1. I can submit my History coursework for my EPQ.		
2. An A* is worth 28 UCAS points.		
3. I will need to dedicate 120 hours to my EPQ.		
4. AO1 Manage the project is worth 20 marks out of 50.		
5. If I work with a friend on a group project we can produce identical REPORTS and PRODUCTION LOGs.		
6. The moderator can't change the mark my supervisor awards.		
7. My EPQ topic must arise from one or more of my A-Level studies.		
8. The final PRODUCT can consist of a long written REPORT plus an artefact or a performance.		

Suggested answers on page 123.

Chapter 1
Starting out

Big journeys start with small steps

From what you have read so far are you still interested in embarking on the EPQ journey?

Once you have decided to undertake this challenging journey, the place to begin is to decide on a topic. This is not something that should be rushed – it is very easy to make a quick decision only to find later that it was not a very rewarding or fruitful topic to study.

This chapter focuses on deciding what to study and beginning your journey.

What's in this chapter

By the end of this chapter you will have produced your PART A: CANDIDATE PROPOSAL and be ready to start the project itself.

The taught element

It is expected that your EPQ should involve about 120 hours of your time. This consists of 90 hours of your own time plus a further 30 hours of support. The 30 hours consists of one-to-one meetings with your supervisor plus a programme of taught skills.

This taught element is not included in your final written record.

What skills?

The taught skills element of the EPQ is designed to help you with the academic and practical skills required to complete your project. AQA suggest that this could include:

- Any skills or techniques that will be required for the safe and effective execution of the project which are not part of the candidate's course of study.
- ICT (information and communication technology) skills that will enhance the production of the report.
- Research skills including the ability to search for and identify suitable sources of information and prior research or relevant work already undertaken.
- Project management skills including time, resource and task management.
- Personal, Learning and Thinking Skills (see right).
- Subject-specific skills.

Evidence of the taught element

Your supervisor is required to outline the details of the taught skills you have covered in your PRODUCTION LOG. The taught skills are listed in the log, there is no requirement to give any more detail.

Here is a typical outline of a programme of taught skills outlined by a supervisor in a student's PRODUCTION LOG, section entitled RECORD OF MARKS:

Outline details of taught skills (specification 2.3 the taught element of the EPQ)

Record here details of relevant skills taught in a class/group and details of relevant skills taught individually to this candidate as described in the specification. Continue on a separate sheet if necessary.

A formal programme of study for all EPQ students was followed. This was taught over the summer and autumn terms in 2013.

Sessions included:
- *Research and study skills.*
- *Note-taking skills, personal learning styles.*
- *Use of visual images in research and note taking.*
- *Manipulating Internet search engines wisely: dos and don'ts.*
- *Plagiarism and how to avoid it.*
- *How to reference, e.g. Harvard style.*
- *How to deliver an effective presentation.*
- *Time management skills.*
- *How to write a report and create an effective plan.*
- *How to write abstracts, summaries and conclusions.*
- *How to critically reflect, analyse and evaluate your work.*
- *Assessment objectives and how to meet them.*

How schools deliver taught skills

A formal taught programme of study for all EPQ students is usually taught over the summer and autumn terms. Although the timing can vary between schools, there should be a total of 30 hours of taught skills.

Whilst it is recognised that each EPQ student will be researching different topics, the taught skills programme will be relevant to all students. The sessions can take place within the school day, in the lunch hour or after school.

Your school may even enlist the help of a local university where a half or whole day can be spent looking at research and referencing skills. A member of staff at the university may deliver this.

Subject-specific skills

If your project involves **working as a team** on a group project then you need to develop skills related to communicating ideas within a group and working effectively to reach agreement on a range of issues. Understanding group dynamics may be important.

If your project involves **primary data collection** then taught skills may include safe laboratory practices or workshop techniques, knowledge of ethical guidelines, data collection techniques and analysis. Knowing how to carry out a risk assessment may also be relevant.

If your project involves a **performance** then you might learn about the format and content of rehearsal notes, initial sketches or other working documents required in the stages of production.

Personal, Learning and Thinking Skills (PLTS)

- **Independent enquiry** – Identification of an appropriate research question, how to explore and examine information and draw conclusions based on reasoned arguments.
- **Reflective learning** – How to review progress and assess key learning experiences.
- **Creative thinking** – Learning how to avoid making judgments too early in the EPQ journey and be open to new ideas and identifying alternative explanations.
- **Self-management** – Adapting to change and demonstrating a degree of autonomy but seeking advice when needed.

EXERCISE 1.1 Taught skills

1. Rehanna is doing a group project with friends Isobel and Harry to organise a sponsored walk on the Clent Hills in aid of the Teenage Cancer Trust.

2. Erik is producing 'Just 22', a play in memory of his great-grandfather killed in World War 1.

3. Michaela is carrying out a project to look at gender differences in children's drawings, she intends to visit a local primary school to study at least 20 children.

4. Curtis is finding out whether he can create the Northern lights in a laboratory.

List **one** subject-specific skill the above students will need in addition to the taught skills listed on the facing page.

Suggested answers on page 123

Suggested scheme of work incorporating taught skills

1 hr lessons	Main content	Materials in this book you could use (there are also exemplars on almost every spread)	Page
1	Introducing the EPQ	Ex 0.1 Benefits of the EPQ Ex 0.2 EPQ consolidation activity	5 8
2	Ideas for topic title	Ex 1.2 Starting to think of a topic Ex 1.3 Generating ideas	13 15
3	A preliminary literature review	Ex 1.4 Evaluating your idea	17
4	Writing the CANDIDATE PROPOSAL	Ex 1.5 Constructing a pre-project proposal form Exemplars: RECORD OF INITIAL IDEAS and PART A: CANDIDATE PROPOSAL	18 19–21
5	Introducing the PRODUCTION LOG and the reviewing process	Exemplars: PLANNING REVIEW, MID-PROJECT REVIEW and PROJECT PRODUCT REVIEW	27–29
6	Plan your time and objectives	Ex 2.1 Time management Ex 2.2 Prioritising Ex 2.3 SMART or not SMART Exemplars: Making a general plan	30 31 33 34–35
7	Communicating changes	Exemplars: RECORD OF INITIAL IDEAS, PLANNING REVIEW, MID-PROJECT REVIEW and PROJECT PRODUCT REVIEW	36–37
8	Using additional management tools	Production timeline, Diary of progress Ex 2.5 Producing a Gantt chart Ex 2.6 Producing a PERT chart	38–39 41 42
9	Dealing with data	Ex 3.1 Quantitative and qualitative	47
10 & 11	Collecting primary data	Ex 3.2 Identifying potential ethical issues Ex 3.3 Debriefing Ex 3.4 Sampling methods Ex 3.5 Questionnaire design Ex 3.6 Assess validity and reliability Ex 3.7 Content analysis Ex 3.8 Experiments	49 51 52 55 57 59 61
12 & 13	A full literature review	Ex 3.9 Consideration of available sources Ex 3.10 Synthesising sources	63 65
14	Being analytical	Ex 3.11 Evaluation sheet Ex 3.12 Being analytical	67 67
15	Understanding peer review	Ex 3.13 Peer-reviewed journals Ex 3.14 Peer review	68 69
16	Avoiding plagiarism	Ex 3.15 Identifying plagiarism	71
17	Preparing MID-PROJECT REVIEW	Exemplars: Good and bad practice	28–29, 37
18	Beginning the REPORT	Exemplars Ex 4.1 Blank page syndrome	75 75
19	Marking exercise	Exemplars I, II, and III	108–121
20	Writing well	Ex 4.2 Powerful paragraphs Ex 4.3 Useful phrases	77 77
21	Writing an abstract	Ex 4.4 Identifying the sections Ex 4.5 Abstracts	79 79
22	Writing the introduction	Ex 4.6 Overview	81
23	Writing the method (required for primary data and artefact only)	Ex 4.7 Writing a concise procedure	83
24	Writing the findings (primary data)	Ex 4.8 Interpreting data	85
25	Writing the discussion	Ex 4.9 Good discussion	87
26	Writing a conclusion and writing the SUMMARY	Ex 4.10 Conclusions Ex 5.1 Annotate a summary statement	89 97
27	Referencing and editing the draft EPQ	Ex 4.11 Referencing Ex 4.12 Checking academic style Checklist	91 92 92–93
28	Preparing PROJECT PRODUCT REVIEW	Exemplars: Good and bad practice	28-29, 37
29	Preparing the PRESENTATION	Ex 5.1 A good presentation Ex 5.2 Adding interest Ex 5.3 Preparing answers Presentation checklist Ex 5.4 A good presentation	97 98 100 101 103
30	Writing the SUMMARY AND REFLECTION	Ex 5.5 Annotate a summary statement Ex 5.6 Reflection	105 107

The skills covered in this book

In **Chapter 1 (Starting out)** we direct your decision making about what to study.

In **Chapter 2 (Manage the project)** help is given with your project planning, including ideas for developing your organisational skills.

In **Chapter 3 (Use resources)** we explain how you can show evidence that you have selected information from a variety of relevant sources, including primary and secondary data. The skills of analysis and synthesis of material are also covered.

In **Chapter 4 (Develop and realise)** we provide some general principles for presenting your report in a fluent and structured way.

In **Chapter 5 (review)** the focus will be on presentation skills and reflective learning.

Project ideas from the past

$\mathbb{M}$ost students will obtain ideas for their EPQ topics from things such as newspaper article they have read, watching a TV programme or documentary, or from an area they have covered in their A-Level studies which they would like to extend. Students may also select a topic from an area they wish to study at University.

You might start thinking by looking at what some other students have done for their EPQ.

'If I were to advise other people who are undertaking the EPQ I would encourage them to research something they are truly interested in, as this would make the experience more rewarding and enjoyable.'

Rohan, EPQ student

Extending your studies

EPQ title: **Are biological factors the primary basis for sexual orientation?**

A student comments:

This topic relates to AS Psychology which I did last year. It is an extension of the 'Relationships in different cultures' section which briefly touches on homosexuality. I also aspire to be a clinical psychologist.

Artefact

EPQ title: **Can I successfully design and make a set of jewelry inspired by Art Deco for a specialist client?**

A student comments:

I plan to study Art and Design at University and my EPQ topic relates to Art Deco design style, which I am particularly interested in, together with the era in which it flourished. I saw the EPQ as a unique opportunity to produce something which I am really interested in and there is no overlap with my A-Level Art.

Reading a newspaper article

EPQ title: **Obama has a dream. What is the legacy of the American Civil Rights movement in America today?**

A student comments:

A newspaper article triggered my idea which has been inspired by my current A-Level courses in Government and Politics as well as my studies in Psychology. Also my personal interest into America and the black community have both contributed to my chosen topic.

Doing your own research

EPQ title: **To what extent are there gender differences in coulrophobia? (fear of clowns)**

A student comments:

I plan to study Psychology at University so I feel what I hope to learn will put me in good stead for when I start my course. As Psychology is not offered at my school this will enable me to deepen my understanding about a psychological topic. I will aim to investigate phobias by collecting primary data from a sample of Sixth Form students at my school to see if there are gender differences in fears of clowns.

A performance

EPQ title: **Just 22 – A play in memory of my great grandfather, killed in World War 1**

A student comments:

This project will tie in with but not overlap with my Performance Studies A-Level and the writing will be supported by what I have learned when studying English and History.

Cross-curricular topic

EPQ title: **The composition of a piece of regency style dance music to be used in a production of Jane Austen's *Pride and Prejudice***

A student comments:

This project aims to combine my three A-Level subjects of Music, English Literature and History The dancing ritual was one of courtship and Jane Austen used the ball to set the stage for character development.

Lizzie and Darcy's relationship began at the Meryton Assembly Ball and I would like to compose a piece which represents the tension of their first meeting.

Some good evaluative titles from the past

A critical analysis of current theories of how the human lifespan can be extended.

With focus on G.L Kittredge's marriage group of tales, how does Geoffrey Chaucer present women in the Canterbury Tales?

Should the care of those suffering with Alzheimer's disease be the responsibility of government?

A critical discussion of the nature and nurture of schizophrenia.

A discussion of the arguments for and against the UK's law on abortion.

A defence of the Kyoto Protocol.

How mental health is represented in the media and thus influences society.

To what extent does England need new laws to be able to deal effectively with defamation, abuse and contempt of court in relation to social media and the Internet?

Is there a life after death?

Projects can come in many forms

- **Design** – A toy, vehicle, website, stage set, blueprint of an invention, etc., plus a research report.
- **Performance** – A concert, play, debate or sport plus a research report.
- **Artefact** – Artwork or costumes for a film or play, working model, video, game plus a research report.
- **Report with findings from an investigation** – Working with disadvantaged people, a scientific study, geography fieldwork or business venture.
- **Critical analysis** – Thinking critically and objectively about a topic. For example, thinking how Shakespeare portrays women in King Lear, or the arguments for and against euthanasia.

Some good titles from past artefacts

How to raise a thousand pounds for a local charity.

Designing a 1960s wedding dress.

Producing a series of fashion photographs based on the 7 deadly sins.

A book of recipes suitable for University students.

A fashion show with recycled materials.

A multiple perspective story of bullying, written by the victim, the bully and the mother.

Writing a short story in Susan Ferrier's style and researching its popularity.

Can I design and make a platform shoe in the style of the 1970s?

Writing a gender-neutral story for preschool children.

EXERCISE 1.2 Starting to think of a Topic

It may help to begin getting your ideas for a topic into focus.

One approach is to go back over your notes for your AS/A-Level subjects or textbook chapters to find a topic. Remember the EPQ involves extending yourself beyond your other areas of study and the project you produce should not be the same as one that could be submitted for a different qualification. For example, it should not be just like an Art and Design project you have done, or a piece of History or English coursework. You need to show that you have done something different.

Use this table to consider topics you have studied and what interests you within these topics and what aspect could be extended.

Remember also that your project can be totally unrelated to your school studies.

Subjects you have studied e.g. AS Level/Year 1 subjects OR Area of personal interest	Topics studied already	How you plan to extend this topic (Your project title must extend beyond the work you are already doing in class)

Things to avoid

The previous spread was just a beginning. Keep your mind open about your ideas and consider some further suggestions, as well as some important guidelines about what not to do.

Moderator comments

Remember: You must work independently. If you are relying too heavily on your supervisor to make decisions for you then this does not demonstrate evidence of independent learning or autonomy.

(Read about supervision on pages 22–23.)

Where to look for topic ideas

News: Newspapers and radio programmes all cover recent events and may stimulate your interest for further exploration of a story.

Internet: There are many reliable educational and current event resources available on the Internet that are excellent sources of ideas for selecting research topics. Keep in mind that because of the open nature of the Internet, many resources vary in quality.

Cross-curricular study: You can explore a topic from a number of different points of view. The EPQ provides an opportunity for cross-curricular study. Keep a specific question in mind, but explore it using ideas and methods drawn from different subjects. For example, if you are studying Mathematics and Religious Studies and History you could explore how Christianity has affected the development of mathematical sciences in Europe during the renaissance period.

Lesson starting point: You cannot choose anything that is part of your current studies (*dual accreditation*) but you can explore a class topic in greater depth. Suppose that you are an A-Level Geography student and you wish to look at the impact of volcanic eruptions and you have only spent about two lessons on volcanoes but found them interesting. You could use this as the starting point for the EPQ by looking in greater depth at the social and economic consequences of volcanic eruptions or look at one specific volcano. In a project of this nature, you could use your knowledge of a particular volcano (such as Yellowstone) as a case study, which helps to give focus to a deeper exploration of the topic in question.

1. Avoid a topic that is overly ambitious

It is not realistic for an EPQ project to be able to cover everything there is to say about a particular topic such as, for example, whether the government should prohibit the sale and consumption of alcohol or whether cannabis should be legalised. It is best to focus on a particular event, time, person or group or place.

For example consider this topic: *The influence of the media on aggressive behaviour.*

Media come in various forms such as television, advertisements, films and commercials. This topic would be too general and broad to research and report on in an EPQ project of 5000 words. Instead, it would be necessary to narrow the focus of the topic to some smaller aspect of media influence.

A better title would be: *The impact of violent video games on male adolescents in the UK.*

The topic has been narrowed and is more manageable because it focuses on a *particular type* of media (violent video games), *time* (current rather than historic), *person or group* (adolescent males), and *place* (focus on UK).

2. Avoid emotive issues

Avoid topics that are linked too closely with issues in your own life. It makes sense to choose a topic that is interesting and personally meaningful but this is not the same as tackling personal issues. For example, some students try to use their EPQ to write about their own experiences with self-harm or cyber bullying. This is not to say that self-harm or cyber bullying should be avoided *per se* but if you are too close to an issue then it is best to avoid this.

The danger with the choice of such a project is that it may stir up emotional issues that may easily get in the way of completing the project. In addition, such projects often lack objectivity. Objectivity means basing your EPQ on facts rather than personal opinion or anecdotal evidence.

3. Avoid a topic in which you have a personal axe to grind

Conducting research demands honesty and objectivity. If you initiate a study to demonstrate that capital punishment should be reintroduced you may not be able to allow yourself the clear-headed reflections required for good research nor acknowledge the possibility that your conclusions may contradict your initial beliefs and expectations.

It is better to begin with a hunch 'I wonder if capital punishment acts as a deterrent to crime?' This will help you to regard the research as an adventurous exploration to shed light on the topic rather than a polemical exercise to substantiate your point of view.

4. Avoid socially sensitive topics

Ethical issues involved in research with human participants are covered in detail in Chapter 3 (see pages 50–51). However, you need to think about this now as well as when conducting research. Selecting a topic or research question can raise issues. Research questions themselves have the potential to be socially sensitive such as 'To what extent is same-sex marriage justified?' or 'To what extent is intelligence racially determined?'

Socially sensitive research is defined by Sieber and Stanley (1988) as 'studies in which there are potential social consequences for or implications either directly for the participants in the research or the class of individuals represented by the research' (page 49). Very few researchers deliberately carry out studies intended to have a negative impact on people. However, they sometimes overlook the negative impact their research might have.

This is not to say that you should avoid these topics altogether but with socially sensitive research the researcher must be careful to avoid bias and error and must make the limitations of their findings clear. In other words, avoid including your own opinion and make sure that that you present arguments both for and against the issue in question.

5. Dual accreditation

'Dual accreditation' means getting credit twice for the same work.

What this means in practice is that you cannot submit the same piece of work for both your EPQ and for an element of one of your AS/A-Level subjects. But even more of an issue is that you cannot base your project on material that you will be examined on because then you would be getting credit twice.

On your PART A: CANDIDATE PROPOSAL form you should make it clear that your chosen EPQ topic does not overlap with your AS/A-Level studies. You could do this in the section which asks you to provide an outline of 'the course of study or areas(s) of personal interest to which the topic relates'.

Your supervisor and centre coordinator should also make a clear statement on the forms PART B: SUPERVISOR'S COMMENTS ON CANDIDATE PROPOSAL and PART C: CENTRE COORDINATOR'S APPROVAL OF CANDIDATE PROPOSAL that there is no dual accreditation.

6. Don't try to be too original

If you choose something obscure or original then you may struggle to find enough material on the topic.

For example, consider this topic: *To what extent are Miley Cyrus and Kim Kardashian effective role models for women?*

Miley Cyrus and Kim Kardashian may be famous and they are frequently featured in celebrity magazines. However, you may not find material that could academically underpin your EPQ. You may wish to broaden the focus and change the title to read: *To what extent does celebrity culture portray positive role models of young women?*

If you broaden the focus of your title then more scholarly information may be found, which can be then shaped to refer to Miley Cyrus and Kim Kardashian.

7. Avoid being too narrow or too broad

If your topic is too narrow you may struggle to find relevant and accessible material. In the initial ideas stage talk about research ideas with your supervisor who may be able to help you by discussing issues that didn't occur to you.

If your topic is too broad, you will find too much information and not be able to focus. Doing some initial background reading can help you limit the scope of your topic. Your supervisor will give suggestions if they think that your topic is too broad.

EXERCISE 1.3 Generating initial ideas

Try a thought shower.

Write a general topic in the centre of the diagram and generate ideas that might extend from that topic. From there you may find some aspect of the topic you would like to explore.

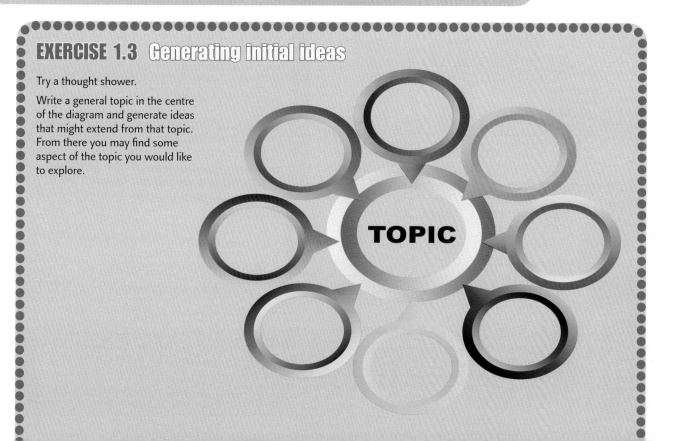

TOPIC

Drilling down

By now you should have had many ideas for your EPQ. It is the time to look in detail at one or two of your ideas.

Finding out more about your topic: A preliminary literature review

A literature review is a systematic consideration of what other people have written or said about your chosen topic. The word 'literature' refers to books, magazines, websites, TV programmes … just about anything.

At this point of your EPQ you should do a *preliminary* literature review. You may now have an idea of what your research question or topic is but you will have an even better idea once you have studied some background literature. This preliminary literature review will be something you can use when completing the PART A: CANDIDATE PROPOSAL form (discussed on the next spread).

You are quite likely to use this material again later on, conducting a more thorough literature review when writing up your project (see pages 64–65).

The diagram below gives some idea of what you might do. An alternative approach is suggested on the right.

A flowchart for doing your preliminary literature review

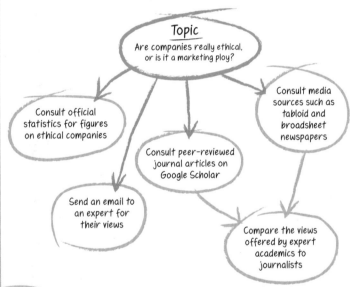

Topic: Are companies really ethical, or is it a marketing ploy?

- Consult official statistics for figures on ethical companies
- Consult media sources such as tabloid and broadsheet newspapers
- Consult peer-reviewed journal articles on Google Scholar
- Send an email to an expert for their views
- Compare the views offered by expert academics to journalists

`My initial research focus was quite narrow as I wanted to investigate whether cannabis was advantageous for fibromyalgia but after some preliminary research I decided that the research focus was quite narrow and I was concerned about finding enough information to be able to write 5000 words.

Changes:

I was concerned about reaching the word limit and so I broadened the title to look at medical marijuana use for pain in general as the original one was too specific.

Harry, EPQ student

A preliminary literature review plan

We have devised a preliminary literature review plan (which you can include in your PART A: CANDIDATE PROPOSAL form).

The example below has been filled in.

Preliminary research idea

Unfair trade: Are companies really ethical or is it a marketing ploy?

What interests you and what may be fertile ground for investigation?

There is a concept called greenwashing which a spin used by companies to say that they are environmentally friendly to try to increase sale when they are not. Greenwashing has increase in response to meet consumer demand for environmentally friendly goods. So are compan as ethical as they claim to be and how fair i fairtrade?

Now think of subsections

Fairtrade, value driven organisations, business ethics, pro-active, socially responsible businesses sustainability, greenwashing.

For each subsection above search for articles. For example, type 'Fairtrade' into a search engine and con whether there is enough material to write a 5000-word project.

Fairtrade website (Fairtrade foundation)

Wikipedia entry on Fairtrade - contains over 117 references which indicate journals whic can be explored further, including Journal Business Ethics, and there are book refere reports and website references.

EXERCISE 1.4 Evaluating your idea

Complete the preliminary literature review proforma below for your initial research idea.

Preliminary research idea

....

....

What interests you and what may be fertile ground for investigation?

....

....

....

Think of subsections

....

For each subsection above search for articles. Consider whether there is enough material to write a 5000-word project.

....

....

Identify the aim of your project Or state a research question, e.g. should the NHS fund smoking-related illness?
Explain how it extends your current A-Level subject areas.
Does the topic relate to your future career/university choice? If so explain how.
Try and describe in 50 words why you are keen to research this topic.
Consider how you can evaluate your sources. Are they reliable or are they likely to give a one-sided viewpoint? If so, what other sources might you use?
Are you going to collect your own data, e.g. carry out interviews or give out questionnaires? There is no requirement that you do this but if the answer is yes, how will you do it?
Is there too much or too little information on your chosen topic?

Your candidate proposal

You should now have now decided on your EPQ topic and have completed some research in order to do this (your preliminary literature review). It is now time to formally propose your project so that it can be approved. You cannot continue until it is approved.

A good place to start is, first, to fill i a pre-proposal form (below). This is not part of the PRODUCTION LOG.

A pre-project proposal form

When formulating ideas for your project proposal you may find it helpful to think of the who, what, where and when questions. Don't worry if you can't answer all of the questions.

A filled-in example is provided.

Think of the what, when and where questions	Exemplar answers for EPQ entitled 'Do the benefits of hydraulic fracturing supersede the enviromental threat that it poses?'
WHO might publish information about this topic? Who is affected by the topic? Do you know of organisations or institutions affiliated with the topic?	I plan to research my project by making reference to: – Peer-reviewed journals – Reputable Internet sites – Published books – Extracts from newspapers.
WHAT are the major questions for this topic? Is there a debate about the topic? Is there a range of issues and viewpoints to consider?	Hydraulic fracturing (fracking) is a highly controversial process by which natural gas can be extracted from shale deposits. The major question I wish to research is whether the benefits of fracking overcome the environmental threat it poses.
WHERE is your topic important: at the local, national or international level? Are there specific places affected by the topic?	'Fracking' is important at all levels – local, national and international. It seems to polarise society into the diehard environmentalists and the supporters of the new technique; this intrigues me and I wish to form an educated decision.
WHEN is/was your topic important? Is it a current event or an historical issue? Do you want to compare your topic by time periods?	This method is currently being used extensively in the USA, the pioneers. It is likely that it will soon be deployed across Europe to reduce prices of gas and offer energy security. The sheer quantities of the resources leaves me wanting to know more.

FELIX'S EPQ ON FRACKING

EXERCISE 1.5 Constructing a pre-project proposal form

Fill in the form for your own idea

Think of the what, when and where questions	
WHO might publish information about this topic? Who is affected by the topic? Do you know of organisations or institutions affiliated with the topic?	
WHAT are the major questions for this topic? Is there a debate about the topic? Is there a range of issues and viewpoints to consider?	
WHERE is your topic important: at the local, national or international level? Are there specific places affected by the topic?	
WHEN is/was your topic important? Is it a current event or an historical issue? Do you want to compare your topic by time periods?	

The formal project proposal

AQA produce a 15-page document entitled CANDIDATE RECORD FORM, PRODUCTION LOG AND ASSESSMENT RECORD (see pdf or Word versions at tinyurl.com/aqaepq02).

- On page 5 of the form there is the RECORD OF INITIAL IDEAS.
- On page 6 of the form there is PART A: CANDIDATE PROPOSAL.

STEP 1: Fill in the first two elements of the **RECORD OF INITIAL IDEAS:**

Your first ideas for the topic/title

Your first ideas for research and development of your project

We have provided some exemplars.

Record of initial ideas (steps 1 and 2)

STEP 2: Discuss your ideas with your supervisor.

We have provided some comments that a supervisor/moderator might make.

STEPS 3, 4 and 5 are on the next spread.

FELIX'S EPQ ON FRACKING

My idea(s) for the topic/title

Do the benefits of Hydraulic Fracturing supersede the enviromental threat that it poses?

My ideas for research and development of my project

Hydraulic fracturing is a highly controversial process by which natural gas can be extracted from shale deposits. I wish to continue my study of Geology at University and this topic will also extend the A-Level course. Engineering geology and mineral extraction are the areas in which the most attention is being focused upon and as a result the most breakthroughs are being made. 'Fracking' seems to polarise society into the diehard environmentalists and the supporters of the new technique; this intrigues me and I wish to form an educated decision upon the topic. It is currently being used extensively in the USA, the pioneers; it is likely that it will soon be deployed across Europe to reduce prices of gas and offer energy security. The sheer quantities of the resources leaves me wanting to know more.

I plan to research my project by making reference to:
- Peer-reviewed journals such as the Journal of Geological Research.
- Reputable internet sites such as Google Scholar and the Geological Society.
- Published books such as 'Reservoir Geomechanics' by Zoback (2007).
- Extracts from newspapers such as the Guardian and the Independent.

Moderator comments

The legal and environmental ramifications of Hydraulic Fracturing is an interesting and controversial topic to research. It is clear from the outset that the student shows an interest in the topic. As the topic is quite new there may be little academic research on the impact of fracturing and so conclusions may be speculative. This will need to be highlighted. Nevertheless, Google Scholar should provide useful avenues for sources. Any newspaper articles should be treated with caution and the student should be ready to evaluate the reliability of these sources. As the topic is controversial the student should also try to present a balanced view and evaluate arguments for and against hydraulic fracturing.

HARRIET'S EPQ ON THE OLYMPICS

My idea(s) for the topic/title

What is the legacy of the 2012 London Olympic Games?

My ideas for research and development of my project

In the run up to the 2012 games we heard a lot about the 'legacy' it was going to create – 'Inspire a generation' was the slogan. Therefore, in my EPQ, I wish to examine several different areas which will reflect how the UK has changed since the London 2012 Olympic Games and whether this promised legacy has indeed come to fulfilment. These areas will include:

- Infrastructure
- Cost and implications of overspend
- Overall sporting participation, has it increased since 2012?
- Legacy from the paralympic games
- Economic benefits
- Emerging new sports
- Does increase in participation rely on successful Olympic performance? Role models, more funding, etc...
- How has disability in sport changed?

Moderator comments

Clear idea of a topic area although the area is quite extensive and it may need to be narrowed down to be more manageable. Impact may be a more appropriate term to measure rather than legacy. So the title may need refinement. The student will need to decide whether to study the main Olympic Games or include the Paralympic Games as well because it may be too ambitious to do the two. The focus of the research may need to be narrowed to look at just a few sporting events.

ALEX'S EPQ ON THE MIDDLE EAST

My idea(s) for the topic/title

What involment has America and Russia had in the Middle East since WW2 and where do they stand today?

My ideas for research and development of my project

Using newspapers from the past few months I plan on finding political positions of America and Russia in the Middle East today, mainly using Syria and Libya as examples of political clashes.

To get the history of political postioning I plan on using Internet sources and books to get a general history of confrontation in the Middle East (including Sunni–Shia relations).

I also plan on talking about the other factors that may be causing such political stress in the Middle East, and how much America and Russia have done to intervene, and how much they have tried keeping the issue at arms length.

Moderator comments

This student's initial proposal shows a lack of preparation. The terms used are vague; for example, what does 'involvement' mean? And the phrase 'where do they stand today?' lacks clarity. 'I plan on talking about the other factors causing political stress' is vague and the student should have clarified what these factors may be.

It is clear that the student has not carried out a preliminary literature review. The student suggests using newspapers from the past few months but fails to specify which ones and the books are not specified either.

Your candidate proposal (continued)

STEPS 1 AND 2: On the previous spread you should have put together the beginning of your RECORD OF INITIAL IDEAS and discussed your ideas with your supervisor.

STEP 3: You must record your supervisor's main comments and advice.

STEP 4: You must record modifications you have made as a result of your discussion with your supervisor.

The spaces on the EPQ form may restrict the amount you can write if you use the pdf form from the website – but there is a version of the form in Microsoft Word which will give you unlimited space. This is available on the AQA website via tinyurl.com/aqaepq02

Record of initial ideas (steps 3 and 4)

HARRIET'S EPQ ON THE OLYMPICS

My summary of the comments and advice from my supervisor

During the first meeting my supervisor commented that she thought 'This is an interesting and topical project'. However, she did add that I will need to decide whether to study the main Olympics or include the Paralympics as well because it may be too ambitious to do the two. My supervisor also said that I may also need to narrow my research to focus on just a few sporting events and also consider where I will find the data and whether the sources are reliable and valid.

In the discussion she concluded that 'Your suggested structure looks fairly comprehensive'.

Modifications I have made as a result of my discussion with my supervisor

In the first stage I had had a few false starts. Initially I was excited about all the different areas which could be examined; however, after delving deeper into the subject and discussing the topic with my supervisor, I quickly realised this topic is vast and the amount of data handling around the Internet large. There was so much 'noise' about the legacy I soon realised it would be a far more meaningful study to narrow my areas of exploration.

I am studying PE A-Level and I eventually wish to take my study of sports to degree level. It is therefore more appropriate for me to focus on the sporting legacy rather than the economic and infrastructural legacy. Also, as a coach and a participant involved in grass roots sport, it is also relevant for me to focus on the main differences seen at club level as well as elite level. Again, when I looked at the vast array of sports competed in at the Olympics, I realised I had to narrow the study still further. It would also be difficult to track and measure all these sports as results between many different sports are intangible. I have decided that the best way to examine this is through comparison of two different sports: swimming and sailing. Both will be interesting to examine post-2012 because in the games itself, one sport exceded medal expectations but the other failed to meet its expectations – has this affected participation further down the line? Has the Olympic 'Inspire a generation' goal been realised?

Moderator comments

The student could have referred to the sources she intends to consult in this section, giving evidence of planning (AO2).

There is evidence of decision making following advice from supervisor (AO3).

FELIX'S EPQ ON FRACKING

My summary of the comments and advice from my supervisor

My supervisor agreed that the legal and environmental ramifications of Hydraulic Fracturing are an interesting and controversial topic to research. She said that she was encouraged by my interest and enthusiasm in the topic, which should help to keep me on track and also my ideas can be developed as I continue to research my topic. As the topic is contemporary there may be little academic research on the area but she suggested that I could use the Internet to search for articles on Google Scholar and look at official statistics. My supervisor advised me to treat newspaper articles with caution especially tabloid ones and try to give a balanced conclusion based on evidence.

Modifications I have made as a result of my discussion with my supervisor

Following the discussion that I had with my supervisor I have taken into greater consideration the orientation of the newspaper articles that I have included in an effort to make the argument more balanced. I have used Google Scholar as a resource to obtain peer-reviewed work, which will make my argument more balanced and more focused. I believe that my project may evolve and change as I do more research, therefore my initial plan may evolve and change as I find new avenues to explore and look into. So despite this initial plan being a rough guide, I believe it will provide me with firm foundations on which to start my research into my question of whether the benefits of Hydraulic Fracturing supersede the environmental threat that it poses. In light of the talk with my supervisor I believe that I have a better understanding of the requirements of the EPQ.

Moderator comments

The student has a clear initial title and plan for the gathering of his sources but includes the caveat 'I believe my project will evolve'. This shows that the student is open to new ideas and the plan may change as new information is uncovered.

STEP 5: Having refined your ideas you are now ready to fill in PART A: CANDIDATE PROPOSAL. Before you do this you can arrange an interim meeting with your supervisor.

PART B: SUPERVISOR'S COMMENTS ON CANDIDATE PROPOSAL is filled in by your supervisor, commenting on your proposal.

PART C: CENTRE COORDINATOR'S APPROVAL OF CANDIDATE PROPOSAL is filled in by the centre coordinator who either approves the project without recommendations, or may make required recommendations, or request a resubmission of the form.

The information in your RECORD OF INITIAL IDEAS and PART A: CANDIDATE PROPOSAL can later be used to contribute to your overall EPQ mark as evidence of planning and management, especially the section on 'my intended product' and the sources to be consulted. Students often complete this form briefly rather than give a list of things they are now going to do, so it is a missed opportunity to improve your mark.

Part A: Candidate proposal

Candidate number

Candidate's full name

Harriet

> HARRIET'S EPQ ON THE OLYMPICS

Part A: Candidate proposal

To be completed by the candidate

> Working title of my Extended Project.
> Present the topic to be researched in the form of a short statement/question/hypothesis with clear focus.
>
> Has the promised legacy of the London 2012 Olympic Games – 'inspire a generation' – been realised?

- my initial resources will be

  In order to address my title I am focusing on just two sports: sailing and swimming. I will formulate some questions to individuals within each sport (Chris Atkins, Vice President of the International Sailing federation and Mandy Garrot from the ASA). This will allow me to expand on my own research (web, sports journals, news articles) with some really interesting raw data. These resources should enable me to reach sound and robust conclusions.

- the courses of study or area(s) of personal interest to which the topic relates

  I study P.E. A-Level and in the future hope to study for a sports degree. This topic also has considerable personal interest because of my own experiences in sport both as a coach and as a performer at grass roots level. The two sports I will assess – swimming and sailing – are comparable as part of the study but useful because I have access to clubs and individuals within these clubs. I am a member of two sailing clubs and Girls Captain and a coach at Northgate Swimming Club.

- my intended product

  My product will take the form of a 5,000 word report with the working title 'Has the promised legacy of the London 2012 Olympic Games – 'inspire a generation' – been realised?'

Moderator comments

The student has now refined her title, which is a clear demonstration of decision making and acting on advice from her supervisor.

Moderator comments

The student has recognised that she will collect primary and secondary data. Although, she has indicated the names of the representatives within sailing and swimming her other resources are quite vague. An indication of specific sports journals would be helpful. She should think carefully about her questions (see pages 54–57 on questionnaire design).

Moderator comments

The student has selected a topic from an area she is interested in and which also she wishes to study at University.

Moderator comments

The candidate has identified her product as a 5,000 word academic-style report rather than an artefact.

Provide details of the courses that you are currently studying

Qualification	Subject	Qualification	Subject
e.g. A-Level, Modern Apprenticeship, BTEC	e.g. Mathematics, English, Leisure & Tourism, Spanish, ICT		
A-Level	Psychology		
A-Level	Physical Education		
A-Level	History		

Notice to candidate   You must not take part in any unfair practice in the preparation of project work required for assessment and you must understand that to present material copied directly from books or any other resources without acknowledgement will be regarded as deliberate deception. If you use or attempt to use any other practice you will be reported to AQA and you may be disqualified from **all** subjects.

Candidate declaration
I certify that I have read and understood AQA's Regulations relating to unfair practice as set out in the notice to candidates above.

Candidate signature

Date   09-10-17

YOUR autonomy and the role of YOUR supervisor

Your supervisor is there to help you shape your ideas and give you advice on how to conduct the research for your EPQ. He/she is not there to teach you the topic you have chosen to investigate. This is your project. Your supervisor is, however, one of the resources that you can call on during your research.

To get the most out of your supervisor you will need to be organised and to take responsibility for the relationship. It is not your supervisor's job to chase you into completing your EPQ, or to tell you how to manage the different stages of the project.

Meetings with your supervisor

You should arrange one-to-one meetings with your supervisor at various key points in the EPQ process. The supervisor should ensure that you have worked as independently as possible. They must:

- **Agree** your EPQ project title with the centre coordinator.
- **Complete** the appropriate supervisor sections in your PRODUCTION LOG (more about this log in the next chapter).
- **Meet** with you for review meetings including: INITIAL IDEAS, PLANNING REVIEW, MID-PROJECT REVIEW and PROJECT PRODUCT REVIEW. Students or supervisors can arrange interim meetings as required.
- **Confirm** that you have delivered a PRESENTATION and provide a record of the questioning during the presentation.
- **Endorse** your completed PRODUCTION LOG to confirm that the evidence submitted for assessment is your own work and has not been submitted as part of any other accredited qualifications.
- **Assess** your work following any standardising and internal moderation procedures required by the Centre Coordinator.
- The supervisor must sign the supervisor declaration to certify that you have worked independently. While your supervisor is a key resource in the completion of your project, ultimately the responsibility for the project rests with you. All EPQ students are expected to be proactive, independent and assertive. So if you need help you will usually have to ask for it.

Don't be a puppet.

How to get the most from your supervisor

The relationship between you and you supervisor is key to the success of your EPQ. In order to get the most out of your supervision you should take control of the process using some of the suggestions below.

DO set ground rules

Let your supervisor know how much contact and support you would like.

Agree a timetable of meetings at the start of your project and stick to this.

Make sure that each meeting has a focus, e.g. deciding an initial title, learning how to perform a literature review.

Turn up on time to each meeting you have arranged. Do not assume that your supervisor is available at all times to see you; they will have other students to see.

Plan together some interim deadlines for the work, (and write these down!) so that you are able to manage your time effectively.

DO take responsibility

Send your supervisor a note before each meeting that can form the basis of your discussions. This could include your research plan, early results of your data collection or draft chapters. This will also show the supervisor that you are managing your project well.

At the end of each meeting with your supervisor agree some action points for you to focus on before the next time you meet.

Keep a record of what you decide in supervision sessions.

DO use the support effectively

Find an appropriate way of mapping and monitoring your own progress; for example, by using a checklist of tasks to be completed. Use this to help the discussions with your supervisor to focus on areas where you need particular advice.

Listen to, evaluate and respond to your supervisor's feedback by making notes and reflecting on what has been said or written.

Apply the feedback to the next stage of your research or writing up.

DON'T go it alone

Avoid saying 'Just leave me to it. I am good at managing my own work and don't need any reminders from a supervisor about where I should be up to, or how much time is left.'

Don't feel you are bothering your supervisor too much – they are busy but willing to help. It is your responsibility to maximise the help they can give you.

Don't feel that your supervisor will mark you down if you pester them too much.

DON'T let your supervisor be too directive

If you are not happy with the way you are being supervised, explain why to your supervisor or discuss the issue with your centre coordinator.

Your supervisor will have attended training and should know not to be overly directive but a gentle reminder to them will not do any harm!

DON'T be disorganised

Don't forget meetings. Even the most organised student may need reminders – use a planner to help you remember what needs to be done by when and include meetings in this planner.

Don't leave everything to the last minute. This will give your supervisor the impression that you are not managing your time effectively.

Recording your supervisor's comments and advice

The moderator needs to see evidence of your autonomy. In other words that you have made the decisions and your supervisor has facilitated this process.

In your PRODUCTION LOG there are several sections where you record your supervisor's comments and advice (in the PLANNING REVIEW, MID-PROJECT REVIEW and PROJECT PRODUCT REVIEW). In these sections it is important to record the advice you have been given but ensure that the decisions are yours.

Let us have a look at some examples where students haven't always got this right.

> My initial idea was to look at whether the September 11th attacks on New York increased the rise of Islamophobia. My supervisor advised me not to do this as there will not be enough information and so he has advised me to do a project on 'How American Democracy has shaped British and American Democracy'. He has suggested this as he has information that may be helpful on this topic.

> My supervisor has helped me to create a good title and has suggested some experiments I can do on whether music affects concentration. She has also suggested the music I should use in my experiments.

> I have decided to do a literature review on whether Churchill really deserved his reputation as a great leader. My supervisor suggested that I restrict my reading to Martin Gilbert's 'Churchill a life' as this is claimed to be the best biography. I have decided that I would like to look at other books and sources on Churchill as I think this one book may not give a broad enough view.

Your supervisor

Your supervisor is there to help you but the moderator must see evidence of your autonomy – it is easy to make it sound as if yo u were told to do certain things by your supervisor; your aim is to act on your supervisor's advice not to do as you are told. Make sure you represent this appropriately in your PRODUCTION LOG.

Moderator comments

The way in which the student has reported the conversation with his supervisor makes it sound as if the supervisor has forced him to change the title, which would not be appropriate. The student should rephrase this comment to show how he has acted on the *advice* of the supervisor - for example, explaining why he felt a change was necessary. This demonstrates the student's autonomy.

Moderator comments

The student makes it sound as if the supervisor has taken all the decisions. This should be rephrased to state the supervisor's comments and how this led the student to make these decisions.

Moderator comments

In this example the student has reported the supervisor's advice but then shown that he has made his own decisions, which is good.

EXERCISE 1.6 Arranging meetings with your supervisor

Email from student to supervisor

Subject: EPQ meeting

Hi Sir, It would be great to have a meeting soon to discuss my EPQ progress, as I think I'm getting along well but I have a few questions. I am free Thursday P1 and P3 and Friday 2 and 4 if these are any good?

Thanks, Sunita

Surita has taken responsibility for arranging a meeting with her supervisor. Having arranged the meeting what else does she need to consider?

Use the information on the facing spread to answer the following questions:

1. How does Surita show that she has taken responsibility?
2. What should she do before the meeting?
3. What might the agenda for the meeting include?
4. What is the advantage of setting an agenda for the meeting?
5. What should she do at the end of the meeting?
6. How can Surita show that she is making her own decisions and showing evidence of autonomy?
7. What does she do if her supervisor is being too directive?

Suggested answers on page 123.

Chapter 2

Manage the project

You have now decided the topic for your EPQ and have had your CANDIDATE PROPOSAL approved. What next?

Obviously you are going to do the project – and this requires management. You must:

1. Manage your time (covered in Chapter 2)

2. Manage collecting data (covered in Chapter 3 – Using resources)

3. Manage producing the final PRODUCT (covered in Chapter 4 – Develop and realise)

4. Manage the review (covered in Chapter 5 – Review)

All of these aspects of your project are done in parallel but we have described them in separate chapters because they map onto separate assessment objectives.

An overview of the later chapters is given on the facing page 'What's ahead in the other chapters'.

A0 1

Assessment objective 1

Assessment objective 1 (AO1) concerns how well you have managed your project. This will account for 20% of your final mark.

The AO1 objectives include:

- Identify the topic.
- Identify project aims and objectives.
- Produce a detailed project plan.
- Complete the work applying organisational skills and strategies to meet stated objectives.

The first two bullet points were dealt with in Chapter 1.

This chapter is concerned with the final two bullet points.

What the moderator is looking for

The moderator is looking for detailed project planning and evidence of monitoring.

This will be demonstrated at various stages of your project:

- RECORD OF INITIAL IDEAS and PART A: CANDIDATE PROPOSAL
- PLANNING REVIEW
- MID-PROJECT REVIEW
- PROJECT PRODUCT REVIEW
- The final PRESENTATION

It is important to have clear *aims and objectives* and discuss how you are going to achieve your objectives.

It is important to be *flexible* and record any changes to your plan and how you have handled these changes.

The PRODUCTION LOG should explain your EPQ *journey*. This is just as important as the PRODUCT itself.

What's in this chapter

Page 26 The PRODUCTION LOG

Your PRODUCTION LOG will be assessed as well as your PRODUCT. The log records the journey.

Page 28 Reviewing the progress of your project

There are **three** important review stages during the production of your project – the PLANNING, the MID-PROJECT and PROJECT PRODUCT REVIEWS.

Page 30 Time management

Key principles will be considered such as threats to time management and prioritising your time.

Page 32 Setting your aims and objectives

An important part of managing your time is being able to set clear and achievable objectives at various stages of your project. Being SMARTA will help you.

Page 34 Making a general plan

A sample production timeline is provided together with a scheme of work to help you to plan your project.

Page 36 Communicating changes to your plan

Being flexible and making changes is a good thing, and these are recorded in the PLANNING REVIEW, MID-PROJECT REVIEW and/or PROJECT PRODUCT REVIEW.

OPTIONAL EXTRAS TO ADD TO YOUR PRODUCTION LOG

Page 38 Management tools: Production timelines, diary of progress, Gantt and PERT

You can go beyond your PRODUCTION LOG, and use other management tools such as a diary of progress, a Gantt chart or PERT chart.

What's in the next chapters...

Part of project management is dealt with in this chapter but you also need to be managing other elements:

Chapter 3 Use resources

In Chapter 3 we focus on how to use primary and secondary sources effectively. This demonstrates evidence of resource management.

Chapter 4 Develop and realise

In Chapter 4 we discuss how to plan your report. This demonstrates management.

As you carry out your research it is important to remind yourself that the time you have at your disposal is limited. It is essential to plan your strategy and think about the overall structure of your project PRODUCT sooner rather than later. For all students this will include a REPORT. Some students use the writing process to help them think through, clarify and develop any early ideas.

Also, your supervisor may wish to see evidence that your project is developing – they may look at your report as well as any other product you are developing. It is important to be prepared to critique and revise your own work several times.

So look at Chapter 4 now – don't leave preparing the final product until the end. Start thinking about it now.

Chapter 5 Review

In Chapter 5 we demonstrate further managements skills – how to manage your PRESENTATION.

The REVIEW documents in your PRODUCTION LOG can demonstrate evidence of planning together with your presentation.

The production log

You may think that your EPQ is about the PRODUCT you hand in at the end (the REPORT plus artefact or performance) – but this is wrong. The journey is equally important – how you have managed the production and the changes you have made. This is recorded in the PRODUCTION LOG that is one of the three items you will hand in at the end of your EPQ (PRODUCTION LOG + PRODUCT + RECORD OF PRESENTATION). The log is part of the 14-page AQA document you have to hand in entitled CANDIDATE RECORD FORM, PRODUCTION LOG AND ASSESSMENT RECORD.

This PRODUCTION LOG demonstrates how you have managed your project from the beginning to the end. There are additional management tools that you can submit along with the PRODUCTION LOG. These are described at the end of this chapter (pages 38–43) – a diary of progress and/ or a Gantt chart, and/or a PERT analysis. These may help you to organise your work from the beginning of the project, so you may wish to read these pages now.

The moderator, when reading your PRODUCTION LOG and REPORT, must feel as if they are on the EPQ journey with you.

Let's start at the very beginning

It is useful to keep track of the forms which have been completed in the production log and the dates which you have completed the forms as part of your overall progress.

Page	Title	Date completed
1	Candidate declaration	3 May 2017
2–3	Submission checklist and Record of marks	
4	Record of initial ideas	12 Sept 2016
6–8	Project proposal and approval (Parts A, B and C)	12 Sept 2016
9	Planning review	19 October 2016
10	Mid-project review	10 January 2017
11	Project product review	1 February 2017
12–13	Presentation record (Parts A and B)	30 April 2017
14	Summary and reflection	1 May 2017

Is this extended project part of a group project?

☑ *No*

☐ *Yes*

If 'Yes', give brief details

Extended Project final title:

Overview of the PRODUCTION LOG

The RECORD OF INITIAL IDEAS records your aims and objectives – this is something you have already completed (page 19 of this book). This can also provide evidence of management (AO1) – many students waste useful space by writing quite brief proposals.

PROJECT PROPOSAL PARTS A, B and C are completed by you, your supervisor and centre coordinator.

Once your project has been approved the next steps are recorded in your PLANNING REVIEW. Make more extensive investigations by reading the sources you have identified and then discuss your plans with your supervisor. You must record their advice in this review.

The MID-PROJECT REVIEW will take place about half way through your project. You should outline your successes and failures and any changes you have made since you started your project. If you are using a supplementary management tool (such as a diary of progress) this is the time to refer to it in your log. Are you on track? Did your literature review take longer than you planned? Are you having difficulty finding enough information? This is all about your journey. Discuss your plans with your supervisor and record this here.

The PROJECT PRODUCT REVIEW takes place near the end of completion of your project. You should again arrange to meet with your supervisor. On the AQA form you should give an honest account of your successes and failures and any changes that you have made since the MID-PROJECT REVIEW. Justify your decisions.

The PRESENTATION RECORD should document your planning and give an account of the EPQ journey. It should not just refer to the PRODUCT itself. Remember to include evidence of your PRESENTATION, such as copies of the PowerPoint slides. If you have filmed your PRESENTATION then include a copy either on a disc or if you have uploaded to YouTube then include the link.

The SUMMARY AND REFLECTION are written at the very end after you have given your PRESENTATION. The SUMMARY is a brief explanation of your PRODUCT – about 150 words. The REFLECTION should summarise the main learning points: any new knowledge that you have gained and have found valuable such as learning how to carry out a literature review, which will be useful at university. It is as important to refer to your failures as well as your successes as these are part of learning. You might also include advice that you would give to students embarking on an EPQ.

Exemplar of a PRODUCTION LOG

We are going to illustrate the PRODUCTION LOG over the next few pages by showing you how two students, Kim and Robert, filled in some of their forms. Both of their final PRODUCTS are given at the end of the book (see pages 108–116).

We start with Kim's PLANNING REVIEW.

The PLANNING REVIEW

Once your project has been approved by your centre coordinator you record your next steps in your PLANNING REVIEW. This can include what sources you will read, how you intend to structure your REPORT or what steps are required to produce your artefact. You can also refer to how you will monitor your progress.

KIM'S EPQ BORN THIS WAY

Planning review

Candidate's full name

Kimberley

Candidate number

To be completed by the candidate. This page records your outline plan at the start of your work.

My next steps in planning, researching and deadlines that I will set myself. What I intend to do, by when, what resources I will use and how I will implement the recommendations of the centre co-ordinator (where appropriate).

I am going to read a variety of peer-reviewed academic articles and selected sections from various books; therefore I will gain a good knowledge of the theories and research that has gone into my chosen topic area of homosexuality. From talking to my supervisor, I also made sure that I knew the criteria needed for measuring nature and nurture outcomes, or an interaction between the two. I am therefore going to narrow down my search in order to meet these specific criteria and keep to the topic of my project.

My summary of the comments and advice from my supervisor

My supervisor gave me some practical advice on producing a project plan with loose target completion dates so that I have an overview to my project and tasks; she advised me to keep a note of all books, journals and sites I decided to draw information from as I would later need to reference them (using the Harvard referencing method which she taught me).

In order for me to meet the criteria of my project title and aim, I would need to define and operationalise the terms 'nature' and 'nurture'. My supervisor recommended that I look at mainly peer-reviewed research and not to focus too much on the BBC documentary 'The Making of Me' – if anything, she said to pick up on the scientific studies carried out in the documentary and research them on the Internet for a more thorough version.

My supervisor further suggested that I attempt to contact Celia Kitzinger – a psychologist who has done a lot of work in the area of homosexuality – by email to ask her questions and/or obtain further information for my project.

Modifications I have made as a result of my discussion with my supervisor and/or the comments from my centre coordinator

Having discussed this with my supervisor, I decided to start Harvard referencing all sources as I've come across them.

I added in a paragraph to my project purely contributing to the definitions of 'nature' and 'nurture' and which sections I plan to look at within each side – this added more depth to my 'Abstract'. I have also put together only peer-reviewed research which I plan to comb through and add into my final project.

I decided against trying to contact Celia Kitzinger because of the lack of time and there is no guarantee that she would reply, so instead I have focused entirely on peer-reviewed articles and books.

Supervisor signature

Date   19-10-16

Moderator comments

Kim has provided an outline working plan with respect to her sources that is strategic. From the outset she recognises that she needs to operationalise the terms 'nature' and 'nurture' which will help her to find suitable material.

Moderator comments

The supervisor has given useful rather than over directive advice on how to manage the project by agreeing some dates for completion. Advice is also given to follow up the sources contained in the documentary that was the inspiration for the project. Although it may be a good idea to attempt to contact an expert in the field, they may not always provide a useful response.

Moderator comments

The changes and clarifications show that Kim has acted on most of the advice of her supervisor and has clearly documented how she intends to proceed with her research.

Kim has made a decision not to contact the expert and she justifies her decision. She might also have considered the views of the expert and decided that the expert may not have provided a balanced opinion.

On this spread we continue to look at exemplars of the MID-PROJECT REVIEW and PROJECT PRODUCT REVIEW. This should help you understand what you will be expected to do.

Moderator comments

Changes to the original plan are communicated and justified in relation to the sensitive nature of the topic.

Moderator comments

There is an indication given of how Kim will evaluate her sources following advice from her supervisor, and there is also a consideration of how she will structure her report.

Moderator comments

Kim has decided to structure her report more clearly following the discussion with her supervisor.

Moderator comments

It is important that the title is agreed here and does not change after the Mid-Project Review.

Moderator comments

The planned steps required to complete the project are clear and relate to the title of nature and nurture.

Mid-project review

Candidate's full name
Kimberley

KIM'S EPQ BORN THIS WAY

> The MID-PROJECT REVIEW gives you the opportunit[y] to review what you have accomplished so far. You can identify your successes as well as the obstacles faced and how to overcome these to advance your work, and use these insights to improve your subsequent work.

To be completed by the candidate.
This page records your outline plan when you have completed your research.

Is my project following my original plan? How has my plan developed?

Initially, I had contemplated doing some thorough primary research into people's views on what causes homosexuality, and from this, I was hoping to highlight some of the misconceptions held by society. Due to the potentially sensitive nature of the task in relation to this particular topic, I decided to use my findings in order to formulate the aim of my overall project rather than specifically including the findings.

My summary of the comments and advice from my supervisor

Specifically, my supervisor has advised me to make sure I evaluate all sources and information found in order to add more depth to my project.

As general comments, she has told me to start considering the structure of my final project as well as any conclusion I have come to regarding the aim of finding out whether homosexual behaviour is caused by biological or psychological factors.

Modifications I have made as a result of my discussion with my supervisor at this stage

I decided to clearly structure my project by adding topic headings, including the abstract, introduction, 'Nature' section, 'Nurture' section and conclusion.

My final title and agreed form of project product

Born this way - are biological factors the primary basis for sexual orientation?

My agreed product is a 5,000 word essay.

My planned next steps to complete my project

To complete my project, I plan to continue researching and gathering resources, whilst dedicating time each week to work on my written report. I plan on finalising the categories I have chosen within the 'nature' and 'nurture' debates so that I can organise my pr[oject into sensible sub-headings.] I [can set out the] arguments within the debate, I then need to draw[...]

> The PROJECT PRODUCT REVIEW takes place when you[r] EPQ is nearing completion. After all your hard work it is time to consider whether you have achieved what you set out to achieve. What have been the successes and failures since the MID-PROJECT REVIEW?
>
> You might want to carry out a gap analysis to list what else you need to do. You might also want to start thinkin[g] of what you will do in your PRESENTATION.

Project product review

Candidate's full name
Kimberley

KIM'S EPQ BORN THIS WAY

To be completed by the candidate.
This page records the (near) completion of your project product.

Moderator comments

The successes are documented together with the changes made in terms of additional detail and research.

Moderator comments

Kim has been advised on the structure of her report, namely further clarification in her introduction and conclusion. This is important advice as it will demonstrate whether the original question has been addressed.

Moderator comments

The clarifications made show that the advice from the supervisor has been taken.

Did my project follow my revised plan (from the mid-project review)?

I have succeeded in organising my project into categories which read clearly and follow on suitably from the previous sub-headings.

To add slightly more detail into the introduction, I decided to include relevant definitions, the need for research into this area, and various historical quotes in order to highlight the original thoughts of psychologists which I planned on either proving or disproving later on in the project having researched more contemporary studies.

My summary of the comments and advice from my supervisor at this final stage

Having looked through my project, my supervisor advised me to include a short paragraph in my introduction allowing the reader to understand what to 'expect' from my project and why, specifically, I chose to focus on the topic. She also suggested that I include short conclusions/summaries after my 'Nature' and 'Nurture' sections, finally rounding off the project with an overall conclusion based on the research I accumulated.

Modifications I have made as a result of discussion with my supervisor at this final stage
Do I need to do anything else to complete my product?

I added more information to the introduction and the three conclusions as advised. I also double-checked that all referencing was present and accurate.

Both Kim's and Robert's final REPORTS are shown in the appendix — see pages 108 and 116.

Mid-project review

ROBERT'S EPQ ON A SPIDER POEM

Candidate's full name

Robert

To be completed by the candidate
This page records your outline plan when you have completed your research.

Is my project following my original plan? How has my plan developed?

I have had some problems gaining access to primary schools but this does not cause any major problems to my project but this is a pity.

But I have given the survey to Sixth Formers, some haven't returned the questionnaires yet.

I have come up with an original idea as there aren't that many positive poems about spiders.

My summary of the comments and advice from my supervisor

Make sure the artefact is strong and the report underpinning the artefact relates to the

Edit and spell check before submission.

Modifications I have made as a result of discussion with my supervisor at this stage

I have created draft versions of my poem and drawings.

I have re-sent my surveys and hand delivered some.

My final title and agreed form of project product

To produce a poem for students in the style of Dr Seuss which will be a short 1,000 word report and the poem will be my artefact

My planned next steps to complete my project

Will come up with a strong idea for my practical piece and do preliminary sketches of characters.

I will create a drafted piece to troubleshoot any problems with the creation of the art.

I will send out more surveys.

Moderator comments

Robert has briefly outlined his failures but more information should have been provided on why he had difficulty in gaining access to primary schools.

Moderator comments

This first statement is vague and should be clearly defined – what is a 'strong artefact'? Robert plans to send out more surveys. This objective is not SMART let alone SMARTA. Robert needs to specify how many more surveys will be sent and how he will decide on who to send them to.

Moderator comments

It is unclear what is meant by a 'strong artefact'. However, the advice relating to the report is useful as frequently students do not link their report to their artefact.

Moderator comments

These comments do not relate to the supervisor's advice about the report underpinning the artefact and Robert seems more concerned with the surveys.

Project product review

ROBERT'S EPQ ON A SPIDER POEM

Candidate's full name

Robert

To be completed by the candidate
This page records the (near) completion of your project product

Did my project follow my revised plan (from the mid-project review)?

I did have some problems completing artefact as the narrative style had to be suitable for children. I had a clear idea of the theme of the poems but had to make sure that it presented spiders in a positive way and that it rhymed.

The illustrations had to be clear. Also my report had to relate to spiders and Dr Seuss.

My summary of the comments and advice from my supervisor at this final stage

To complete artefact to a high standard and begin planning my presentation make sure I refer to the EPQ journey in my presentation.

Modifications I have made as a result of discussion with my supervisor at this final stage. Do I need to do anything else to complete my product?

I have begun the presentation using my written report as a stimulus for my slides as it acts as a summary of my project and the research I did. I have also begun to plan out the final version of my poem including finalising illustrations.

Moderator comments

Robert has not proofread the text in this log and there are typographical errors. Robert does not comment on the need for his report to relate to his artefact and there is no further mention of his surveys.

Moderator comments

The advice relating to the PRESENTATION is important as some students are tempted just to refer to their PRODUCT in the PRESENTATION rather than their EPQ journey.

Time management

Time management concerns pacing yourself. It's a bit like running a marathon rather than a sprint. You need to realise you are in for the long haul. You have to spread your work over a period of time and maintain your level of interest. It is important to know how to use your time effectively.

Moderator comments

Many EPQ students say, in their SUMMARY AND REFLECTION, that they wished that they had managed their time better. This includes starting their reading and literature review earlier, for instance using the summer break to start the research.

Many students fail to anticipate busy times within their school schedule such as writing the UCAS personal statement and mock exams. Furthermore you may be involved in various extra-curricular activities. During these busy times research for the EPQ may need to be put on hold.

Threats to effective time management

Everyone can become a better time manager but you need to recognise where the problems may arise. There are significant benefits from improving this skill for both your own research and as a skill you can offer employers.

- **Lack of objectives**   If your aims and objectives are not clear from the outset then this can result in wasted time finding irrelevant information.

- **Lack of information or clarity about the task**   If you do not fully understand what each task requires then you may not leave yourself sufficient time. For example, the PRODUCTION LOG cannot be written at the end – you must do it as you go along.

- **Disorganisation**   Not having a routine or system makes managing your time and life more difficult. Effective students are not necessarily workaholics; you don't have to put in more hours, but rather just use your time more efficiently.

- **Unforeseen crises or difficulty juggling multiple commitments** Your computer crashes or you have lost your memory stick. Your best friend has just broken up with their boyfriend and needs a few hours of your time. You may also have to juggle other commitments such as sport or Duke of Edinburgh's Award. All of these mean that your high priority goals (e.g. your EPQ) suffer.

- **Perfectionism**   You want your work to be of the highest and most groundbreaking standard but this is not realistic and may prevent you completing the project.

- **Performance-debilitating circumstances**   You work in busy or unsuitable locations and therefore are unable to concentrate on what you are doing.

- **Procrastination**   You look and feel very busy, but in reality are only doing the less important tasks needed to complete your project (such as emails and referencing). Procrastination is the vice of people who like to think about doing work rather than actually doing it. Procrastination comes from the Latin word for tomorrow and it can be best defined as putting off doing something until tomorrow that could be done today.

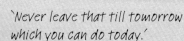

'I like work; it fascinates me. I can sit and look at it for hours.'

Jerome K Jerome – *Three men in a boat* (1889)

'Never leave that till tomorrow which you can do today.'

Benjamin Franklin (1770)

EXERCISE 2.1   Time management

Read the extract below from a student PRODUCTION LOG.

Can you identify the main issues with this student's time management (refer to the list above)?

After my initial panic of losing my memory stick with 2,000 words of my project and I hadn't backed it up I had to start again. Upon near completion of my project I realised that the sources contained in my bibliography lacked variety and all came from the same source of media. I hadn't kept a list of references as I went along and so I had to rush to complete the bibliography at the end. I also realised quite a way into the project that the title was too descriptive and vague and so I added some more evaluative sections. Due to the added complications of homework and University Open Days, I didn't quite keep to schedule and was a week late completing my research. I still had to complete my references, I also realised I was under the word count and so had to add some sections. This could have been avoided if I had managed my time better.

Suggested answers on page 123.

> 'Time is a dressmaker, specialising in alterations.'
>
> The writer Faith Baldwin (1945)

Effective time management

Your initial plan for your EPQ may end up in shreds but there are a number of key principles that you can utilise to help you improve your time management:

- **Have clear objectives**   Knowing the aims of your research will clarify your objectives.

- **Devise a good plan**   Make sure to include clear milestones and deadlines in your plan, and stick to them.

- **Classify tasks by urgency and importance**   Tackle those that are both important and urgent first.

- **Use a diary and timetable key activities**.

- **Don't let other people distract you**   Manage other people's expectations and make your priorities clear to them.

- **Focus on one thing at a time**.

- **Review each activity before you leave it**.

- **Reward yourself**,   i.e. decide to check Facebook after you find a reference, or allow yourself the rest of the evening off once you finish the draft of a chapter.

Prioritising

It is difficult to manage your time effectively if you are not clear about your purpose, aims and objectives.

You need a sense of priority – deciding what needs to be done next. There are elaborate schemes in textbooks on time management and prioritising.

To arrive at your priority rating for different tasks ask yourself two simple questions.

- How important is it?

- How urgent is it?

A priority may have different mixes of these two ingredients.

Choose your own reward

EXERCISE 2.2   Prioritising

Review your priorities at present.

In the 1st column below start by listing five tasks that need to be done.

In the 2nd column grade them in order of importance: A = very important, B = less important and so on.

In the 3rd column grade them according to urgency: 1 is very urgent and so on. Now relist them in the box underneath according to their scores with A1 being the top priority

Priorities	Order of Importance (A, B, C, D, E)	Urgency (1, 2, 3, 4, 5)

My priorities for the next steps of my project

Setting your aims and objectives

An important part of managing your research project is setting your own clear and achievable aims and objectives. This is valuable as it will help you focus on the things that matter to your research and future plans.

An *aim* is a general statement of what you intend to achieve in your PRODUCT, such as to investigate the relationship between social deprivation and achievement. An *objective* is a specific statement of what you want to achieve.

All planning is thinking forward in time, though there is always a limit to how far ahead it is possible to plan at any one time.

'It is wise to look ahead in time, but foolish to look further than you can see.'

Winston Churchill

Objectives: What do you want to achieve?

What is it that you *actually* want to achieve in this EPQ project? Remember that completing your EPQ is a journey and a process.

Look at your first ideas for your research proposal as a starting point. As your research progresses you will amend the objectives of the project as you uncover new knowledge.

Setting short-term objectives and providing evidence of these are key parts of your EPQ journey. Objectives should be definite in the sense of being well defined. In your **PRODUCTION LOG** you need to make sure that your objectives are SMART.

Below is a tool to help you do this.

GOAL SETTING

Specific
Measurable
Achievable
Realistic
Timely

SMART: A tool to evaluate your objectives

SMART is an acronym credited to both Peter Drucker (1955) and G.T. Doran (1991), although it is difficult to identify whether either of these two were actually the first people to use the term 'SMART' with reference to objectives.

The SMART acronym refers to writing objectives that are specific, measurable, achievable, realistic and timely. Using these criteria you can critically evaluate the objectives that you have set yourself. For every objective you set, confirm it meets the SMART criteria.

Specific	Measurable	Achievable
Objectives should address the 5 Ws: Who, what, when, where and why Make sure the goal specifies what needs to be done with a timescale for completion. Use action verbs: Compile, create, design, develop, implement, produce, analyse, apply, change, determine, differentiate, identify, perform, etc. Avoid jargon and words/phrases that are vague, misleading or ambiguous. For example: • Using the phrase 'do more reading' is not specific enough. Instead you should write 'I need to read Chapter 1 by the end of the week' or 'I will identify and read two relevant journal articles'. • Using the phrase 'deal with outstanding questionnaires' is ambiguous. It could mean 'not yet dealt with or resolved' or 'exceptionally good questionnaires'. Instead you could write 'follow up remaining questionnaires'.	Objectives should be measurable so you can check whether you have achieved them and are actually making progress. This can include numeric or descriptive measures that define quantity, quality, cost, etc. Focus on observable actions. Some examples of measurable objectives: • Write a 500-word introduction by the end of the week. • Produce five questions for my mid-project review with my supervisor by Friday week. • Interview 10 participants as part of my pilot study.	Ask yourself whether, with a reasonable amount of effort and application, the objective is achievable. An objective is achievable if is within your control and influence. • Is there previous research in the area? If so then it is, in principle, possible. Otherwise it may not be achievable. • Are the necessary resources/equipment available, or is there a realistic chance of getting them within the time frame originally outlined? • If you plan to submit an artefact, ask yourself if you can you develop the artefact you have planned, for example can you produce the film or fashion show? • If you depend on expert advice, will you get a response? Setting objectives that are too low or unachievable will reduce your motivation.

Statue of Winston Churchill

EXERCISE 2.3 SMART or not SMART

Identify whether these objectives are SMART or not SMART:

1. Do some Internet research.

2. Start to plan my project.

3. Design a questionnaire consisting of 10 questions by the end of the week.

4. Use a variety of resources.

5. Contact some experts in the field.

6. Identify the number of female characters in Chaucer's *Canterbury Tales* by the end of the month.

7. Create a graph to show the total number of people in England and Wales applying for payday loans in the last two years.

Write the following objectives so that they are now SMART:

1. Proofread my project and edit as required.

2. Contact Professor Chivers, the expert in the field.

3. Check out the Internet site Google Scholar.

4. Read about supervolcanoes.

Suggested answers on page 123.

Performance objectives can be even SMARTA

Some people have added a final 'A' for 'agreed'. According to Trainer (2012) this additional A 'is essential because when setting objectives each party must agree to the objectives for there to be any benefit'.

In the case of the EPQ you need to agree your objectives with your supervisor.

Realistic	Timely
Whilst objectives should be realistic this does not mean that they need to be easy. They can be objectives that are quite demanding but not so much that the chance of success is small. Realistic objectives take into account the available resources such as skills, time and equipment. Consider the following: • Is it possible to achieve this objective? • Who is going to do it? • Do I have the necessary skills to do the task well? Make sure that you are being realistic. You can get feedback from your supervisor to help you do this. Setting learning targets in this way will, through experience, gradually improve your ability to manage your own self-development and learning. For example: Should I read five original research articles or just two of them? It may be realistic in the time you have available to limit the number of articles you read.	This refers to a deadline, date, milestone or time when the objective will be accomplished or completed. This timescale should be included in the objective so as to make it measurable. A deadline helps to create the necessary urgency, prompts action and focuses your mind. If you do not set a deadline this can reduce your motivation and your sense of urgency to perform the task. Ask yourself if the objective can be accomplished within the deadlines that have been established, bearing in mind other possible competing demands which may cause delay. For example: The introduction section will be completed by the end of October.

Turning your objectives into a plan

Once you have identified what you want to achieve (your objectives) you need to start the process of turning these into a plan. Look again at each objective and ask yourself:

• What is stopping me from achieving this objective?

• Why haven't I achieved it already?

• What/who will help me to achieve this objective?

Answering these questions will help you to put together a viable project plan, not just for doing the research, but for developing the skills you need to complete it successfully.

Making a general plan

The timeframe for you to complete your EPQ is quite different from the relatively short deadlines you are used to, for example like a deadline for an essay or piece of homework in your A-Level subjects. You have months to complete the EPQ and therefore it may be hard to pace yourself unless you formulate a general plan.

On this spread we present two different approaches to time management produced by EPQ students.

`From going through the EPQ process I would advise people to make a detailed plan using their objectives because this will make the process of planning your time a whole lot easier.'

Ailish, EPQ student

`If I was to give advice to someone else considering an EPQ it would be to make sure that they know exactly what they are going to do before they start and that time management is very important. I organised my time by having specific deadlines that I had to meet as well as the mid-project and end-of-project deadlines.'

Harriet, EPQ student

Moderator comments

Rosie has demonstrated clear evidence that she is tracking her progress against the timescales which she has set herself. A deadline helps to create the necessary urgency, prompts action and focuses your mind. Timely objectives provide clear evidence of management for AO1.

Exemplar 1

ROSIE'S EPQ SPACE ODYSSEY

Not having a routine or system makes managing your time and life more difficult. Unforeseen circumstances and juggling multiple commitments can mean that your EPQ suffers. Therefore it is useful to set deadlines for each phase of your project. Although such deadlines may need to be altered slightly during the course of your EPQ, this work plan will provide a useful structure to enable you to stay on track.

The plan below provides a structure for you to set deadlines and monitor your progress. In column 1 Rosie has listed all the tasks to be completed, starting with the INITIAL IDEAS. In column 2, Rosie has allowed three days to complete this task and will identify the deadline for this task, for example November 5th. If she achieves this deadline she can indicate it with a tick in the third column. If she does not complete it by the 5th she will write the date when she does complete it. Hitting one deadline late means having less time for future deadlines but this plan has some slack in it so she should be able to catch up.

EPQ title: **Is 2001 A Space Odyssey the best film ever made? A critical analysis.**

To Complete	Time allowed	Intermittent deadlines	Achieved?
Initial ideas	3 days	November 5th	
Part A: Candidate proposal	3 days		
Planning Review	1 day		
Research: watching films	3 months		
Research: film criticism	1 month		
Research: wider social/ cultural sources	1 month		
Analyse all sources	3 weeks		
Plan and do interview	3 days		
Mid-Project Review	3 days		
Plan Written Report	1 week		
Write-up	3 weeks		
Project product review	3 days		
Summary	1 day		
Plan for presentation and display	2 weeks		
Presentation Record Part A	1 day		
Rehearse presentation	1 day		
Presentation and display	1 day		
Summary and reflection	1 day		
Contents	1 day		
SUBMISSION			

You can include a plan in the appendix of your project as additional evidence of planning and monitoring. Your should refer to this plan in your PRODUCTION LOG (at PLANNING REVIEW, MID-PROJECT REVIEW and/or PROJECT PRODUCT REVIEW). Such plans provide excellent evidence of monitoring against timely objectives – one of the SMART criteria (see previous spread).

Exemplar 2

JACK'S EPQ ON RED IN FILMS

It is important to ensure that you have enough time for all of the individual sections of your EPQ in order for you to complete it by your submission deadline. The detailed time plan below lists all of the individual sections of your PRODUCTION LOG and also includes other elements of planning and research. The tasks for each element are listed, for example research involves creating a book list and evaluating sources. When you have completed the activity for each element you can record the date (and give yourself a pat on the back).

EPQ title: **Why is the colour red sinister in film?**

Element	Task to complete	Date completed
PLANNING PROJECT	Produce Gantt chart	
	Organise a schedule for completing work	
	Produce a system of notes	
	Review research	
RESEARCH	Initial research – is the project viable?	
	Commence actual research	
	Create a book list	
	Induction to the University library, and search for relevant material	
	Internet search	
	Consider different routes to develop: religious, mythological, historical, psychological …	
	Compile a list of films to watch	
	Watch films – links? similarities? motifs?	
	Film Studies books – the aesthetics of film	
	Email the British Film Institute, have they got any suggestions?	
	Email a film studies Professor at University	
	Evaluate sources – reliable? relevant?	
PRODUCTION LOG	Record of initial ideas	
	Part A: Candidate proposal	
	Planning Review	
	Mid-Project Review	
	Project product review	
	Presentation Record Part A	
	Summary and reflection	
WORK TO RECEIVE	Project Proposal Part B	
	Project Proposal Part C	
	Presentation Record Part B	
ACTUAL PROJECT	Written Report	
	Slide Show	
	Presentation	
	Display and Q&A	

Take a good look at when you could commit time to spend on your EPQ. Look for slots of between 30 minutes and two hours as research has shown that your brain starts to slow down when you have been working for more than two hours.

In particular consider times when you are sitting around doing very little – you might be able to turn this into study time. If you travel to school or college by train you could do some work on the train. But also leave some clear chunks of time for you to relax, keep fit, go shopping, watch TV, etc.

You should try to stay committed to the structure you create. But try to be realistic as well, you may wish to review your study timetable every few weeks to see if it is working for you. Take account of when you are at your best to study. Do you work well early in the morning or late at night? Think, too, about where will be the best place to study, whether it is a study area at college/school, a library or computer room, or a quiet place where you live.

Try to be realistic and do not aim for the impossible. There will be busy times within your timetable such as extra-curricular events and even UCAS applications, mock exams which may have to take priority and so adapt your timetable accordingly.

Communicating changes to your plan

It is important that any changes to your initial plan are communicated fluently. In the RECORD OF INITIAL IDEAS, PLANNING REVIEW, MID-PROJECT REVIEW and PROJECT PRODUCT REVIEW there is a section where you should communicate any changes to the plan you made at the start of your project.

We looked at examples of these four forms on pages 19–20 and 27–29. Let us look again at examples of these forms and focus on how students have communicated changes.

Moderator comments

This exemplar shows how Henry has made changes from his first ideas to understand the journey of the black community in the US. The discussions with his supervisor led him make changes. He now has a narrower and more manageable scope for the investigation.

Moderator comments

This exemplar shows how Henry's initial title continues to evolve as the research progresses. Consequently the title is now more focused. He has also become more focused on how he intends to conduct his research.

Failures: 'I found that some of my internet research was unreliable. Although this was no real hassle it did mean some extra work to do quickly if I wanted to complete my project to the deadline.'

Changes: 'I decided to use other more reliable sources such as peer-reviewed journals and also books written by respected authors in the field.'

Huw, EPQ student

HENRY'S EPQ ON CIVIL RIGHTS

RECORD OF INITIAL IDEAS

My idea(s) for topic/title: **How has the journey of the black community in America changed?**

My ideas for research and development of my project

Ever since campaigning for the 2008 presidential election in the United States began, I have been fascinated with the journey of the black community in the US. I want to explore the story of African-Americans and understand their path to their lives today, from the days of slavery and segregation to now, with a black man as President. I want to understand all aspects of the Civil Rights Movement and how the works of Martin Luther King Jr and Rosa Parks propelled the problem of racial equality into the public and political spotlight.

My summary of the comments and advice from my supervisor

After reading my first ideas for my project, my supervisor was optimistic and interested in how I would further develop my research. She commented on how my title links positively with my interest in politics; however, she did say that my title needs to be narrowed down as the time frame for the 'journey' seems like a huge undertaking from slavery to the present day. She advised me to investigate which century has been the most interesting and focus the basis of my project around it.

Modifications I have made as a result of my discussion with my supervisor

After a meeting and discussion with my supervisor, we have mutually agreed that it would be beneficial for my project's time frame to be narrowed down, focusing more so on the Civil Rights Movement of the 1950s onwards rather than the days of slavery dating back to the 15th and 16th century. However, I have decided that I will begin my project with an introduction to Abraham Lincoln's Presidency and the American Civil War (1861-1865) as I have learned that this is what many experts consider the true beginning of the Civil Rights Movement.

PLANNING REVIEW

My next steps in planning, researching and deadlines that I will set myself. What I intend to do, by when, what resources I will use and how I will implement the recommendations of the centre co-ordinator (where appropriate).

I plan on reading various different books, articles and Internet research websites in order to gain a further insight into the American Civil Rights Movement. These sources will derive from both an academic and non-fictional nature. I will research further into the works of inspirational figureheads such as Rosa Parks and Martin Luther King Jr, whose courage and determination brought about social change in the United States on an unprecedented scale. I will look at the federal government's role in the Civil Rights uproar and evaluate their intervention techniques and their effectiveness in bringing about racial equality. I plan on gaining statistics from respected sources that clearly show the inequality in the United States. I am going to look at various economic indicators such as the average wage, life expectancy and the percentage of whites and blacks living in poverty to gain a clear image of the disparity in the US. I will also look at African-American representation across all three branches of the political system, including the Executive, Congress and the Supreme Court and question how racial equality can be a reality when representation in the highest political offices is inadequate.

In order to keep to the timescales I will use a Gantt chart which will help to determine whether the project is on schedule at various points such as the mid-project review.

My summary of the comments and advice from my supervisor

'How has the journey of the black community in America changed?' was my initial title for my Extended Project. After a meeting with my supervisor she has questioned this heading which was very broad and open. We have agreed that I need to narrow down my title in order to get an accurate and detailed project. We have also agreed that I need to keep a strict record of all the books and sources I have used throughout my project and has advised me to use the Harvard method of referencing which is both tidy and highly respected. Finally she has said I need to present an analytical account rather than simply a narrative description which is a potential trap I could fall into.

Modifications I have made as a result of my discussion with my supervisor and/or the comments from my centre coordinator

As a result of the discussion I have had with my supervisor, I have made some slight changes to my project so far. Firstly I have changed my title to 'I have a dream… To Obama' in which I will describe and evaluate the Civil Rights Movement from the fruition stage it entered in the 1960s to the election of President Barack Obama in 2008. However, I have decided that in order to gain a detailed understanding of the whole Civil Rights Movement, I must describe some of the landmark times such as the Presidency of Abraham Lincoln (1860-1865) and the segregation laws that came into place at the end of 19th century. I have also begun to keep a diary of the sources I have used and started to order them in the Harvard style of referencing in order to keep a tidy and presentable record.

Never ignore a problem

'Research is, by its nature, unpredictable.'
Gary A. Cziko (1989)

Don't be tempted to try to ignore a problem, or hope that it will go away. Also don't think that by seeking help you are failing as a researcher.

Once you start to gather relevant sources for your project in the course of your literature review you may find that the research project is not developing as you had hoped. This happens frequently during the course of EPQ research so do not be overly concerned if you have encountered a problem. Try to gauge what it will take to resolve the situation.

Changing the title is not normally the answer, although modification of some kind may be useful. Remember you can change the title as the EPQ evolves but you can't change or shape your title to fit in with the finished PRODUCT at the end.

If you encounter an intractable problem during the course of your research you should arrange to meet your supervisor as soon as possible. Give them a detailed analysis of the problem, and always value their recommendations. The chances are they have been through a similar experience and can give you valuable advice.

You are encouraged to record any problems or changes in the MID-PROJECT REVIEW and PROJECT PRODUCT REVIEW where there is a space on the form for you to communicate such changes.

Finally, it is worth remembering that every problem you encounter, and successfully solve, is potentially useful information in writing up your research. So do not be tempted to dodge any problems you encountered when you come to write-up. Rather, carefully highlight these problems in your REPORT and show the moderator how you overcame them. It's all part of the journey.

MID-PROJECT REVIEW

JAMES'S EPQ ON MEDIA EFFECTS

EPQ title: **To what extent does the media affect children's beliefs about teenagers and what those children are like as teenagers?**

I plan to find out what children believe about teenagers. I will do this by giving children in primary school questionnaires about teenagers that I will design myself.

I will research teenagers in the media and look at research studies into children's development into teenagers.

By MID-PROJECT REVIEW this student had experienced difficulties:

I had difficulty in finding a primary school to visit which had time in their busy teaching schedule to allow the children to complete questionnaires. I therefore decided to change my title to 'Female Heroines in children's literature'.

Moderator comments

James had difficulties gaining access to participants and therefore had to change the focus (and title) of his project. It is very late to do do this because he has to start the approval process all over again.

MID-PROJECT REVIEW

TOM'S EPQ ON FRANCO

EPQ title: **Franco's Spain. From dictatorship to democracy**

In order to research this I am going to look through history text books, journals, encyclopaedias, newspaper archives and to speak to relatives like my father who lived through it.

By MID-PROJECT REVIEW this student had experienced difficulties:

I thought of using newspapers from the time as this source would show important events at the time. But the newspapers have shut down and the archives don't go back that far. I might have to rely on ones that are written in the 21st century.

Most of my other sources are from historians who have written various other books on the same subject, which means they have mostly an unbiased point of view. At the beginning I didn't know where to start so I looked at websites and got information from there about books. I looked at the information and the author and went from there and used the books' bibliography to get more authors.

Initially I thought I would do some research and then plan my essay depending on what I found but when I started it seemed harder to pinpoint what I needed and so I wrote a plan with what I wanted in the essay specifically for each section.

Moderator comments

In this example Tom has a problem with access to information (secondary data) which he seems to have overcome and documented this in his log. Tom also documents his problems composing his essay as a whole. He worked out a plan of the different sections to be covered.

PROJECT PRODUCT REVIEW

WESLEY'S EPQ ON LINCOLN

EPQ title: **Does Abraham Lincoln deserve the title of Great Emancipator?**

By PROJECT PRODUCT REVIEW this student is able to reflect about how his project objectives had changed.

One of the unforeseen obstacles that I have had to overcome was coming to a balanced conclusion and overcoming my biased judgment of Lincoln. Before I started the project I watched the 2012 film Lincoln and after seeing the character brought to the screen as well as my prior knowledge I empathised with him. I was sure that I would end up agreeing with the statement. It came as a shock when I examined more critical interpretations of him. During the course of the research I weighed up all of the different interpretations of Lincoln and in order to have a more balanced account of whether Lincoln was the great emancipator I tried to present arguments for and against the idea and avoided my own opinion in an attempt to arrive at a more balanced conclusion.

Moderator comments

Wesley communicates how his idea about Lincoln has evolved during the course of the research. Many EPQ students may think that they have the answer to the EPQ question before they start and set out to support this. This should not happen. You should avoid your own personal opinion and be objective, stating arguments for and against and then come to a balanced conclusion. This is exactly what Wesley does successfully.

EXERCISE 2.4
Making changes

Four students below describe problems they encountered. Suggest what changes they might make to deal with their problems:

1. *I wanted to look at the criminal justice system in Europe but found that this was too overwhelming.*

2. *I was worried about reaching the word limit.*

3. *I was concerned that I would go over the word limit.*

4. *I wanted to interview a local MP about his views on the badger cull but he did not respond to several of my emails.*

Suggested answers on page 123.

Management tools: production timelines and diary of progress

In order to demonstrate evidence of management some students include additional project management tools such as production timelines and/or a diary of progress. An example is shown on this spread. The student initially states the areas she aims to investigate and then uses production timelines (initial, secondary and final). She also includes a diary of progress and diary of issues.

Although additional management tools are optional, they provide excellent evidence of management. But remember you should refer to these additional management tools in your PRODUCTION LOG.

Megan's EPQ is based around an article in *The Guardian* by Michael Chessum (10 July 2012). This article considered whether the privatisation of higher education and marketisation of Universities will force out bright working-class students.

Megan used an additional management tool which begins with the areas which she wishes to investigate and then an initial production timetable is constructed with key dates and tasks to be completed.

KEY WORDS

Primary data is information observed or collected directly from first-hand experience.

Secondary data is information used in a research study that was collected by someone else or for a purpose other than the current one.

MEGAN'S EPQ ON UNIVERSITIES

Avenues to investigate

Do higher tuition fees force out poorer students?

What are the social and economic reasons for wanting to study at University in the first place?

What were the political reasons for increasing tuition fees?

What are the tuition fees at top universities compared to non-Russell group?

How many students from middle- and working-class backgrounds are applying to university?

- *Choice of A-Levels.*
- *Transition between college and university.*
- *Choice of university – Russell group, standard, old polytechnic.*
- *Choice of subject.*
- *Length of course.*
- *Part-time and summer jobs.*
- *Consideration of options other than university.*
- *Accessibility for all (including less well off, international or mature students).*
- *Gender issues male versus female applications.*
- *Could also consider Open University/part-time study.*

Initial Production Timetable

Dates	Research	Action
25th Sept – 15th October	Research the exact details of how the fees have changed in the past 5 years. Create some primary data from 50 students in YR13 at local Sixth form and FE colleges to see if they are applying to university.	Create a graph to demonstrate change in fees and any changes in overall applications. Compose and begin to distribute/gather questions for students. Respond to replies from universities and summarise what they're saying. Gather in, and pull together, data from students.
17th October – 10th December	Identify wider consequences of working-class students not applying to University – look into youth employment, apprenticeships, the deficit itself, etc.	Compile tables and graphs to show possible trends.
4th January – 1st February	Continue with research on questions above.	Mid-project review, discuss progress with your supervisor once a good part the project has been done.
2nd February – 2nd March	Finish off research.	
25th March – 9th April	Analyse and compile findings and write essay.	
10th April – 14th April	Complete essay, create presentation and finish record book.	Project product review to review successes and failures.

Secondary Production Timetable

Date:	To do:	Notes/To continue with:
9th March – 30th March	Collect primary data Contact more colleges. Contact secondary. Contact more current University students. Collect secondary data Demographic data on existing University students, such as socio-economic background, gender. Find out the most popular long courses.	Complete secondary data collection a identify patterns in the data and draw conclusions. Finish writing and distributing primar data collection methods. Data comparisons. Look at each indicator each day next week.

Tuition Fees

Diary of progress

3rd Sept – Recorded initial idea.

14th Sept – Initial meeting with supervisor, to discuss my project title. Complete record of initial ideas.

16th Sept – Revised project aim following advice from supervisor, came up with some questions I want my investigation to answer, wrote production timetable, and began to draft questions I wanted to ask students.

17th Sept – Part A: Candidate proposal

26th-27th Sept – Created an online questionnaire.

10th Oct – Planning review

17th Oct-10th December – Collected data from online questionnaire.

4th-30th Jan – Continued with research, mid-project review.

27th Feb – Having finished and published my online surveys, I realised that I had no way of organising the data I was collecting. Most of the responses are text answers, so can't be compiled into a simple chart, so I decided to make a 'page' for each question asked, and then copy the received answers onto each of these pages.

7th March – Having contacted about ten sixth form colleges from around the country, some of them had emailed saying that they could not help, because they had no way of asking their students to fill out my questionnaire. However, some have been of more help, offering to circulate the link to their HE students. Whether or not these students continue to fill out my questionnaire remains to be seen, it is, however, a step in the right direction!

9th March – I logged on to my survey account, and was somewhat surprised to see over 100 replies, of which half had been filled out by students from two colleges in Norfolk and Suffolk that I had contacted. The lesson being that, although some colleges won't help, some clearly will. So I plan on contacting a few more colleges today, to see if I can get some replies from the more northern and western counties, and perhaps from London, Wales and Scotland too, to ensure that my questionnaire covers a range of students.

I pulled together my secondary data, and [...] [...]rs. I realised that I needed to manipulate these numbers somehow, to co[...] [...]centages and index numbers. Use 2007 as an index, as this [...] [...]n discussed politically.

UCAS groups subject[...] [...]ta for this, and calculated the change across t[...] [...]s different in terms of employability as E[...] [...]bjects, and to consider the impact of this [...]

11th March – Emaile[...] [...]eady contacted.

> Do not make the mistake of thinking that 'the more I write, the better Grade I will get'. A diary such as this may not necessarily help your final mark. Only produce a diary if you feel it will help your organisation. Lengthy diaries do not impress the moderator – it may even irritate a moderator who has to wade through extra material that has little value. It is perfectly possible to get an A* with just a good quality PRODUCTION LOG, but these extra planning tools can helpful if used appropriately.

Diary of issues

25th Sept – I wanted to make an online questionnaire for current A-L[...] way of collecting data, and from a wider source, as the link could be[...] start building a questionnaire, only to be told half an hour later by a[...] questions, or I could only have 50 responses etc. So I had to re-start[...] would actually give me a template that was suitable for my purpose,[...] presented by Google.

28th Oct – Having put my questionnaire on the Internet via social fee[...] good and helpful results. However, via sites such as Facebook, I have[...] group – all from the same part of the country, whilst those who have[...] the university system. To make my results more valid I need to find a[...] a range of areas.

I also think I need to find students to talk to who have not gone to Uni[...] enough number of these students may be difficult.

I had also stated in my introduction that I wanted to investigate the br[...] this is an extremely wide question which is difficult to research, especi[...] employment may have arisen but this cannot be directly attributed to[...] I need to make this area of my investigation more focused to come to[...]

6th March – Pulling together my data confirmed my worry that my sur[...] more from a wider range of people – I cannot use this data yet becaus[...] range of people. I plan to do this firstly by contacting colleges across th[...] of the people who answered my survey are from affluent backgrounds[...] cost of transport, as well as the places they comes from, is evidence of[...] paper surveys, to give to a wide range of students across the college, k[...] come from less affluent areas of the city. My twin sister who attends th[...] posted the link to my survey on social media sites, asking for people to[...] Hopefully a combination of these ideas will make my survey more valid[...] students feel about the fees.

Having looked at the way in which data is collated on UCAS, it became[...] and the change in the number of applicants, for every single university[...] university even for one indicator was going to take hours, whilst the co[...] 10 Russell group universities, 10 standard universities and 10 former p[...] to investigate. This makes the task much more manageable, and will pr[...]

9th March – I do still think the fact that the students who are most likely[...] problem; however, I do not know how I can get round this situation. Per[...] survey, which I will have to take into account when putting together my[...]

Finally I feel a bit disorganised, having realised that my production time[...] added to it to make a more accurate, better one for between now and m[...]

13th March – I realised that the total data definitely contained details of a[...] colleges.

The **initial production timetable** (on facing page) contains objectives that meet the SMART criteria. The student has used specific words such as compile, create and analyse. Also the objectives are timely – there are specific timeframes in which the tasks need to be achieved.

The secondary production timetable (on facing page) contains timely objectives for the period 9th March for three weeks. Specific action verbs such as 'complete' (rather than 'do') are used. However, some rather too general ones are also used, such as 'contact more colleges' (how many?) and 'more current University students' (what counts as a more current student?). These points could be SMART.

A **diary of progress** (on this page) is also provided which details key dates and gives a clear indication of the activities taking place.

A **log of issues** is provided next with dates and the student gives a candid account of obstacles faced. This provides clear evidence of monitoring your objectives.

A **final production timeline** to finish the project is provided showing key dates and activities.

Final production timetable to finish project – as of 1st April

Date	To do:	Notes/To continue with:
1–7th April	Draw conclusions from primary research regarding transition from college to University (gap year etc.) – see if there is any data on UCAS available for this, although I don't think there is. Collect data from primary research from questions relating to jobs and accommodation (living choices) – as usual, put together into an essay plan with main conclusions and any graphs created. Ensure essay plan is completed, including main concluding paragraph, additional factual research to put in the introduction.	Research and essay plan finished – plan which graphs need creating.
8–14th April	Write introduction and section regarding total applications. Create graph to show change in total applications, index for change since 2006 to show long-term trend.	Written a rough introduction, will need editing but might be easier to do this end. First section on total apps written. Planned list of graphs – create with each relevant section.
15th–20th April	Write section regarding choice of university. Graphs to show percentage change in applications to each University.	Didn't have time to do graphs, do tomorrow.
21st April	Write section regarding choice of subject.	Finished both sections.
22nd April	Write sections related to living choices and transition from college to University – include graphs for employment and for % who defer entry. Write final conclusions to essay. Proofread.	25th – introduction edited, essay all finished, proofreading completed.
24th April	Proofread essay and edit as required. Write first section of project product review. Meet with supervisor for project product review. Produce presentation. Talk to supervisor about this, and change it following any advice given.	As of Friday, presentation has been planned and formed in rough, needs finishing over weekend and into next week (add graphics, more detail to slides).

Management tool: Gantt

To be an effective and efficient researcher you will need to plan your research project carefully to make the most of your time and research opportunities. Your plan will need to be revised over time as your research develops.

The plan will help you quickly identify if you drop behind your targets, giving you the chance to make the necessary adjustments to ensure you complete your research.

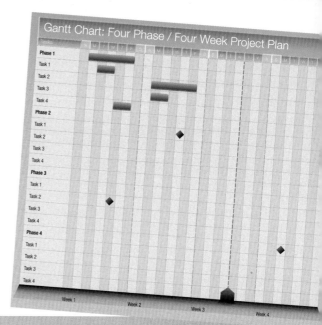

Gantt Chart: Four Phase / Four Week Project Plan

Week 1   Week 2   Week 3   Week 4

Project management tools: Gantt and PERT

On this and the following spread we look at tools – Gantt and PERT – that can be used to help you schedule and manage complex projects.

They allow you to monitor the achievement of project goals and help you to see where remedial action needs to be taken to get a project back on course.

By deciding to use one of these project management tools you will be able to provide the moderator with the evidence that you have applied organisational skills and strategies to meet your stated objectives.

A word of caution

Simply including a Gantt chart, PERT diagram, or diary of progress will not show evidence of monitoring unless you refer to it in your PRODUCTION LOG.

The Gantt chart

A Gantt chart is a horizontal bar chart that shows the timing of each task. Examples of simple Gantt charts are shown above and on the facing page. Originally Gantt charts were prepared laboriously by hand; each time a project changed it was necessary to amend or redraw the chart and this limited their usefulness – and continual change is a feature of most projects. Nowadays, however, with the advent of computers and project management software, Gantt charts can be created, updated and printed easily. Today, Gantt charts are one of the most popular and useful ways of showing activities displayed against time.

A Gantt chart is drawn with many columns.

In the first column of the chart is a list of the activities involved in the completion of a project.

Along the top is a suitable time scale.

A bar represents each activity; the position and length of the bar reflects the start date, duration and end date of the activity.

This allows you to see at a glance:

* What the various activities are.
* When each activity begins and ends.
* How long each activity is scheduled to last.
* Where activities overlap with other activities, and by how much.
* A start and end date for the whole project.

The Gantt chart will help you to visualise the schedule and determine a completion date. During the project, you will be able to determine whether the project is on schedule at various points such as the MID-PROJECT REVIEW. If changes occur, you can utilise the Gantt chart to determine how the changes will affect the completion date.

The first Gantt chart was devised in the mid 1890s by Karol Adamiecki (left), a Polish engineer who had become interested in management ideas and techniques. Some 15 years later Henry Gantt (right), an American engineer and management consultant, devised his own version of the chart and it was this that became widely known and popular in western countries. Consequently it was Henry Gantt whose name was to become associated with charts of this type.

EXERCISE 2.5 Producing a Gantt chart

Below is a list of tasks.

Fill these tasks in the correct order on the first column of the blank Gantt chart on the right.

In the remaining columns indicate when each task might be done.

Tasks:

- Write references and bibliography
- Draft a conclusion
- Final copy
- Plan structure and main content of my essay
- Write general notes on my findings
- Plan and prepare presentation
- Analyse relevant sources
- Research and select various sources
- Gather research on the media
- First draft
- Second draft

Suggested answers on page 123.

Work breakdown: Task to be completed	Week							
	1	2	3	4	5	6	7	8
1								
2								
3								
4								
5								
6								
7								
8								
9								
10								
11								

Preparing a Gantt chart

Many students use a Gantt chart in addition to their PRODUCTION LOG to demonstrate evidence of planning. A Gantt chart is useful for most EPQ projects where the tasks are sequential. The first step in creating a Gantt chart is to list all of the tasks that are required for the project down the left-hand side. One way to create this list is to use a work breakdown structure, a technique for splitting tasks into sub-tasks and creating a task hierarchy.

If you use a Gantt application you enter a date each time a task is finished. Any change in the timing of a task affects all the tasks that depend on it. If a task runs ahead of schedule, the Gantt application automatically recalculates the dates of all the tasks that depend on it in order to take advantage of the time gained. Conversely, if a task is delayed, all the tasks that depend on it are automatically rescheduled, which may or may not impact the overall end date of the project.

By using the Gantt display you can easily add or remove tasks, set or adjust the duration of tasks (length of bars), link tasks (for example, to make one task follow immediately after another), and add constraints (for example, to specify that a task must end no later than a given date).

Linking tasks in a Gantt chart

Project plans normally require tasks to be performed in a specific order. For instance, the initial ideas stage comes before writing the candidate proposal. To achieve this, the Gantt application lets you link tasks so that they depend on each other. By default, tasks are usually linked in a 'Finish to Start' relationship (dependency), which means that the first task you select (the predecessor task) must end before the next task you select (the successor task) can start, and so on.

This is typically represented on the Gantt chart by lines with arrowheads joining each task to its successor (as shown in diagram below). The arrowhead indicates the direction of the link: it goes from the predecessor to the successor.

Gantt charts using Excel

There are various software packages that can create Gantt charts, but one that is more widely used is Microsoft Excel, see tinyurl.com/aqaepq05. There is also GanttProject which is free to use and includes PERT.

Below is an EPQ specific Gantt chart to demonstrate the initial planning stage of an EPQ project. This chart clearly demonstrates the student's activities over a nine-day period leading up to developing an initial title. Notice linking lines between predecessor task and successor task.

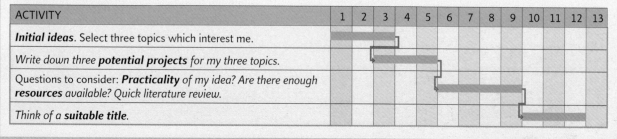

ACTIVITY	1	2	3	4	5	6	7	8	9	10	11	12	13
Initial ideas. Select three topics which interest me.													
Write down three **potential projects** *for my three topics.*													
Questions to consider: *Practicality of my idea? Are there enough* **resources** *available? Quick literature review.*													
Think of a **suitable title.**													

Management tool: PERT

Another planning and monitoring tool is the Program Evaluation Review Technique (PERT). Primarily, the PERT chart identifies the critical path for a project – and so the system is also called the Critical Path Method (CPM).

The critical path is the sequence of tasks to be accomplished with no slack time allowed. In other words, if any task on the critical path takes longer than expected, the end date of the project will be affected.

PERT was developed by the US Navy in the 1950s to manage the Polaris submarine missile programme. A similar methodology, the Critical Path Method (CPM) was developed for project management in the private sector at about the same time.

Thoughts from a moderator

The success of a PERT or Gantt chart depends on how it is used. Just including a detailed PERT/Gantt chart doesn't necessarily add to your project (or your mark). It is a tool for you to use to help keep your project on track.

For some students it is more of a hindrance than a help because the overhead of keeping it up to date can quickly exceed the value it provides.

However, if you do find it helpful, use it, but make sure you refer to it in your PRODUCTION LOG to show the moderator that you are monitoring the timescale of your EPQ.

Fortunately, project management tools such as Microsoft Project or GanttProject can be used to show both the Gantt and the PERT view. So you input your data and can get both views. Therefore a project manager would not necessarily need to make two separate diagrams.

The PERT system

This method is particularly relevant if your EPQ requires that various tasks are completed at one particular point in time – for example, if you are arranging a charity fashion show or a number of people are involved in doing a group project.

What is PERT?

PERT is a model for project management designed to analyse and represent the tasks involved in completing a project. It is similar to a Gantt chart but more complex. It is used to analyse the tasks in a project, especially the time needed to complete each task, identifying the minimum time needed to complete the total project. It allows you to look at optimistic, pessimistic and expected estimates. In practice you would rarely do a PERT analysis by hand; you would use a computer tool such as Microsoft Project.

Why do PERT?

For the same reasons that Gantt charts are useful, PERT is useful. It is a diagram that shows the sequence in which tasks will take place and their inter-dependencies and it includes various estimates of task duration. A PERT chart defines and makes visible dependencies between the tasks. It helps identify the critical path, plus early start, late start and slack time for each activity. It provides for situations where project durations are reduced due to better understanding of dependencies, leading to improved overlapping of activities and tasks where feasible.

EXERCISE 2.6 Producing a PERT chart for a fashion show

On the facing page are a list of activities for a fashion show. Decide which order you would place them in the PERT diagram below by assigning a letter from the PERT chart to each activity. For example, if you think activity A is 'print tickets' than place the letter A next to print tickets.

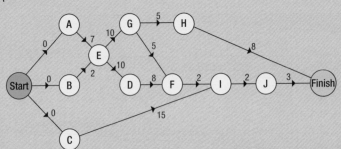

In order to be able to use PERT you need to follow these steps:

1. Create an activity network of tasks to be completed (on left) and a list of each activity and how long each will take (on right). The total amount of time to arrange the fashion show is 18 weeks.

2. Find the critical path for the activities by considering which activities should be started first. For instance, would you print programmes before you know how many tickets have been sold? Can you make the costumes before the models have been chosen?

3. Since the timescale is short you may need to work on some activities in parallel.

PERT versus Gantt: Building a shed (an artefact)

Let's look at how you would use PERT to plan the building of a shed. Then we will compare PERT and Gantt management of this project.

A PERT diagram for building a shed

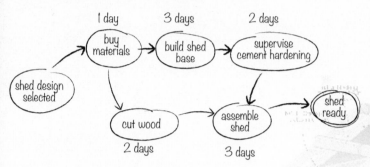

In order to be able to use PERT you need to form an activity network. This is a way of illustrating what tasks need to be completed and how long each task takes and in what order the tasks need to be completed. Clearly when building a shed the base will need to be completed before the roof is erected. The above network diagram shows the relationships (arrows) between the main activities (rectangles) that are required to build a shed. The following information fleshes out some of the activities in the above diagram:

The **cut wood** activity can be carried out in parallel to the **build shed base** and **supervise cement hardening** ones – this of course assumes that you have different teams working on each set of activities.

Critical path

The dark arrows shows what is known as the Critical Path (Buy materials ▶ Build shed base ▶ Supervise cement hardening ▶ Assemble shed). The Critical Path is the sequence of activities that occupies the most time in order to complete your project. Any delay in this sequence of activities will impact the overall timeframe of your project. Therefore, you should carefully monitor all activities on this path.

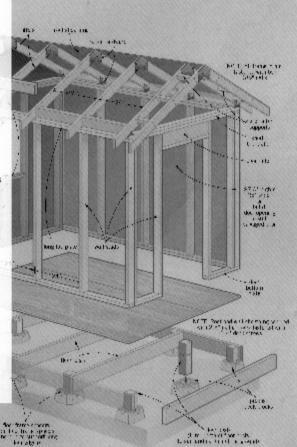

Letter	Activity	Duration
	Arrange seating	3 days
	Print programmes	2 days
	Hire models	7 days
	Make costumes	10 weeks
	Book venue and date	2 weeks
	Advertise	5 weeks
	Sell tickets	10 weeks
	Rehearsal	15 weeks
	Make scenery and props	8 weeks
	Arrange refreshments	2 weeks

A Gantt chart for the build shed project

Name	Begin date	End date
Buy materials	4/1/15	4/1/15
Build shed base	4/2/15	4/4/15
Supervise cement harden...	4/5/15	4/6/15
Cut wood	4/2/15	4/3/15
Assemble shed	4/7/15	4/9/15

Comparing Gantt and PERT charts

A Gantt chart does not show the relationships between the activities of your project whereas the PERT chart does. The PERT chart is sometimes preferred because it clearly illustrates task dependencies. On the other hand, the PERT chart can be much more complicated to compose. Of course you can use both techniques to show how you monitor your project.

Suggested answers on page 123

Chapter 3

Use resources

'**Resources**' are 'a stock or supply of materials, ideas and other assets that can be drawn on by a person in order to function effectively'.

In Chapter 2 you learned about the management of your project. In this chapter we will focus on how to manage the resources that you use.

This includes:

- Critically selecting, organising and using information from a range of sources, including primary and/or secondary sources.
- Analysing and demonstrating the understanding of any links, connections and complexities of the topic.

AO2

Assessment objective 2

The second skill in the mark scheme is 'use of resources'. This will account for 20% of your final mark.

The AO2 objectives include:

- Obtain and select from a variety of resources.
- Analyse data.
- Apply information relevantly.
- Demonstrate understanding of appropriate links.

What the moderator is looking for

- Evidence is required of *detailed* research, using a *wide* range of sources.
- It is important that your research material, taken from different sources, should be *synthesised* together, i.e. combined in a meaningful way.
- Both the sources and the material should be critically *analysed,* i.e. strengths and limitations identified and/or explained and interpreted (what does the data mean?).
- Candidates should reference their written work and provide a bibliography (a list of all the books, articles, websites referred to with details of how they can be obtained).

What's in this chapter

Primary and secondary data

When you do your EPQ you will need data (information). You need facts to achieve your project aim and objectives.

Such data can come from a variety of sources or 'resources'. It will be either:

- Primary data, and/or
- Secondary data.

There is no requirement to use primary data in your study but many students do.

> **A reminder:** If you wish to do a piece of coursework in one of your A-Level subjects, make sure the topic is completely different from anything you will be examined on – otherwise this would count as dual accreditation.

Primary data

Primary data is information observed or collected directly from first-hand experience.

You do not have to use primary data or sources in your EPQ but many students wish to. You must be rigorous in designing your methods to collect primary data.

Collection of primary data is discussed on pages 48–61.

Secondary data

Secondary data is information used in a research study that was collected by someone else or for a purpose other than the current one.

For example, using published data or data collected in the past. In a sense a literature review is a form of secondary data.

Collection of secondary data is discussed on pages 62–71

Triangulation

Triangulation is the process of comparing the results of two or more different studies of the same thing to see if they are in agreement. The studies have often used different techniques, for example if studying pupil–teacher interactions the researcher may use both observations and interviews of pupils and teachers, i.e. two sources of data. You can also use data that you have collected (primary data) to confirm previous research (secondary data) or compare several different secondary sources.

Consider the following research question: Do adopted children experience problems with peer relationships when they reach school?

The issue could be explored from three different perspectives, the teacher, the parent and the pupil, in order to increase validity (the genuineness of your findings). Although triangulation of evidence can be time consuming and often beyond the scope of the collection of the primary data for your EPQ, it reduces the chance of one-sided evidence.

Triangulating sources of secondary data would form a useful avenue for evaluation.

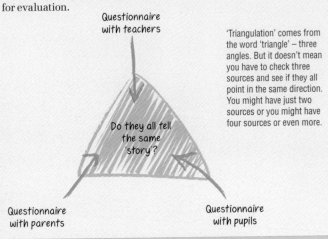

'Triangulation' comes from the word 'triangle' – three angles. But it doesn't mean you have to check three sources and see if they all point in the same direction. You might have just two sources or you might have four sources or even more.

Using primary or secondary data

Do you use primary or secondary sources or both? If you use both this is called dual methodology. Students using primary data will also use secondary data but you can conduct an EPQ with just secondary data.

There are some key issues to consider in terms of resources. If you are collecting primary data you must consider the ethical treatment of your participants (this is covered on the next spread). When using secondary data, there are no ethical considerations in terms of the data itself. However, the nature of the data you use may be socially sensitive and you should be aware of this (see discussion on page 49).

Also remember that your EPQ is a piece of academic work. Writers need to stay current with the language which is sensitive to diverse groups because what was acceptable terminology yesterday may not be acceptable today (Ruderstam and Newton 1992).

Data analysis

Whatever kind of data you are collecting, you do need to analyse it – and analysis depends on the kind of data you have collected from primary or secondary sources.

The data can be quantitative or qualitative:

- **Quantitative** data represent how much or how long, or how many, etc., there are of something; i.e. a behaviour is measured in numbers or quantities.

- **Qualitative** data cannot be counted or quantified. They may be words or pictures and express what people think or feel – though you can also get quantitative data in words about what people feel! The main criterion for being qualitative is that the data is non-numerical.

The way you analyse your data depends on the kind of data it is – there is quantitative data analysis and qualitative data analysis.

Quantitative data analysis

Quantitative data are summarised using measures such as the mean, median or mode. These are called measures of central tendency and express the average:

- Mean – Add all numbers and divide by the total number of items.

- Median – Arrange numbers in order and identify the middle number(s).

- Mode – The value or item that appears most often.

Measures of dispersion are also useful when summarising quantitative data:

- Range – The difference between the highest and lowest number and add 1.

- Interquartile range – Divide the data into four and give the range between the first and third quartile. This removes the influence of extreme values.

- Standard deviation – The spread of the data around the mean. Calculate this using a calculator or Excel.

Probably the most important measure to use is graphical representation because this allows the reader to see your results at a glance:

- Bar chart or histogram – The height of each bar shows the frequency of the item. It is best to display measures of central tendency rather than individual scores.

- Frequency graphs (see top right) are used when the data are continuous and therefore can be joined by a line.

- Scatter diagrams – Used for correlational data.

Using graphs allows you to see the results at a glance

A graph allows you to 'eyeball' your findings and draw conclusions. You can see at a glance from the graph below that more young adults lived with their parents in 2013 than in 1996 and this trend has been steadily increasing since 2002.

Young adults aged 20–34 living with parents in the UK, 1996–2013

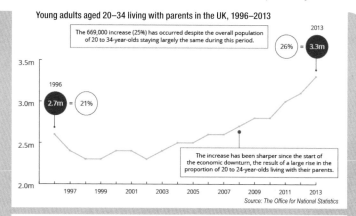

The 669,000 increase (25%) has occurred despite the overall population of 20 to 34-year-olds staying largely the same during this period.

2013 — 26% = 3.3m

1996 — 2.7m = 21%

The increase has been sharper since the start of the economic downturn, the result of a large rise in the proportion of 20 to 24-year-olds living with their parents.

Source: The Office for National Statistics

Qualitative data analysis

If you ask people questions that require answers in words, you will have a mass of data requiring qualitative analysis. If you gather information from different books or websites you will have the same problem. This method of analysis is also suitable for pictures.

Qualitative data is summarised by identifying repeated themes. Qualitative analysis is a very lengthy process because it is painstaking and iterative – every item is carefully considered and the data is gone through repeatedly. The main intention is to impose some kind of order on the data.

There is no one method to use but the following gives some general guidelines:

1. Read and reread the data dispassionately, trying to understand the meaning communicated and the perspective of the author or participants.

2. Break the data into meaningful units – small bits of text that are independently able to convey meaning.

3. Assign a label or code to each unit. These labels/codes are categories for analysis and may be drawn from existing theory or may emerge in your mind as you have read the data. Each unit may be given more than one code/label, i.e. may belong to more than one category.

4. Combine simple codes into larger categories/themes.

5. A check can be made on the emergent categories by collecting a new set of data and applying the categories. They should fit the new data well if they represent the topic area investigated.

6. The final report will be based on the categories, using examples and quotes to illustrate these categories.

Computer programs have been developed to help the process of qualitative analysis. Such programs can search for common words or phrases, or they allow the researcher to code text or pictures. Examples include ATLAS.ti and code-a-text.

EXERCISE 3.1 Quantitative and qualitative

Here is the quantitative description of the picture on the left:

- Picture is 10" by 14"
- With frame 14" by 18"
- Weight 8.5 pounds
- Surface area of painting is 140 sq. in.
- Cost £300

Your task: Write a qualitative description.

Suggested answers on page 123.

Primary data: Ethical issues

Primary data are collected by the researcher(s) themselves. The primary data may be triangulated with secondary sources to reach conclusions.

Remember there is no requirement for you to collect primary data.

Perhaps a good starting point is to consider ethical issues because you will be interacting with live participants.

We may often assume that we know what is right and wrong.

`On the other hand, if morality were nothing more than commonsense, then why are there so many ethical disputes and issues in our society?`

David B. Resnik (201

Ethical considerations

Ethics

The topic of ethics concerns standards of behaviour that distinguish between right and wrong, good and bad, and justice and injustice. Some ethical standards are highly general and apply to all situations, such as being honest or being helpful to others. Other standards apply to specific situations such as medical ethics or ethics when conducting research. We are concerned with the latter.

Invasion of privacy? Tea Room Trade

Humphreys (1970) carried out research into the practices and social interactions of gay men meeting up in a public toilet for sex. He posed as a gay man and acted as a 'watchqueen' – a person who acts as a lookout in exchange for watching sexual activity. Humphreys' role as a watchqueen enabled him to observe 'hundreds of acts of fellation' (page 178). This in itself raises a number of ethical issues but this was exacerbated by the fact that, in order to find out more about his participants' backgrounds, he took their car number plates and used a contact in the police to find out where they lived. 'Fortunately, friendly policeman gave me access to the license registers without ...being too inquisitive about the type of market research in which I was engaged' (page 193). He then allowed a year to lapse, changed his appearance and posed as a health worker to interview the men in their homes. Humphreys concluded that most of the stereotypes about gay men were untrue and that their public sexual practices were not harmful to anyone. He also demonstrated that many of the males were married and lived 'normal lives'.

Humphreys believed that blatant deception was justified by the scientific benefits of the research. However, Von Hoffman (1970) disagreed by saying 'there are certain areas of personal life which are not the domain of "snooping" social scientists' (page 215).

Ethical issues

An 'issue' is something that raises discussion or conflict. An ethical issue is a conflict between what a researcher wants and the rights of participants. They are conflicts about what is acceptable. For example, a researcher wants to collect meaningful data but this may mean having to deceive participants about the aims of a study. A participant may understandably feel insulted by such deception.

Informed consent

Participants should give permission or consent before they agree to take part. 'Informed' means that they know exactly what the aim of the study is and what they will be required to do. You should also inform them of any potential risks. TV programmes often contain a prior warning such as: 'there is some flash photography', 'there are scenes that some viewers will find disturbing'. These messages give viewers prior warnings of the risks involved and the option to switch channels.

In general you should not provide incentives for the participants to take part and certainly no coercion!

Deception

The problem with fully informed consent is that knowing the aims of a study may affect the honesty of participants – they may behave differently if they know what the researcher is investigating. Therefore researchers sometimes do not tell participants about the true aims of a study or mislead them in some way. In some cases this is only a minor issue, for example saying that a study is about social relationships but not saying that attitudes to obedience are being examined.

Participants can be debriefed at the end of the study (discussed on the next spread) and told what the study was actually about, but this may not make up for any feelings of being cheated. Even with debriefing participants' right to fully informed consent has been negated by the deception.

The British Psychological Society publishes information on ethics and standards in research with human participants.

See tinyurl.com/aqaepq06

Right to withdraw

Even if a participant has signed a consent form before the study they must be made aware that they are free to withdraw from the study at any time. This means that, if they do become uncomfortable about the procedures, their well-being is assured.

It is difficult for a participant to really anticipate what will be involved, even if it has been fully described to them. Furthermore, a researcher may not fully anticipate what will happen. As McNamee *et al.* (2007) comment, 'the nature of the problem to be investigated is fluid, incompletely determined at the beginning of the study, and subject to change as the study progresses' (page 135). As such, it is a challenge to foresee and plan for the ethical concerns that might have arisen during the time of a research study. The right to withdraw compensates for this.

Participants must also be able to request that the data they have given be removed from the study. Even if pseudonyms or a coding system is employed the right to withdraw data must be respected.

Below is an example from an EPQ project where the student explains how the right to withdraw was included:

Children in the study were encouraged to give voice to their perceptions and feelings about how their learning difficulties affect their time in schools, and the behaviours which they display. By its very nature, this process invoked emotive memories and feelings. Bringing their behaviours into conscious thought processes may have also invoked heightened levels of emotional awareness. The extent to which these types of possible risks may occur was impossible to quantify or anticipate in full prior to the start of the project; a point which was magnified due to the longitudinal nature of such qualitative research (Economic and Social Research Council 2006). In anticipation of difficulties in this regard, participants, parents and the schools were, at the outset, given information on their right of withdrawal from the processes of this research.

EXERCISE 3.2
Identifying potential ethical issues

Consider the following EPQ topics. Does the topic raise any ethical issues and if so identify the issues raised?

1. A questionnaire to investigate attitudes towards (hydraulic fracturing).

2. An observation study to investigate whether people buy more 'Big Issue' magazines when it is sunny compared to when it is raining.

3. A small-scale survey to investigate whether teenagers have taken class A drugs.

4. An experiment to investigate magnetic field patterns.

5. An questionnaire which asks primary school children whether they have nightmares on a regular basis.

6. An experiment to investigate the effect of nitrous oxide on teenagers.

7. Examining the effects of alcohol in respiration in yeast.

8. To investigate whether alcohol decreases reaction time in PE students who are playing table tennis.

Suggested answers on page 123.

BBC News 2/1/2014
The lawyer who revealed that crime writer Robert Galbraith was actually *Harry Potter* author JK Rowling has been fined £1,000 for breaching rules of confidentiality.

Protection of participants

The researcher should assess the level of risk involved in their study as they have a duty not to cause either physical or psychological harm to their participants. Ethical guidelines state that participants must not be exposed to harm greater than they would experience in everyday life. At the outset the participants should be informed of potential risks but some reactions may not be anticipated.

Physical harm is more clear-cut and might include intrusive interventions such as the administration of drugs or other substances, vigorous physical exercise, or techniques such as hypnotherapy. The majority of participants would not encounter such interventions in the course of their everyday life.

Psychological harm is more difficult to clarify. For example, there would be minimal risk involving brief questionnaires that ask about favourite TV programmes. On the other hand, questions relating to parental alcoholism or illegal behaviour may pose greater risk in that the questions make the respondent feel uncomfortable. Embarrassing participants or making them feel foolish constitutes psychological harm.

Here is some guidance on research that would normally be considered to involve more than minimal risk:

- Research involving concealment or deception – research where there is deliberate concealment or that which is conducted without participants' informed consent.

- Participant groups where permission of a gatekeeper is normally required – ethnic or cultural groups, native peoples or indigenous communities, young children in school or those with a learning disability, cognitive impairment or mental illness.

- Data collection involving access to records of personal or confidential information – genetic or other biological information, concerning identifiable individuals.

- Sensitive topics – sexual behaviour, illegal or political behaviour, experience of violence, abuse or exploitation, mental health, gender or ethnic status, addiction, etc.

- Questionnaires should not imply that it is normal or right to belong to a specific ethnic group or to have a particular sexual preference or engage in a particular lifestyle. This unintentional sexism may creep into the design of a study at various levels (McHugh *et al.* 1986).

- Research that would induce psychological stress – asking sensitive questions, for example, may cause anxiety or humiliation.

Anonymity and confidentiality

A distinction should be made between anonymity and confidentiality. Anonymity means that no one, including the researcher, knows your identity. Whereas confidentiality means that the researcher will preserve your identity by using a code or pseudonym.

Making data 'anonymous' means removing the participant's name. However, you will often need to take more than this basic step to protect a participant's identity. Removing a name may not be enough because, when pieces of information are presented together (such as age, job title and strongly expressed opinions), it may become easy to identify someone.

On the other hand, participants may want to be identified. Grinyer (2002) suggests that in some research contexts, it is possible that participants may be keen for their own voices to be acknowledged, and are happy for their identity to made known alongside their contribution to the research.

If participants explicitly state that they wish to be identified then a guiding principle is that participants need to be in control of the disclosure of their identity and their contribution.

Privacy

Privacy refers to a person's right to control information about themselves. Both confidentiality and anonymity are related to this – it is your right to decide who gets to know what about you.

Protecting privacy is sometimes difficult in observational studies, for example when observing people in a public park. There is an assumption that it is acceptable to record the behaviour of others if they are in public but there is no universal agreement about what constitutes a public place (read about the Tea Room study on the facing page).

Primary data: Dealing with ethical issues

When conducting your own research you need to balance your requirement to conduct meaningful research against the rights and feelings of your participants. On the previous spread we have discussed some of the ethical concerns facing researchers. One of the ways of dealing with such issues is to avoid certain kinds of research. However, in any study, even those that are ethically quite sound, there are steps that must be taken to protect participants.

Before the study: Gaining informed consent

A consent form should contain the following information:

- **The rationale for the study** including aims or research questions. If you are not giving this information at the outset you must ensure that your study has gained approval from your supervisor.

- **Why the participants have been selected** to take part.

- **Information about their right to withdraw** at any time during the study or to withdraw their data at the end of the study.

- **Information of what they are required to do.** They must be provided with sufficient information to be able to make an informed decision as to whether to participate.

- **Details of how data will be stored.** For example, whether their information will be held anonymously or how their confidentiality will be protected. The storage of data will need to comply with the **Data Protection Act (1998)**. The Act states that anyone who uses data has to follow strict rules that are called 'data protection principles'. Anyone who uses data must ensure that the information is: kept for no longer than is necessary, kept safe and secure, used for the intended purposes and used fairly and lawfully. The Act also has stronger legal protection for sensitive information including ethnic background, sexual health, criminal records and religious beliefs.

Whose consent?

You should first of all seek the consent of headteachers or heads of department who known as *gatekeepers*.

However, this is not sufficient, you must a obtain the informed consent of the partic

In the case of individuals under the age of you must also gain informed consent from parents.

Here is a exemplar form seeking informed consent from a gatekeeper

RORY'S EPQ ON SEBD

Dear Headteacher

I am writing to you to seek your consent to conduct a study in your school.

Rationale
This study will explore concepts of Drama and Social, Emotional and Behavioural Difficulties (SEBD). In applying a range of methods including field notes taken during classes and recordings of discussions with students, it will look to give voice to the students' experiences and perceptions of Drama. We want to put the child at the centre of the research.

Aims
To listen to, appreciate, and interpret the perceptions and experiences of secondary school pupil s with SEBD to Drama.

To identify areas of similarity and difference, between cases, in their experiences of Drama.

Case Study Procedures
Various data collection methods will be used over the course of five to six weeks. Methods are likely to include both informal conversations, and formal interviews discussing a variety of issues regarding the thoughts of children about Drama and how they perceive it as affecting their behaviour. As part of this research Drama lessons will also be observed and field notes will be taken. In some instances, photographs may be taken during Drama lessons and used during interviews and focus groups as mediating artefacts which will help improve the information gleaned from the interactions with the participants. Some information on your school (i.e. behaviour policy, etc.) will also be useful in this case.

Possible Risks, Discomfort, Safety and Injury
There are no direct physical risks associated with this study other than those normally associated with participation in Drama. If children involved in this study experience pain, discomfort or injury they should notify their class teacher.

It is possible that reflecting upon and discussing their behaviour might make the children feel uneasy. The discussion of past experiences may also do this.

If this is the case, the child is encouraged to make this clear to the researche immediately who will then endeavour to make every effort to alert relevant persons at your school to this fact. This will be discussed with the child and their parent/guardian at the onset of this research. If the children involved have any thoughts or concerns as a result of this process then they will be encouraged to discuss these with the researcher, the Special Educational Needs Coordinator, or the Educational Welfare Officer.

Benefits
The children involved may feel that the self-reflective process embedded in procedure is beneficial to their own behaviour. By taking part in this researc your school will be helping us to increase the knowledge base of this subje area, which may benefit the children in the future.

Can the participant stop taking part?
The children identified by your school as being suitable to engage in this research can change their mind and decide to withdraw from this project any time.

What information will be collected, and how will it be used?
Data will be collected using the procedures outlined above and will then analysed for the purposes of an Extended Project at High Clare School. will likely include notes taken by the researcher, transcripts of conversatio (both formal and informal) and notes made by the children.

If any work resulting from this research is published then no identifiable characteristics of either your school or the participants will be made pub Pseudonyms will be used for both your school and the participants invo copy of the completed results will be given to you if you ask for them.

Please keep this information sheet for your records; you can, however, questions about the project at any time. Please contact me directly usi contact details below.

Many thanks for your support,

Rory Jones (EPQ student)

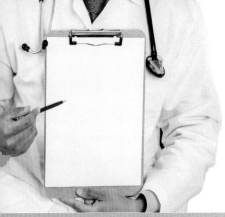

EXERCISE 3.3 Debriefing

On this spread we have given the informed consent and debriefing forms that would be used for the staff in the school where data was being collected.

A debriefing form would also be needed for the students. Use the elements listed below left to produce a suitable debrief for a study where a questionnaire on dreams had been given to teenagers aged 12–18.

Remember to use simple language throughout. Your purpose is to inform not to confuse the participant.

After the study: Debriefing

A 'briefing' is when a person is given details of an event that is about to happen; a 'debriefing' involves giving the details of an event after it has happened. The need for debriefing arises mainly because a researcher has not fully revealed the aims of the study beforehand because these may affect the participants' behaviour.

The need for debriefing might also be because an initial briefing was simply not possible – for example, if you are observing the behaviour of people in the street. After you have observed them you might stop and explain what you did (you might have photographed them or simply written down what they did). This could not have happened beforehand and therefore informed consent must be sought retrospectively.

Elements to include in a debriefing form

Debriefing may be written or oral but should contain various points including:

- The title of the study.
- Thank the participant for their time.
- Provide a full explanation of the purpose of the study and how the findings will be used (if you weren't able to when asking for informed consent).
- If you have used deception or concealment, carefully explain the nature and reasons for deception.
- Confirm that their results are confidential or anonymous.
- If participants are uncomfortable about any procedures, remind them that they have the right to withdraw their data.
- If the study involves any kind of possible stress, the participant must be informed of possible counselling they can receive.
- Participants must be informed that, should they require further information about the results of the study once it is completed, they can contact you. Provide up-to-date contact details. You should also include details of your supervisor or centre coordinator should a participant wish to express concern about the study.

...onsent form to be signed

...ease read the following statements carefully. Sign only when you have agreed ...ith all of the statements and when you have had any relevant questions ...nswered.

...have read the information sheet for the study, and the full details of the data collection procedures have been explained to me. I am clear about what my school's involvement will be in this study and I am aware of the purpose of the study.

I trust that results will only be used in complete confidentiality and for the academic purpose of this study.

I have received copies of what information will be sent to parents, including the introductory letter containing the parental consent form and the participant consent sheet.

I am satisfied that the results will be stored securely, remain confidential, and if published will not be linked to this school or the children within it in any way.

I hereby give my full consent for the study to be undertaken providing written consent of the involved participants and their parents is also obtained.

Name .... (Head Teacher)

Signature .... Date ....

Name .... (Special Educational

Needs Coordinator)

Signature .... Date ....

Name .... (Head of Drama)

Signature .... Date ....

Here is an exemplar debriefing form

RORY'S EPQ ON SEBD

EPQ title: To what extent does drama influence children with behavioural difficulties?

I wanted to write to you to formally thank you and your staff for their support during my research at The Big School.

I have worked across many departments during the past six weeks and have had contact with a lot of members of staff. Everyone has been very accommodating and supportive and for that I extend my thanks. Special thanks must also go to Mr Thomas and the Drama Department for their daily support and interest in my work. I would also like to express my gratitude to the three participants – Beth, Tom and Sally – for their involvement and maturity throughout the process.

As promised, I will share with you a copy of my results if requested. For reasons of anonymity and confidentiality I will only be able to do this once I have completed my EPQ but will honour my commitment to you once this is complete. Once again, many thanks for your support.

Best wishes,

Rory Jones EPQ Student

Primary data: Sampling

'Sampling' is the process by which you select the participants in your study. According to Shipman (1981) sampling is 'the systematic way of choosing a group that is small enough to be convenient for data collection and large enough to be representative of the population from which it has been selected' (page 59).

Selecting a sample

In order to consider whether a sample is representative you need to clearly define your target population – that is the group of people at whom the research is aimed. If you wish to investigate the attitudes of UK teenagers then this is the group you need to represent in your sample. If you are just interested in urban UK teenagers then your target population is just people in that age group who live in cities and you should sample from that group.

In reality, samples tend not to be representative. For example, you might take a sample of teenagers in your school and claim this represents all British teenagers. Such claims may not be justified and need to be explained. For instance, you might argue that the students in your school represent a range of socio-economic groups and cultural groups and thus are representative of the UK in general.

Shipman (1981) suggests that the problem of real representativeness of samples applies to many subjects, 'the historian has to be wary of generalising about a past population from evidence left by the rich who could afford to leave written records...the criminologist [relies] on criminals who had been caught rather than those who were successful in getting away with crime' (page 60).

If the entire target population is relatively small, such as pupils in a school who suffer from social emotional and behavioural difficulties (SEBD), then the researcher can include the entire population in the study. This type of research is called a census study because data is gathered on every member of the population. No method of sampling is required.

Under normal circumstances the target population is too large for the researcher to attempt to study all of its members. In this case a method of sampling is required. Sampling methods are broadly classified as either probability or nonprobability.

Probability sampling

- **Random sampling** is where each member of the target population has an equal chance of being selected. A random technique is used, such as the lottery method where all names are in a hat or tumbler and the required number are drawn out.

  However, if the target population is large it is often difficult or impossible to identify every member of the population, so a subset is selected and then it is not a truly random sample. A further issue is that of those people identified, some people will not take part so you do not end up with a random sample.

- **Systematic sampling** is when every nth name (e.g. 5th or 20th) is taken from a list such as an electoral register or a telephone directory (the target population).

- **Stratified sampling** is a method commonly used when surveying people's opinions for market research or opinion polls. Participants are selected according to their frequency in the population. Subgroups (or strata) within a population are identified (e.g. boys and girls, or age groups: 10–12 years, 13–15, etc). Participants are obtained from each of the strata in proportion to their presence in the target population. A researcher first identifies the relevant strata and their actual representation in the population. Random sampling is then used to select participants from each stratum.

  Here is an example of how it can work. If your target population is a school of 700 pupils, you might identify year groups as your strata. The number of students in each year group will determine the sample randomly selected from the year group. This means that if there were twice as many students in Year 8 than Year 12 you would select twice as many in the sample for Year 8.

KEY WORDS

Population All the people in the world.

Representative In sampling, a sample selected so that it accurately stands for or represents the target population being studied.

Sample A selection of participants taken from the target population being studied and intended to be representative of that population.

Sampling The process of taking a sample. Can be either probability or nonprobability.

Target population The group of people that the researcher is interested in. The group of people from whom a sample is drawn. The group of people about whom generalisations can be made.

EXERCISE 3.4 Sampling methods

Identify the sampling method in each of the studies below:

1. A questionnaire was given to a group of students in a local comprehensive school, selected by placing all the students' names in a container and drawing out 50 names.

2. A group of Psychology students interviewed shoppers in a local shopping centre about attitudes towards dieting.

3. A researcher put a notice on the noticeboard in the sixth form common room asking for participants who have an hour to spare.

4. A researcher selected the first five names in each class register for every school he visited.

5. Various subgroups in the population were identified and then members from each subgroup were randomly selected.

Suggested answers on page 123

Nonprobability sampling

In nonprobability sampling some members of the target population have no chance of selection.

The advantage of nonprobability sampling is that it can be a more economical way of obtaining participants. For example, if people volunteer for a study they are less likely to subsequently withdraw. However, the degree to which the sample differs from the target population remains unknown in nonprobability sampling.

- **Convenience (opportunity or availability) sampling** is when the sample is selected because the participants are available or convenient to obtain. An example of this is when you select the first ten people you find to complete your questionnaire. These ten people may be those who happen to be in the Sixth Form common room at the time. This is probably the most common method used in research.

- **Self-selected (volunteer) sampling** is when participants will put themselves forward to take part. They may respond to an advertisement on a school noticeboard or in a newspaper asking for volunteers. In the latter case there is the potential for a more varied sample of participants – on the other hand the typical profile of the readership will be a significant biasing factor.

  A particular danger with the representativeness of a self-selected sample is that there may be something unusual about those who volunteer. They may, for example, be especially keen to please the researcher.

- **Quota sampling** is the nonprobability equivalent of stratified sampling. Convenience sampling is then used to select the required number of participants from each stratum. This differs from stratified sampling, where the strata are filled by random sampling.

  Consider this example: A market researcher is given a list with the type of persons to contact based on their gender, social class and age. The interviewer will have a quota of each type of respondent she has to interview. She might be asked to interview five working-class women aged 25. She will then go to an area where she will find women who fit this category. Bias can occur with this type of sample as it can depend on the judgement of the interviewer to fill her quota so she may approach certain types of people who will look more welcoming rather than approach a mother with four demanding children.

- **Snowball sampling** is useful when a researcher wishes to find participants who belong to particular groups, such as people with eating disorders or people who have travelled to Africa. Imagine a large snowball rolling down a slope getting bigger and gaining momentum as it does. This analogy can help to explain this sampling technique, which relies on referrals from initial participants to generate additional participants. One participant can recommend other similar individuals. However, the problem is that the sample may ultimately not represent a good cross-section from the population because it is friends of friends.

The position of the researcher – insider/outsider status

Insider researcher

When carrying out research the researcher may be located within the community they are studying, e.g. a homosexual male studying same-sex marriage or a heterosexual male studying same-sex marriage. Both scenarios will raise the issue of bias versus neutrality.

It has been widely argued that the researcher must be part of the social group he or she is researching in order to truly understand participants' experiences. For example, when studying religious groups, ethnic minorities or disabled people – if you are an outsider then you will not be able to fully comprehend or represent their experiences (Charlton 1998).

Asselin (2003) suggests the insider researcher should gather data with her or his 'eyes open' and assume that she or he knows nothing about the phenomenon being studied. Asselin points out that, although the researcher might be part of the culture under study, he or she might not understand the subculture. For instance, a female researcher studying premenstrual syndrome may not have experienced this condition in the same way that other women have.

Outsider researcher

A different perspective is taken by Tinker and Armstrong (2008) who argue in favour of an outsider status approach when conducting research. They maintain that in some cases, being on the outside 'can provide a valuable sense of distance, which can allow the researcher an insight into other people's social worlds' (page 58).

Tinker and Armstrong give four ways in which outsider status can be used to elicit rich and meaningful data from respondents:

a) Elicit detailed responses.

b) Minimise the respondents' fear of being judged.

c) Ask some questions that a researcher from the same cultural group may not feel able to.

d) Maintain a critical distance from the data.

Outsider status can serve to place the respondent in a position of an expert, which will serve to empower them. Respondents may also be more willing to share things with an outsider for less fear of being judged.

While they acknowledge that outsider status could potentially limit a researcher's understanding of the material, it can also improve data analysis by allowing the researcher to maintain a sense of critical distance from the topic of investigation.

(Adapted from Tinker and Armstrong 2008 page 58)

Primary data: Self-report techniques

If you do wish to collect primary data you must be quite rigorous in the methods you use. One of the most common methods used by students is questionnaires. The next few spreads provide guidance about how to ensure your questionnaire (or interview) is fit for purpose.

At the beginning you should establish some aims for your data collection, i.e. stating what you intend to find out.

You might also include one or more hypotheses. See page 61 for more about aims and hypotheses.

Self report: Questionnaires and interviews

Questionnaires and interviews are both called 'self-report methods' because people tell you their thoughts and feelings – whether they give you truthful answers is another matter.

A well-designed questionnaire can gather information in an economical way from a range of people. However, a poorly designed questionnaire may produce invalid results. Research based on your own measuring tool that has been hastily thrown together may lack validity and will be of little scientific value. The safer option may be to use an existing questionnaire (or psychological tests on intelligence or personality), which have been pre-tested for reliability and

validity (see information on page 57). Many of the same principles apply to interviews.

There are a number of key steps in the design and use of questionnaires and interviews that we will consider:

1. Develop the questions to be asked (see below and facing page).

2. Design a good questionnaire (see facing page).

3. Conduct a pilot study (see page 56).

4. Test the reliability and validity of the questionnaire (see page 57).

5. Decide on your participants (see pages 52–53).

Questionnaire versus interview

A questionnaire has a fixed set of questions that are generally answered in writing without the researcher present. A questionnaire can be delivered in person with the researcher asking the questions, but this becomes more like an interview because some interaction between respondent (person answering the questions) and questioner is inevitable. For example, the respondent might ask for a question to be explained and then the questioner may unconsciously influence the answer given.

There is one special advantage of using questionnaires: Once you have designed your questionnaire, you can then give it out to a large number of people relatively easily. This means you may collect a large amount of data.

There is one special advantage of interviews: The interviewer can adapt questions in response to the answers given, which may allow unexpected information to be collected and/or information that is in greater detail.

Developing good questions

A leading question steers a person toward one answer rather than another. For example, if I ask you 'Do you get headaches frequently' and then asked about how many you get every week, what would you say?

When researchers asked people this question they found the average answer was 2.2 headaches per week. But when they asked a slightly different question 'Do you get headaches occasionally?' (instead of saying 'frequently') people estimated an average of just 0.7 headaches. The way the question was asked affected the answer given, i.e. it was a leading question.

When designing open or closed questions there are three guiding principles:

1. **Clarity** Questions need to be written so that the reader (respondent) understands what is being asked. There should be no ambiguity. *What does ambiguity mean?* Something that is ambiguous has at least two possible meanings. For example, 'Did you see the girl with the telescope?' could mean 'Did you see the girl when you were using the telescope' or it could mean 'did you see the girl who was using a telescope'. There are other factors that reduce clarity:

   - Avoid jargon, colloquialisms or slang – ensure that the question wording caters for all levels of literacy. Some words may be unfamiliar such as the acronym ASBO. Also remember for some respondents English may be their second language.

   - Avoid double-barrelled questions, such as 'Do you suffer from sickness and headaches?' Ask for one piece of information at a time. 'Do you suffer from

sickness?' and 'Do you suffer from headaches?'

   - Avoid double negatives – in other words don't ask respondents whether they agree with a negative statement, as in the case of asking people to agree or disagree with the statement 'Capital punishment should not be abolished'. Use the positive 'Capital punishment should be abolished'. The latter is much less confusing.

2. **Bias** The way questions are worded might lead a respondent to be more likely to give a particular answer (as in a leading question, see box on left). The major problem is *social desirability bias*. Respondents prefer to give answers that make them look more attractive, nicer, more generous, etc., rather than being totally truthful. For instance, they say that they read *The Times* rather than *the Sun*. Socially desirable answers are also more likely with sensitive questions, for example asking people about use of illegal drugs or sexual practices; people will answer in more socially accepted ways. Bias

can be minimised if the questions are worded carefully, for example 'How many times have you broken the law by responding to an important text on your mobile when you were driving?' could be rephrased 'How many times have you prioritised sending a text when driving in order to obey the law?'

3. **Analysis** Questions should be designed with analysis in mind. Once a researcher has collected in all data, the answers need to be summarised so that conclusions can be drawn. There are two broad categories of questions:

   - *Closed questions* have a fixed set of answers and collect quantitative data because the answers can be counted.

   - *Open questions* collect qualitative data because the answers will differ from one person to the next and cannot be counted.

(Quantitative and qualitative data are discussed on page 47.) A questionnaire can contain a mix of open and closed questions. The same is true for an interview.

...sign a good questionnaire

...good questionnaire should contain good questions (obviously). Some ...her things to consider when designing a good questionnaire:

Order of questions It is best to start with questions that will encourage respondents to keep going.

- Start with easy rather than difficult questions that require quite a lot of thought.
- Start with questions that don't make respondents feel anxious or defensive, such as personal questions. These are best left until they have relaxed.
- Start with factual rather than abstract questions so that respondents don't give up straightaway.
- Start with relevant questions so they feel the questionnaire is worthwhile.
- Start with closed format questions which are less taxing to do.

Variety In order to maintain the respondents' interest and to improve the response rate, a variety of question formats could be employed.

Response set This is the tendency for people to respond in the same way to all questions, regardless of context. For example, a tendency to say 'yes' or to circle a middle value. In order to avoid a response set with, for example, a Likert scale (see below) you could switch the positive and negative sides of the scale so it was sometimes agree to disagree and sometimes disagree to agree. Also if you present an even number of options it prevents the respondent from circling the middle value in the Likert scale.

Filler questions It may help to include some irrelevant questions to mislead the respondent from the main purpose of the survey. This may improve their honesty and reduce *social desirability bias* because they are less aware of what you are really trying to find out.

Distributing your questionnaire You can either hand the questionnaires to respondents for them to complete and ask them to return it to you. Alternatively, they can post it back or email. SurveyMonkey is an easy way to create and publish a survey online. It includes step-by-step guidance (see www.surveymonkey.com).

EXERCISE 3.5 Questionnaire design

Identify at least FOUR possible problems with this questionnaire and TWO positive points.

....

Student questionnaire

Student name:

Age: 11–12 13–14 14–15 16–17 18+

Academic year (please circle): 7 8 9 10 11 12 13

Boarding house (please tick):

Baxter	[ ]	Witley	[ ]
Potter	[ ]	Dudley	[ ]
Harris	[ ]	Foster	[ ]
Maybury	[ ]	Prospect	[ ]

Rate the subjects you are currently studying:

	Really like it		It's OK			Hate it			
....	10	9	8	7	6	5	4	3	2	1
....	10	9	8	7	6	5	4	3	2	1
....	10	9	8	7	6	5	4	3	2	1
....	10	9	8	7	6	5	4	3	2	1
....	10	9	8	7	6	5	4	3	2	1

What do you think makes a good lesson?

Suggested answers on page 123.

Examples of closed questions

Choice of categories

'What is your relationship status?'

Single [ ]   Married [ ]   Civil partnership [ ]   Living together [ ]

Divorced [ ]   Separated [ ]   Widowed [ ]

Likert scale

'Capital punishment would reduce crime.' Circle your answer:

Strongly disagree... Disagree... Don't know.. Agree... Strongly agree

Differential scales

'How would you rate the sixth form enrichment lecture on the rise of the Roman Empire?' Circle the number that represents the extent to which you agree with this statement:

Extremely interesting 1 2 3 4 5 6 7 8 9 10 Extremely dull

Checklists

'Circle the A-Level subject choices you are interested in.'

Maths, Geography, History, Law, Sociology, Psychology, Biology

Ranking

'Please rank each animal in terms of fearfulness.' (1 = most fearful, 8 = least fearful)

Rat, rabbit, dog, cat, bird, fish, snake, slug

Examples of open questions

How would you describe your relationship status?

Do you think that capital punishment reduces crime? Explain your answer.

Which animals scare you?

Advantages of open questions	Advantages of closed questions
The data obtained from an open question can be more detailed and gives more insight into respondents' attitudes.	Quantitative data is obtained which is easier to analyse because the answers can be added up and expressed using graphs and other descriptive statistics (such as the mean and range).
The respondent is able to expand on their answer to a question such as 'Are you in favour of capital punishment? Please explain your answer.' This encourages thought and allows freedom of expression.	Quicker for respondents, which may improve the response rate to the questionnaire. With open questions respondents may be put off by having to provide lengthy explanations for their answers.

Disadvantages of open questions	Disadvantages of closed questions
Less literate respondents may be discouraged.	The permissible responses are restricted so a respondent may not be able to give the answer that best represents their experiences or thoughts. They are forced into a particular kind of answer.
Time consuming for respondents to complete.	The respondent is unable to expand on their answer.
Time consuming to analyse and difficult to summarise; a researcher may misinterpret the response.	Acquiescence or response set may occur where a participant will answer 'don't know' to all questions.

Primary data: Self-report techniques (continued)

On this spread we will consider ways to review and improve your questionnaire (or interview). We start with a pilot study and then consider how to test reliability and validity.

KEY WORDS

Pilot study It is a small-scale preliminary investigation carried out before the main study to detect any problems or ambiguities so that adjustments can be made. It is sometimes also called a feasibility study.

Why carry out a pilot study?

In order to find out if there are any problems with the design, instructions for participants or the measuring instruments used. Any revisions can then be made before the final study.

Reliability Reliability is consistency. If you use a ruler to measure the height of a chair and then find, the next day that the measurement was different, you would probably think the chair must have changed because you would expect the ruler to be reliable (consistent). If the fluctuation were due to some change in the ruler it would be pretty useless as a measuring instrument – not dependable, consistent or reliable.

Any tool used to measure something must be reliable.

Consistency can be measured within a set of scores or items (internal reliability) and also over time – we would expect the same person to produce the same answers if tested a second time (external reliability).

Validity The concept of validity refers to whether an observed effect is a genuine one. This includes the extent to which a researcher has measured what he/she intended to measure (internal validity) and the extent to which the findings can be applied beyond the research setting to other people and/or to other situations (external validity).

Use Excel to calculate a correlation coefficient to check reliability

Excel is a Microsoft Office spreadsheet application, which is on most computers.

- *On an Excel sheet enter your data in two columns.*

- *To obtain the correlation coefficient, place the cursor in an empty box and type '=correl('. This is now the formula box.*

- *Then click on the top of one column and drag the cursor to the bottom of that column so the column is selected. The values for this column should appear in your formula box. The formula should look something like this: =correl(a6:a13*

- *Type a comma in the box.*

- *Repeat with the second column of data.*

- *Finish with a closing bracket. The formula should now look something like: =correl(a6:a13,b6:b13)*

- *When you press return the correlation coefficient should appear in this box.*

- *If you have 20 pairs of data and correlation coefficient of +.38 or −.38 is good (a negative number means there is a negative correlation). A lower figure means that the two sets of data are not well correlated. You can use the table on the right to check how good the correlation coefficient is.*

To see a scatter diagram click and drag your cursor from the top left to the bottom right of the two columns. From the toolbar menu select 'chart' and select 'XY scatter'.

Pilot study

You will now be aware of the complexity involved in designing questionnaires and so a pilot study should be conducted to address any ambiguities in the questionnaire before you go on to use the questionnaire in your actual study. You don't want to find yourself with 100 filled-in questionnaires only then to discover that most of the respondents couldn't make sense of some of the questions.

Stage 1

Select a small sample that is representative of the target population to take part in your trial run. This will usually involve no more than five participants. The pilot study may address a number of issues that can then be resolved prior to the main study:

- Check that instructions and ethics forms (consent and debrief) are easy to understand. Instructions should be 'standardised' so they will be exactly the same for each participant.

- Check that the questions in the questionnaire are understandable and did not confuse any of your test sample.

- If a test is used, check that the questions are not too easy, which results in a ceiling effect – everyone does well and gets top scores showing no differences. Alternatively, you might find a floor effect – the questions are too hard and everyone scores almost zero.

- Check that you are sufficiently skilled in the procedures.

- Check the correct operation of equipment.

You could also assess the reliability of the questionnaire at this stage by doing a test-retest (see facing page).

Stage 2

Make any changes necessary and then repeat the pilot study with a new sample to recheck your changes.

The table below tells you what values are considered significant in relation to the number of pairs of data you have (N).

Significance table	
N =	Correlation coefficient needed for significance
4	1.000
8	.643
12	.503
16	.429
20	.380

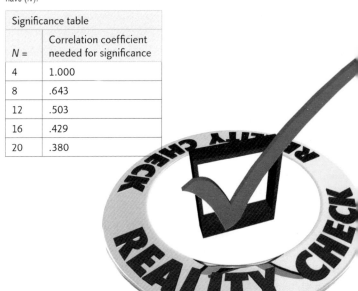

EXERCISE 3.6 Assess validity and reliability

Go online and check out a few psychological tests. Try to assess their validity and/or reliability as we have done for the SPQ on the right:

- **What stress type are you**? Some people are 'Type A' whereas others are 'Type B'. Complete a questionnaire here: tinyurl.com/aqaepq07
- **Are you extraverted or introverted**? See tinyurl.com/aqaepq08
- **Emotional intelligence** can be assessed at tinyurl.com/aqaepq09

Considering reliability

Internal reliability

Internal reliability relates to whether questions on the test are measuring the same thing. You may have deliberately included some filler questions (e.g. lie scale items, see bottom right of this page) and these should be discarded when assessing internal reliability.

The most commonly used method is called *split-half reliability*. This is calculated by comparing two halves of a test, questionnaire or interview. This can be done by placing question 1 on Form A and question 2 on form B and so on. Or the questions can be divided using a random method.

Therefore you end up with two forms of the same test. Each form should yield the same score if the items on the test were consistent. The two scores can be compared by calculating a correlation coefficient (you can do this using Excel as shown on the facing page).

To improve low internal validity you should remove the test items that produce the least similarity. You can do this by removing certain items and seeing if there is a stronger correlation with the remaining items.

External reliability

When testing external reliability the key thing to remember is you must use the same people and the same questions. For example, the same interviewer must interview the same person twice using the same questions, and then the outcomes are compared. If the interview is reliable your result will be the same if you do it a week later.

This method is called *test–retest reliability*. The two scores can again be compared by calculating a correlation coefficient.

The interval between test and retest must be long enough so that the participant can't remember their previous answers but not too long because then their thoughts or feelings or even abilities may have changed and we would expect their scores to be different.

Low external reliability may be due to a number of factors. For example, a poorly trained interviewer may not be consistent in the way they are asking questions and this may lead to different answers. Therefore the interviewer needs better training.

Or it might be that the test items or questions are ambiguous and therefore participants are not consistent in the answers they give. Therefore the questions should be examined again.

Considering validity

Internal validity

On the previous spread we mentioned ambiguous questions, *leading questions* and *social desirability bias*. All of these will affect the validity of a questionnaire – if a person is not able to give an answer that reflects what they truly feel or think then the data collected will lack validity.

External validity

On pages 52–53 we considered sampling – the issue of who do you give your questionnaire to. If you only give it to A-Level students this will restrict the validity of your questionnaire. Your findings will only apply to this group of people (low *population validity*).

External validity also involves the question of whether the findings can be generalised beyond the research setting, most importantly whether 'social scientific findings are appropriate to people's everyday natural setting' (Bryman 2001) – responding to questions on a questionnaire may not reflect how an individual would respond to the same situations in everyday life. This is called *ecological validity*.

Testing spider phobia

You can use pre-existing questionnaires on the Internet such as a spider phobia questionnaire (SPQ) which can be accessed at www.mun.ca/biology/bpromoters/spider_questionnaire.php

The SPQ contains 31 questions, for example:

> Question 19. The way spiders move is repulsive.

> Question 21. If I came across a spider when cleaning an attic I would probably run.

Internal reliability: use the split-half technique.

External reliability: use the test–retest method.

Internal validity: consider whether any of the questions are ambiguous or leading, and whether any of them might lead to a *social desirability bias*. You might also consider whether the questions actually relate to spider phobia.

External validity: consider what groups of people you can generalise the findings to. Can we generalise the findings to young children or adults? Can we generalise the findings to people in France or China?

Ecological validity: responding to questions about spiders on a questionnaire may not reflect how an individual would respond in real life if they actually saw a spider. Consider if you were asked 'I would not walk into a room where there was a spider' you may respond 'yes I would' but if you walked into your bedroom and actually saw a large spider on the ceiling you may have to remove it before you went to sleep.

A lie scale

One way to assess whether people are telling the truth is to include a few questions that act as 'truth detectors' to test truthfulness. For example, asking 'Are you always happy?' The truthful answer is 'no' but a person who wishes to present themselves in a positive light (social desirability bias) may be tempted to answer 'yes'. Respondents who lie on a high proportion of lie scale items may not be giving truthful answers on the rest of the questionnaire.

Primary data: Observational techniques

T he most obvious way to investigate what people do is to observe their behaviour – if you ask people what they do they may be dishonest or may simply not know what they do. Observation allows a researcher to obtain direct evidence.

Recording data

When we watch somebody perform a particular action we see a continuous stream of action rather than a series of separate behavioural components. In order to make a reliable and objective record of what we observe we need to break this stream of behaviour into a set of component behaviours. For example, when observing infant behaviour you can divide this into component behaviours such as smiling, crying, sleeping, etc., or when observing facial expression you can create a list of different expressions.

This set of component behaviours is referred to as *behavioural categories* or a *behaviour checklist*.

Sometimes each behaviour is given a code to make recording easier and then the method is called a *coding system*.

When you make observations you then count occurrences of the component behaviours.

Behavioural categories should:

- Be clearly operationalised and objective. The observer should not have to make inferences about the behaviour, for example having a category such as 'being happy' and having to say 'he's smiling and therefore must be happy'. All categories should be directly observable.

- Cover all possible component behaviours and avoid a 'waste basket' category for all behaviours not covered elsewhere.

- Be mutually exclusive, meaning that you should not have to mark two categories at one time.

Observing bears in a zoo

Jordan and Burghardt (1986) undertook a study of black bears in a zoo in order to determine whether the presence of observers altered the animals' behaviour. They did this to establish whether naturalistic observations of animals were in fact 'naturalistic' – if the animals' behaviour was affected by the presence of observers then it wasn't so natural after all.

In this study they selected two bear enclosures in parks in the USA, one at Dollywood, Tennessee (less observed by people) and the other at Tremont, Pennsylvania. They found a much higher activity level at Tremont where the bears had more human contact.

You could conduct your own observational study at a zoo based on some of the procedures of this study. The researchers spent one hour each day making recordings over a two-and- a-half year period. Observations were recorded every 30 seconds (time sampling) using a behaviour checklist/coding system similar to the one below.

Behaviour checklist and coding system for recording postures and locations of captive black bears
Activity level 1: Reclining postures
    Lying on back (P6)
    Lying on front (P7)
    Lying on side (P8)
    Lying/sitting in a tree (P28)
Activity level 2: Sitting or standing
    Standing on all fours (P3)
    Standing on two feet (P29)
    Sitting erect or semi-erect (P4)
Activity level 3: Bipedal standing and slow locomotion
    Standing on two feet while touching an object (P1)
    Walking on all fours (P11)
    Rolling over (P18)
Activity level 4: Vigorous activity
    Running (P19)
    Ascending (e.g. trees) (P24)
    Descending (e.g. trees) (P27)
    Running a short distance and then walking (P32)
    Jumping (all legs off ground) (P35)

Sampling procedures

In an *unstructured observation* data is recorded continuously – every instance of the behaviour seen or heard by the observer is recorded (possibly using behavioural categories). This is possible to do if the behaviours the researcher is interested in do not occur very often.

In many situations, however, continuous observation is not possible because there would be too much data to record. Therefore there must be a systematic (structured) method of sampling observations:

- **Event sampling** Counting the number of times a certain behaviour (event) occurs in a target individual or individuals. For example, counting how many times a person smiles in a 10-minute period.

- **Time sampling** Recording behaviours in a given time frame. For example, noting what a target individual is doing every 30 seconds. The researcher may tick items in a checklist.

Some other things about observations

Naturalistic and controlled

In a *naturalistic observation* the researcher does not interfere in any way but merely observes the behaviour(s) in question. The researcher may use behavioural categories or a coding system to record observations (as on the left).

In a *controlled observation* behaviour is observed but under conditions where certain variables have been organised by the researcher. For example, the bears' environment might be changed to see how that affected their behaviour (as at Tremont in the example on the left).

Overt and covert

If a participant is aware of being observed (*overt observation*) they may alter their behaviour so validity is reduced.

This can be overcome by making observations without a participant's knowledge (*covert observation*), such as using one-way mirrors. This may raise ethical issues regarding invasion of privacy.

Participant and non-participant

In some observations the observer is also a participant in the behaviour being observed (*participant observation*) which is likely to affect objectivity. More often the observer is not a participant (*non-participant observation*)

Considering reliability

Observations should be reliable, as with all methods of collecting data. We need to feel confident that if the observations were repeated with the same participants the data would be the same (i.e. consistent).

One way to check reliability is to compare the observations made by two observers. If they are reliable they should produce the same record. The extent to which two (or more) observers agree is called *inter-rater reliability* or *inter-observer reliability*.

This is calculated by dividing the total agreements by the total number of observations. A result of +.80 or more suggests good inter-observer reliability.

Considering validity

Internal validity

Observations will not be valid (or reliable) if the behavioural categories/behaviour checklist/coding system is flawed. For example, some observations may belong in more than one category, or some behaviours may not be codeable. The result is that the data collected does not truly represent what was observed.

The validity of observations is also affected by *observer bias* – what someone observes is influenced by their expectations. This reduces the objectivity of observations.

External validity

Observational studies are likely to have greater *ecological validity* than some other kinds of research because they involve more natural behaviours.

Population validity may be a problem if, for example, children are only observed in middle-class homes.

Evaluation of using observations

Advantages	Disadvantages
What people say they do is often different from what they actually do so observations may be more valid than, for example, questionnaires.	The observer may 'see' what he/she expects to see. This is called observer bias. This bias may mean that different observers 'see' different things, which leads to low inter-observer reliability.
Observations provide a means of conducting preliminary investigations in a new area of research, to produce hypotheses for future investigations.	If participants don't know they are being observed there are ethical problems such as deception and invasion of privacy.
Naturalistic observation gives a more realistic picture of spontaneous behaviour, therefore higher ecological validity.	If participants know they are being observed they may change their behaviour.

Content analysis
(a kind of observation)

If you have a newspaper article or a series of TV programmes that you wish to analyse to identify key themes, content analysis is a way of doing this. A *content analysis* is what it says – the analysis of the content of something.

Content analysis is a form of indirect observation; indirect because you are not observing people directly but observing them through the artefacts they produce. These artefacts can be TV programmes, books, songs, paintings, etc.

EXERCISE 3.7 Content analysis

For this activity you are going to do a content analysis of children's picture books to examine how books expose children to natural environments and animals.

Step 1: Read the abstract from *The Human–Environment Dialog in Award-winning Children's Picture Books* (see tinyurl.com/aqaepq10)

Step 2: Select at least two illustrated books to analyse. The books should relate to animals and also environments (some books, such as an illustrated alphabet, might not have any environments).

You could consult the list of Caldecott Medal award winners – a prize awarded annually to the most distinguished American picture book for children (see tinyurl.com/aqaepq11).

Step 3: For each animal in the book place a tally mark in the appropriate position in the table below.

One tally is shown for a book with a cat lying by the fireside.

		Animal			
		Wild (lion, tiger, etc.)	**Domesticated** (dog, cat pet rabbit, etc.)	**Anthropomorphic** (animals acting like humans)	**Total**
Environment	**Natural** (not created by humans)		I		
	Built (spaces entirely made by humans)				

Step 4: Draw conclusions

- What trends in the presentation of the animals in various *environments* did you see in your book?
- What trends in the presentation of animals did you see in your book?
- Based on the evidence you collected, what messages about the environment would a child receive from these books?

Alternative – analyse the way men and women are portrayed in children's books or children's films or popular songs.

Primary data: Other research methods

You may be planning an experiment, correlation or a case study. In which case the taught element of your EPQ may cover what you need to know. If not, on this spread, we provide some basic information.

KEY WORDS

Confounding variable A variable that systematically varies with the IV and therefore may explain the results instead of the IV under test.

Extraneous variable 'Nuisance' variables that muddy the waters and make it more difficult to detect a significant effect.

Ecological validity Being able to generalise a research effect beyond the particular setting in which it is demonstrated.

Validity refers to whether an observed effect is a genuine one.

Note that not all studies conducted in a lab are experiments. Controlled observations are conducted in a lab. And some studies conducted in the 'field' are just field studies not field experiments.

Experiments

The key feature of an experiment is that it can demonstrate a cause-and-effect relationship. For example, it can show that noise actually *causes* people to do lower quality homework or that high temperatures *cause* aggression.

The reason why this is possible is that, in an experiment an independent variable (IV) is directly manipulated by the experimenter in order to observe its effects on the dependent variable (DV). This means that any change in the DV was *caused* by the IV as long as there were no confounding or extraneous variables.

Observation and self-report

The IV and DV in an experiment may be measured using observation or self-report measures. For example, if we want to find out if high temperatures cause aggression we could use:

1. Observation: Put some people in a room that is normal in temperature and other participants in a room that is quite hot (the IV is the temperature of the room) and observe participants' behaviour (DV).

2. Self-report: Measure the DV (aggression) by asking participants questions about their current emotional state.

Correlations

Studies that use a correlational analysis allow a researcher to determine whether there is a relationship between two co-variables. No causal relationship can be demonstrated.

Investigations

There are some occasions when a study doesn't fit into any of these categories. There is no IV or DV, or co-variables. It's just an investigation.

Evaluating experiments and correlations

Type of study	Advantages	Disadvantages
Lab experiment To investigate causal relationships between an IV and DV in a special environment where all variables can be controlled.	Well controlled, therefore the effect of confounding/extraneous variables can be minimised, thus higher validity. Can be easily replicated (repeated) because all variables are identified and controlled, demonstrating validity.	The task or environment is contrived, and/or participants may be aware they are being studied and therefore the behaviour measured is not 'everyday' behaviour. Investigator may unwittingly communicate expectations and influence participants' behaviour
Field experiment To investigate causal relationships between an IV and DV in more natural ('everyday') surroundings.	Less artificial, and therefore usually higher ecological validity. Participants are often not aware that they are participating in an experiment and therefore their behaviour is more 'natural'.	Less control of extraneous variables, reduces validity. The task used may be quite artificial, reducing ecological validity. More time-consuming and thus more expensive
Natural (quasi) experiment The IV varies or differs without the action of the researcher – in other words something else has caused it to change but not the experimenter. The DV may be measured in a lab.	Allows research where IV can't be manipulated for ethical or practical reasons. Enables psychologists to study 'real' problems such as the effects of a disaster on health (increased ecological validity).	Cannot claim to demonstrate causal relationship because IV not directly manipulated. Participants may be aware of being studied, thus reducing validity.
Correlation Co-variables either increase together (positive correlation) or, as one increases the other decreases (negative correlation). There may be *intervening variables* that can explain why the co-variables being studied are linked.	Can be used when it would not be ethical or practical to conduct an experiment. If the correlation is not strong then you can rule out a causal relationship. If the correlation is strong then further investigation is justified because there may be a causal link.	Cannot show a cause-and-effect relationship. People often misinterpret correlations and assume that a causal relationship has been identified whereas this is not possible (for example, the correlation between smoking and cancer does demonstrate that smoking causes cancer).

Where to begin?

The beginning of any study involves stating your *aims* – describing what it is you intend to investigate in your research study. For example:

- In this study I am going to investigate why some people are more helpful than others.

In experimental research you also produce a *hypothesis* (or several hypotheses). This is a statement of what you believe to be true. It is what you aim to demonstrate. For example:

- Women are more helpful than men. (directional hypothesis)
- Younger people are less helpful than older people. (directional hypothesis)
- Younger people are different from older people in terms of helpfulness. (nondirectional hypothesis)

In a correlational study a hypothesis is also stated but this time it states a correlation rather than a difference. For example:

- Helpfulness is related to age. (nondirectional hypothesis)
- Helpfulness increases with age. (directional hypothesis)

Operationalisation

Variables in a hypothesis must be operationalised, i.e. defined in a way that they can easily be tested. For example, instead of saying that the DV is 'helpfulness' an experimenter must specify a way to measure this, such as measuring how long it takes for a participant to go to help a woman who fell over.

What happens at the end?

Once you have collected data, the last step is to use a statistical analysis:

- **Descriptive statistics** involve the use of graphs – such as representing mean values in a bar chart or drawing a scatter diagram.
- **Inferential statistics** allow you to calculate whether your findings are significant (see page 84). You may find a difference between women and men in terms of helpfulness but is it so small that it does not represent a meaningful difference? Guidance on the use of inferential statistics can be found in specialist books, for example Cara Flanagan's *The Research Methods Companion for A-Level Psychology*.

Case studies

A case study is the detailed study of one case (!) – but the case could be one person, one group of people (such as a family or a football team or a school) or an event.

A case study may be conducted within a short space of time (one day) or may follow the case over many years.

The key feature of a case study is that a lot of information is collected about the case and this is likely to involve a variety of techniques – interviews, psychological tests, observation, and even experiments to test what an individual can or can't do.

The information may be collected from the case being studied or from other people involved, such as family and friends. The information is likely to be qualitative but may include quantitative data, too.

A case study may be about unusual individual(s) or events, such as a person with brain damage, or may be about 'normal' people or events, such as a day in the life of a typical teenager.

Evaluation of case studies

Advantages
The method offers rich, in-depth data. This means that information that may be overlooked using other research methods may be identified.
Can be used to investigate instances of human behaviour and experience that are rare (for example, mental illness) or cases which could not possibly be created in research laboratories (for example, cases of damage to specific areas of the brain).
The complex interaction of many factors can be studied, in contrast with experiments where variables are separated out.

Disadvantages
Most case studies take a long time for the collection and analysis of data, which means they require time, effort and money.
It is difficult to generalise from individual cases as each one has unique characteristics and/or because we can't make before and after comparisons.
It is often necessary to use recollection of past events as part of a case study and such evidence may be unreliable because people's memories are inaccurate.
Researchers may lack objectivity as they get to know the case, or because their theoretical biases may lead them to interpret the data less objectively.
There are important ethical issues such as invasion of privacy and confidentiality – many cases are easily identifiable because of their unique characteristics, even when real names are not given.

EXERCISE 3.8 Experiments

One picture is a composite of the left side of Cara's face and the other a composite of the right side of her face. Some psychologists believe that the left side of your face (connected to the right side of your brain) should be better at displaying emotion.

1. What is the aim of this experiment?
2. What is the IV?
3. What is the DV?
4. How is the DV operationalised?
5. How could you assess the reliability of the DV?
6. State a hypothesis for this study.
7. If participants do select the right hand photo more often, what would you conclude?
8. Explain why it might be better to have several pairs of photos constructed in a similar way.

Suggested answers on page 123.

Secondary data: Range of sources available

The Internet contains a vast amount of academic resources. It is therefore not surprising that it is becoming increasingly popular as a research tool.

It is important to note that the moderator will check your references section and, even if your references are entirely Internet based, this will not matter as long as there are a variety of sources.

What is important is that the Internet is used carefully and critically. An article written by a columnist in a newspaper or a blogger on the Internet will not have been subjected to the scrutiny involved in published academic research. Textbooks and academic journals are subject to a process called *peer review* where other academics express their views on the accuracy of the information (peer review is discussed on pages 68–69). You should be mindful of this. Anyone can put anything they want on a website; there is unlikely to be any review or screening process.

It is important to critically evaluate Internet-based sources – and indeed apply the same to any sources you use.

Wikipedia

As you will probably know, Wikipedia is a free online encyclopedia. Wikipedia is not wicked, but relying solely on Wikipedia may not be advisable, as you will be marked on the range of *sources that you select.*

Also be warned that in some academic circles Wikipedia is not regarded very highly because it is written collaboratively by volunteers from all around the world. Anyone with Internet access can make changes to Wikipedia articles (read http://en.wikipedia.org/wiki/Wikipedia:About).

On the other hand there are editors who regularly review all material to check accuracy. It is also the case that the number of users acts as a kind of peer-review system.

Whose website is it?

.edu is used by many educational institutions.

.gov many government sites use this extension.

.org tends to be sponsored by non-profit organisations, some of which are reliable sources and some of which are very biased.

.com have commercial or corporate sponsors who probably want to sell you something.

The Internet

Here are a few basic guidelines to remember when conducting Internet research:

- Cross check – You should always cross check Internet sources against other sources such as journals, books and encyclopedias. This is a good way to make sure that the material is reliable and authoritative.

- Be selective – You can easily be overwhelmed by the amount of information that is available on the Internet. Before you start your search, think about what you're looking for, and if possible formulate some very specific questions to direct and limit your search.

- Use peer-reviewed subject directories and search engines – These are excellent places to start your academic research on the Internet. INFOMINE and Academic Info are good examples of high quality peer-reviewed subject directories containing links selected by subject experts.

- Use a variety of search engines – Major search engines such as Google and Yahoo differ considerably in how they work to find different things for you. It is therefore a good idea to always use more than one search engine.

- Use a specialised search engine – Beaucoup includes 2,500 + search engines and directories. Alternatively, the Search Engine Colossus International Directory of Search Engines includes search engines from 230+ countries around the world. Google Scholar also gives access to academic abstracts, although you may have to pay a fee for access to the full article.

- Record accurate details of the sites you search – It is necessary to keep track of the sites that you visit primarily to refer to them in your references. In order to get the Internet address right (it is easy to make a transcription error when writing complicated Internet addresses) save in your favourites. This also will help if you need to revisit the site.

You may wish to use the table below in order to keep an accurate record of the Internet sites you visit. You can include it in your report, in the appendix.

Title of page	
Author/ organisation	
URL (full address starting with http:// which can be copied from the address bar in your browser).	
Date of publication/last update (usually at the bottom of the page).	
The last date you accessed the information.	
Where you have used the material.	

Other credible sources

A-Level textbooks

A-Level textbooks can also be a useful starting point to look for further references at the back of the textbook. However, the moderator will expect you to do research beyond your A-Level texts. If your references section just contains A-Level textbooks then this is not going to demonstrate a range of resources.

Books

You will not be expected to read the entire book when conducting a literature review. Instead, search the book for relevant information by examining the preface and table of contents. If there is a relevant section or chapter then read this section, which may throw up other useful avenues to explore. You can also search inside some books on Google Books using key words and sometimes the contents page will be available. Some books will have been peer reviewed (see the next section) and are therefore reliable sources of information.

Academic journals

There are thousands of scholarly journals publishing over one million research papers each year. They differ from 'popular' magazines because they contain in-depth reports of research. The articles are written by academics and are peer reviewed. These can often only be accessed from a University library though more and more are becoming open access online.

The abstracts of such articles are provided on Google Scholar and provide a brief overview of the aims, method and conclusions of the study.

Newspaper articles

Newspapers and magazines provide information on current happenings around the world; they also provide information for research, entertainment and leisure. According to Njeze (2013) 'most students read newspapers to broaden their knowledge and keep abreast of the recent developments and to enhance their academic performance' (page 2). McMane (2001) observed that newspapers are an inexpensive way to enhance classwork by providing the basics for studying different subjects from basic literacy to the highest level of critical thinking. Most newspapers have websites where current and past articles can now be accessed online.

TV programmes

A documentary may provide a useful source of information or may even provide inspiration for an EPQ topic.

Watch out

Don't assume that everything you read is true. Check more than one source.

Here's an example:

It was reported that Gordon Brown liked to wake up to the band 'The Arctic Monkeys'. This was a misquote. In an interview with 10-year-old children on Channel Five, he was asked if he was a fan of the Arctic Monkeys. Brown replied 'At least with the Arctic Monkeys they'd wake you up in the morning because they are so loud'.

This appeared in a newspaper as 'Brown wakes up to the Arctic Monkeys'.

Less credible sources include: blogs by organisations that may have an ulterior motive such as an article about the Badger Cull written by the League Against Cruel Sports.

EXERCISE 3.9 Consideration of available sources

Use the table below to consider which sources would be relevant for your EPQ topic.

Source	Example of source suitable for your topic	Would this be a good source to use? (Yes or no)	Justification for your decision
Internet			
Wikipedia			
Textbook			
Book			
Academic journal			
Newspaper article			
TV programme			

Secondary data: Using different sources

For assessment objective 2 (AO2) the moderator is looking for:

- Evidence of detailed research, using a wide range of sources.
- The research material should be synthesised together.

'Synthesis' means to combine two or more entities together to form something new or to form a connected whole.

So you must use different resources AND try to synthesise them together. One way to do this is to conduct a literature review.

Using different sources

Consider the following EPQ title 'To what extent can bullying lead to tragedy?'

This EPQ was inspired by a Channel 5 documentary *Bullied to death: The tragedy of Phoebe Prince*, broadcast on 23 September 2013. Fifteen-year-old Phoebe Prince moved with her family from Ireland to America in September 2009. In January 2010, after months of bullying at the hands of school classmates, Phoebe hanged herself.

There are various other reports of this case. One article on Slate.com was a different version of events to that presented by Channel 5 (see tinyurl.com/aqaepq13). This article was written by Emily Bazelon who argues that 'the story of Phoebe's death is more complicated than the narrative that had taken hold in the media'.

This shows how important it is not to rely on just one source. Using information from various sources will help you critically evaluate the sources that you have used. The next spread provides more detail on evaluation.

Moderator comments

The EPQ does not demand that a literature review is carried out but, by conducting a literature review, you will show the moderator that there are clear links between the aims and objectives of your EPQ and previous published research in your chosen field.

Furthermore, the literature review can also demonstrate to the moderator how and why you have selected some resources and disregarded others.

You should decide whether a literature review is appropriate for your discipline.

According to Rudestam and Newton (1992) a common misunderstanding is that a literature review is a `laundry list of previous studies with sentences or paragraphs beginning with words, "Smith found...Jones concluded"'.

Synthesising your sources: A literature review

The term 'literature' refers to what has been written or said about a particular topic – books, articles, videos, and so on. You may have conducted a brief literature review when deciding on your aims for the project but now is the time to consolidate this review.

Ridley (2008) provides a comprehensive definition of a literature review:

'[An] extensive reference to related research and theory in your field, where connections are made between source texts that you draw on...it is an opportunity to show that you have engaged with and responded to the relevant body of knowledge underpinning your research' (page 2).

The purpose of a literature review is to convey what knowledge and ideas have been developed on a topic. It also aims to establish the strengths and weaknesses of the literature to date.

Ridley makes a very helpful point when she states that the literature review is an 'ongoing activity which begins when you pick up your first book or article related to your research and continues until you finish the final draft' (Ridley 2008, page 3).

'The literature review is not a compilation of facts and feelings, but a coherent argument that leads into the description of the proposed study' (Ruderstam and Newton 1992, page 47).

Carrying out a literature review

When your supervisor has approved your title you can then begin to find information for your literature review. In the end you may not use everything you have read but, to begin with, read widely and make notes.

Put the notes to one side and then from memory construct a logical plan.

- A literature review is like a funnel. It begins quite wide – you may use a few paragraphs to discuss the general area of study.
- Then narrow down to the specific area of your project and review expert evidence that is relevant.
- You may group items together, for example writers who share one view and then writers who share a different view. You can also include evaluation of the previous literature.
- The review should lead logically to your aims.

What the literature review should NOT be

- A descriptive list that just summarises one piece of literature after another. Do not begin each paragraph or sentence with the name of a researcher.
- A compilation of facts and feelings: 'In my opinion capital punishment is justified', or 'I feel that animal research is cruel and unnecessary'.
- An exhaustive list of everything you have read. You must be selective.
- You should not include irrelevant material. For example, if your project aims to address whether Henry Kissinger was an effective politician, is it relevant to know about his childhood? Rather than writing everything you know about Henry Kissinger select relevant literature on his effectiveness as a politician.

An example of a bad literature review

EPQ title: **To what extent do we seek partners of the same levels of attractiveness?**

Psychologists have proposed various explanations for interpersonal attraction:

1. Evolutionary: We seek partners who are physically attractive, possibly because this is evidence of their good reproductive potential. Features considered attractive: a good complexion, white teeth.

2. The matching hypothesis: We actually seek a partner whose physical attractiveness matches our own physical attractiveness.

Studies on the matching hypothesis include:

Walster et al. (1966) carried out a study called the 'Computer Dance experiment'. About 400 students were invited to a freshers' week dance and told they would be paired with a similar partner (in fact they were paired randomly and judges rated each student in terms of physical attractiveness). At the end of the dance students were all given questionnaires including a question about whether they would like to see their partner again. Walster et al. found that students were most likely to want to see a physically attractive partner again rather than one who was more of a match.

Walster and Walster (1969) repeated the study and they did find support for the matching hypothesis probably because this time the participants spent time together beforehand and were given a choice of who to partner. This time they did prefer someone who matched their own perceived physical attractiveness.

Silverman (1971) conducted an observational study of couples in public places (such as bars and theatres). The couples were between 18 and 22 and unmarried. Observers independently rated the couples on a 5-point scale and found high similarity between members of a couple. The observers also noted that the more similar the attractiveness, the happier the couple were rated in terms of the degree of physical intimacy (e.g. holding hands).

Murstein (1972) asked couples who were engaged or going steady to rate their own and their partners' attractiveness on a 5-point scale. Independent judges also rated the participants' attractiveness. The similarity ratings for couples were compared with ratings made of randomly paired couples. Murstein found that real couples were significantly more similar than the randomly paired couples.

> JUSTIN'S EPQ ON ATTRACTIVENESS

Moderator comments

Why is it bad? It is organised by listing relevant studies with no attempt to link or synthesise this information.

In addition it does not attempt to evaluate the studies.

The example on the right places each study in context and relates them to each other (i.e. synthesises them together) rather than just saying 'Walster did a study ..' and Silverman did a study …'. The better example also leads logically to the aims and states these clearly.

EXERCISE 3.10 Synthesising sources

The first step, when synthesising information, is to determine how your sources are alike or different, whether they agree or disagree and whether they reach the same conclusions. As you identify connections, remain objective and present quotations to illustrate key points.

Read the following two passages on euthanasia.

1. Write a one-sentence summary of each source's position on the topic.
2. List one point of agreement.
3. List one point of disagreement.

Passage 1: Many religions have a strong view on whether euthanasia is morally right or wrong. Pope John Paul II said 'It is suffering, more than anything else, which clears the way for the grace which transforms human souls'. Allowing euthanasia undermines the commitment of doctors and nurses to saving lives. Euthanasia affects other people's rights, not just those of the patient.

Those who believe this think that suffering is part of the moral force of the universe, and that by cutting it short a person interferes with their progress towards ultimate liberation. M Scott Peck, author of *The Road Less Travelled*, has written that in a few weeks at the end of life, with pain properly controlled, a person might learn 'how to negotiate a middle path between control and total passivity, about how to welcome the responsible care of strangers, about how to trust and maybe even, out of existential suffering, at least a little bit about how to pray or talk with God' (Verkaik and Laurance 2002).

Passage 2: According to a report in *The Independent* newspaper (March 2002) many people think that each person has the right to control his or her body and life and so should be able to determine at what time, in what way and by whose hand he or she will die.

And behind that lies the idea that human beings are independent biological entities, with the right to take and carry out decisions about themselves, providing the greater good of society doesn't prohibit this. Allied to this is a firm belief that death is the end. However, euthanasia affects other people's rights, not just those of the patient Supporters of euthanasia say these are good reasons to make sure the euthanasia process will not be rushed, and agree that a well-designed system for euthanasia will have to take all these points into account (Peck 1978).

Suggested answers on page 123.

An improved version

We have used a similar study in Appendix III. Below we have identified how this material synthesises the evidence to produce a much better literature review. Read the complete version on page 117.

'Love is often nothing but a favourable exchange between two people who get the most of what they can expect, considering their value on the personality market' (Fromm 1955)

… Relationships start with interpersonal attraction. Psychologists have proposed various explanations for interpersonal attraction. One view is that we seek partners who are physically attractive ….

An alternative view is the matching hypothesis, which suggests that people aspire … Based on Lewin's (1935) level of aspiration theory, the matching hypothesis suggests that we actually seek a partner whose physical attractiveness matches our own physical attractiveness. … Walster et al. (1966) suggested that people are attracted to those of a similar level of physical attraction to their own ….

The matching hypothesis focuses on physical similarity but, as Price and Vandenberg (1979) found, couples can be similar in other ways …. Buss (1989) studied men and women in 37 different cultures and found that men sought partners with youth and physical attractiveness and valued fertility … So matching may involve more than matching for physical attractiveness alone.

Walster et al. (1966) tested this hypothesis in a study called the 'Computer Dance experiment'. … However, this study was criticised because it didn't relate to real life relationships very well. When Walster and Walster (1969) repeated the study they did find support for the matching hypothesis ….

Further support for the matching hypothesis has been found in studies of real life couples. Silverman (1971) conducted an observational study of … Murstein (1972) asked couples who were engaged or going steady ….

As online dating is increasingly common as a way of meeting people Shaw Taylor (2011) conducted a series of studies to investigate whether the matching hypothesis applied to online dating ….

All of these studies support the matching hypothesis in a variety of different settings and in relation to couples in varying stages of a relationship.

Aims

The aim of this study is to replicate Murstein's research, adapting the original design. Instead of actually asking participants to rate their own attractiveness, this study will use photographs of married couples and require participants to rate the attractiveness of the people in the photographs. We would expect couples to be similar (matching) in attractiveness because they have chosen each other. They should go for someone of a similar level of attractiveness rather than someone who is much more or much less physically attractive.

Secondary data: Being analytical

For assessment objective 2 (AO2) the moderator is looking for critical *analysis* of both your sources and your own comments.

Analysis means to examine something in detail but not descriptively – you are aiming to evaluate.

There are many different ways to produce analysis/evaluation. On this spread we have considered two of them:

1. Analysis method 1: Considering conflicting arguments.

2. Analysis method 2: Considering the value of the sources used.

Example project

JENNY'S EPQ ON YELLOWSTONE

I have decided to research on whether the 1-in-10,000 odds that an eruption will occur in the next 100 years as reported by The Huffington Post is accurate or not, and what the impact on the climate, human life, and all of nature will be if it were to erupt. This leads me to my EPQ title 'What would the impacts on human life be if the supervolcano Yellowstone were to erupt in our lifetime?'.

I will also examine previous supervolcano eruptions, what led to their formation and their eruption, and hope for any future life to thrive. To do this I will gather information and evidence from a range of papers, geological records and websites, magazines and books.

You can either evaluate your sources in the body of the REPORT (as shown on the right) or you can add a supplementary sheet such as the one below. This can work well if you provide a thorough justification for the reliability of your sources.

Analysis method 1: Considering conflicting arguments

Jenny might evaluate her arguments about a supervolcano eruption in the following way:

However, the apocalypse type disaster which many scientists and media outlet have been reporting since the discovery of the supervolcano may be scrutinise by recent research. The global impacts are indicated to be less severe, due to th composition of the magma that the Yellowstone supervolcano contains. It conta little sulphur, and although it is inevitable that aerosols will prevail from the eruption, the likelihood of a severe temperature change has now been doubted New models suggest that life on Earth would not face any kind of extinction fro the eruption, and the only mass loss of life would occur in those that are in clos proximity to the blast. The geological record also provides evidence of there bei no extinction events at the time of super eruptions, apart from the bottleneck th occurred during the Yellowstone event. However, a bottleneck does not mean extinction, and so scientists are now predicting that life on Earth would weath the extinction fine, although major setbacks would occur.

Analysis method 2: Considering the value of the sources used

	Source 1:	Source 2:
Source	Wolchover, Natalie (2012) *Life's Little Mysteries. What if the Yellowstone supervolcano erupts?* [Online] Available at: www.lifeslittlemysteries.com/2518-yellowstone-supervolcano-eruption.html	Book written by Popper, K. R. (1979) *Of Clouds and Clocks.* Objective knowledge, an evolutionary approach. OUP.
Author's background	Natalie Wolchova is a science writer for Staff Writer – Simons Science News at Simons Foundation. She has no formal qualifications so this may reduce the validity of her claims but she is studying for a degree in Physics.	Karl Popper is generally regarded as 'one of the greatest philosophers of science of the 20th century' (Stanford Encyclopaedia of Philosophy), so we could say that this source is very reliable.
Date published	2012	1979 Although dated it is still regarded in high esteem. Furthermore, *Clocks and Clouds* is an American University undergraduate research journal that publishes articles on the cutting edge of political science, international relations and public policy.
Depth of reviews	Not peer reviewed.	Peer reviewed by reliable sources.
Sources cited	Credible sources including: Michael Rampino, a biologist and geologist at New York University, Stephen Self, director of the Volcano Dynamics Group at the Open University, Jacob Lowenstern, scientist-in-charge at the Yellowstone Volcano Observatory.	Credible sources including Comptom, Hume and Eddington.
Objectivity	Simons Foundation is a non-profit organisation, therefore the report is likely to be objective as it has not received funding from large powerful organisations.	Popper's philosophical views had many supporters but also opponents. An early adversary of Popper's critical rationalism was Karl-Otto Apel and also Houck questioned Popper's idea of falsification.
Justification for reliability	Natalie Wolchova is a science writer at Simons Foundation which is a non-profit organisation, therefore the report is likely to be objective as it has not received funding from large powerful organisations.	On balance, Karl Popper's body of work and reputation among scientists suggests this is a very reliable source.

EXERCISE 3.11 Evaluation sheet

Use the evaluation checklist at the bottom to evaluate the extract from the following article:

The pill that could slow aging: Researchers reveal groundbreaking study to extend lifespan and improve health of the elderly (*Daily Mail*, Mark Prigg, 28/2/2014)

Extract: A groundbreaking new study could hold the key to living longer and remaining healthy in old age. US researchers found a protein called SIRT1 extended the lifespan of mice, delaying the onset of age-related health problems. It also improved their general health, lowering cholesterol and even warding off diabetes. Although the study was carried out in mice, researchers say it could eventually be used in humans. Researchers led by Dr. Rafael de Cabo of the National Institute on Aging at the National Institutes of Health tested the effects of a small molecule that activates SIRT1, called SIRT1720, on the health and lifespan of mice. 'Here, we show for the first time that a synthetic SIRT1 activator extends lifespan and improves health span of mice fed a standard diet,' says Dr. de Cabo.

The investigators found that SRT1720 supplementation led to decreases in total cholesterol and LDL-cholesterol levels, which might help protect against heart disease, and improvements in insulin sensitivity, which could help prevent diabetes. SIRT1 and its sister protein SIRT2 are known to play an important role in metabolism across a wide range of species. They are involved in DNA repair and gene regulation, and may help to prevent diabetes, heart disease and cancer. The animals were given the supplement from the age of six months and for the rest of their lives, alongside a standard diet.

However, experts warn the study is still at a very early stage, and had not yet been tested in humans.

Source evaluation sheet: Checklist to evaluate sources

Tick one item in column 1, 2, or 3 and provide evidence

Factors to consider	Column 1 Least reliable	Column 2 Possibly reliable	Column 3 Most reliable
1. Type of source	Unfamiliar website Tabloid newspaper	Published material	Official websites, institutional sites, academic journals
2. Author's background	No credits provided	Educated on topic	Expert in the field
3. Date published	None	Outdated	Recently revised
4. Depth of reviews	Controversial reviews	Good public response; general approval	Peer reviewed by reliable sources
5. Sources cited	None	Credible sources	Citations referencing other well-cited works
6. Objectivity	Clearly biased	Sponsored source	Balanced, neutral

Suggested answers on page 123.

Evaluation checklist

One way to consider the value of your material is to analyse the sources it has come from (method 2).

1. Type of source – What makes a source credible or not is explained on page 64.

2. Author's background – A source is more credible if the author has credentials, is regarded as an expert in the field and has published other reputable works.

3. Date published – Check the date the research was published. Are the findings still current or is a more recent version of the work available?

4. Depth of reviews – Find reviews for the source. You may be able to check reviews online and see how and why others criticised the source. If there is significant controversy surrounding the validity of the source, you may wish to avoid using it, or examine it further with a sceptical eye.

5. Sources cited – If the article cites other reliable sources then this is a sign of credibility. It is, however, sometimes necessary to verify that the other sources also show a pattern of credibility and are used in context.

6. Objectivity – If the author is financially connected with the subject then the source may not represent all views. For example, if someone is an employee of Shell Oil company writing about the benefits of drilling for oil in the Arctic National Wildlife Refuge, then you should treat conclusions with caution.

EXERCISE 3.12 Being analytical

In the examples below, are the opening sentences analytical or are they just descriptive? Write A or D beside each.

1. Castro's men had distributed leaflets about the strike in the early morning of the 9th and made some effort to communicate details of the strike to the Havana public.

2. The uptake of breastfeeding is often linked to the wealth of the family, even in developed countries.

3. However, it has been argued that positive discrimination such as all women shortlists does not normalise the presence of women MPs or provide good role models.

4. One of the most controversial and contemporary issues surrounding this area is the change in attitudes towards Islam.

5. Castro clearly demonstrated strong leadership during the battle of La Plata.

6. At this stage the embryo is producing thousands of brain cells.

7. Lying behind the aqueous humour is the iris, a ring of pigmented cells.

8. There are multiple ways in which the media can be used in favour of a certain organisation and Christian fundamentalism is no exception.

Suggested answers on page 123.

Secondary data: Peer review

The academic community evaluates the validity of published work through the system of *peer review*. Peer review (also called 'refereeing') refers to the assessment of academic work by others who are experts in the same field (i.e. 'peers'). The intention of peer review is to ensure that any research that is conducted and published is of high quality.

How can you use peer review when evaluating sources?

This is an extract from an A* EPQ

'I have decided to concentrate on peer-reviewed research articles which involves the assessment of scientific work by others who are experts in the same field. The intention of peer reviewing is to ensure that any research conducted and published is of a high quality, thus allowing a means of establishing the validity of scientific research. However, peer review is not without criticism and according to Bordens and Abbott (2008) it can serve to preserve the status quo. However, there are also advantages to peer-reviewed articles in that it can prevent fraudulent work entering the public domain.'

This student states at the outset that she has used peer-reviewed articles in her EPQ. She also recognises the limitations of peer review. Throughout her project she also evaluated her sources.

What you can learn on this spread is the importance of peer review and the advantages and disadvantages.

The Oxford English Dictionary *defines peer review as:*

'Evaluation of scientific, academic, or professional work by others working in the same field.'

The value of peer review is based on the assumption that it provides a valid measure of the quality of a piece of research. When a research article has been written it will be submitted for publication. Before it can be published in an academic journal it is reviewed by members of the journal's editorial board. This board consists of reviewers who are experts from various universities and organisations. The reviewers will judge the quality of a research article based on the following factors:

- Originality of the research.
- Soundness of the research methodology.
- Quality of the writing.

Peer review and academic journals

The process of peer review begins when a research paper is being considered for publication in an academic journal. The editor sends the article to other experts in the field (who are generally unpaid). The expert critically appraises all aspects of the study and returns it with their recommendations as to whether the work is of acceptable quality. If not, researchers are asked to revise their work and resubmit the paper. This ensures that high standards are maintained.

The process of peer review is quite lengthy. It can take on average eighteen months for a peer-reviewed article to go from submission to publication. The reason why it takes so long is that very few articles are accepted without the need for revisions and so may be resubmitted several times before being accepted for publication. This means that research of the highest quality is entering the public domain.

A downside to the length of time is that the information disseminated through peer-reviewed journals is often several years old by the time it is published. Nevertheless, academics consider the quality of information far outweighs the need for rapid publication.

Peer review and books

Any reputable publisher takes steps to ensure that their published material is reliable and sound. Once an author hands in a finished manuscript the publisher sends this out to one or more experts to review the text. Comments are made about the accuracy of the manuscript as well as the quality of the writing and research. The author is then required to make changes before publication (see our thanks to our reviewers at the front of this book!).

Peer review and the Internet

The sheer volume and pace of information available on the Internet means that new solutions are needed in order to maintain the quality of information. Scientific information is available in numerous online blogs, online journals and, of course, Wikipedia (an online encyclopedia).

To a large extent such sources of information are policed by the 'wisdom of crowds' approach – readers decide whether it is valid or not, and post comments and/or edit entries accordingly. Several online journals (such as *ArXiv* and *Philica)* ask readers to rate articles. On *Philica* papers are ranked on the basis of peer reviews. On the Internet 'peer' is coming to mean 'everyone' – perhaps a more egalitarian system.

EXERCISE 3.13 Peer-reviewed journals

Find five academic journals that may be relevant to your EPQ topic and list them here.

Name of journal	Why is it relevant to my research?	How can I evaluate it using the peer review strengths and weaknesses?

The strengths of peer review

The intention of peer review is to ensure that any research that is conducted and published is of high quality. Peer review also guards against fraud, plagiarism (see next spread), falsification of data and fabrication of data.

Academic journals provide an important archive of comprehensive, up-to-date and authoritative information in a given scholarly field. They are published periodically and build into yearly volumes that serve as a permanent record of research. Universities keep these in their libraries and also subscribe to online publications. Some journals accept research from various areas, e.g. the journals *Nature* and *Science*. In psychology, the *British Journal of Psychology* accepts and publishes studies from many different fields whereas some journals are extremely specialised, e.g. the *Journal of Personality and Individual Differences*.

Academics have argued that without peer review they would be inundated with information. Research on informal communication among scientists also suggests that much of what is discussed among scholars turns out to be journal articles (Schafner 1994).

Finally publication determines ownership of intellectual property. According to Guédon (2001), a journal can serve like a patent office for ideas. By publishing in the journal, academics can establish ownership of their intellectual property.

The limitations of peer review

There are many difficulties with the process. First of all it isn't always possible to find an appropriate expert to review a research proposal or report. This means that poor research may be passed because the reviewer didn't really understand it.

Anonymity is usually practised so that reviewers can be honest and objective. However, it may have the opposite effect if reviewers use the veil of anonymity to settle old scores or bury rival research. Research is conducted in a social world where people compete for research grants and jobs, and make friends and enemies. Social relationships inevitably affect objectivity. Some journals now favour open reviewing (both author and reviewer know each other's identity).

One of the major criticisms is that peer review maintains the status quo and prevents potentially revolutionary research from being published. One reason for this is science is generally very conservative and resistant to large changes in opinion. If the results of a study do not fit with the accepted existing knowledge, peer reviewers may reject the proposed publication.

The 'file-drawer' problem

This refers to a bias towards publishing studies with positive results. A positive result is where a research hypothesis has been supported. However, negative findings tend to be either rejected or are never submitted for publication. For every study showing positive findings, there could be a hundred with negative results stuffed in university filing cabinets (hence the name file-drawer) in this way our understanding of a subject becomes distorted.

Fraud

Proven cases of fraud are a rarity, but there have been a number of high profile instances.

Here are some recent famous cases of professional misconduct. In each case the individuals published research for a considerable amount of time before they were discovered.

- *Hwang Woo-suk's fraudulent cloning case: http://news.bbc.co.uk/1/hi/4763973.stm*
- *Andrew Wakefield and the MMR controversy: http://news.bbc.co.uk/1/hi/health/8700611.stm*
- *Mark Hauser who invented data for his monkey research: http://www.thecrimson.com/article/2013/9/27/mark-hauser-publishes-book/*

EXERCISE 3.14   Peer review

EPQ title: **Should people pay for NHS treatment they need due to their lifestyle choices?**

The National Health Service (NHS) has a huge job on its hands – to treat and care for a total population of 62.7 million people. This is an increase of 12 million people since the founding of the NHS in 1948 after the Second World War. Despite the obvious need for extra funding, there has been a call for £20 billion[1] worth of savings to be made by 2014 due to the 2008 recession – debated to be the greatest crisis since The Great Depression. Jeremy Hunt, Secretary of State for Health, has to carefully plan the £105 billion NHS budget per year, but with demand increasing by 4% a year and admissions to Accident and Emergency increasing by 5%[2], this is an ever growing difficult task. The NHS must cater for everyone's needs including: hospital admissions, doctors' surgeries, prescriptions, medication and many more essentials. With the United Kingdom being a more economically developed country, it has been hit with a new wave of diseases caused by lifestyle factors. As exercise decreases, car ownership increases, processed foods become more readily available and alcohol and drugs become more glamorised, the number of self-inflicted diseases has increased. This, alongside longer life expectancy, is testing the NHS and, with the biggest baby boom for 40 years[3], will continue to. While many are quick to give answers and suggestions, NHS cuts are a battle between, ethics, politics and economics and cuts may not be the only way to save money. This EPQ will examine arguments for and against whether the NHS should pay for treatment people need due to their lifestyle choices. I plan to carry out my research by reading peer-reviewed articles, journals and books. I will also use the Internet, but only reliable sites. I am also going to find the opinion of a doctor and perhaps a politician to compare their views and why this may be.

[1] Gov.uk, Making the NHS more efficient and less bureaucratic

[2] 24 Hours in A&E, Channel 4

[3] CNN Money

1. Write a brief narrative (2–3 sentences) that outlines your first impression of the draft introduction on the left.

2. Explain whether the title draws you into the paper.

3. Indicate what you *like* about the draft (positive/encouraging feedback).

4. What suggestion(s) can you make to improve the introductory paragraph?

5. Has the author used secondary/primary data to support their assumptions?

6. In the main body of the introduction, are there parts that are confusing?

7. How clear is the writing? If there are places that seem wordy or unclear, how might the author revise to address those problems?

Secondary data: Avoiding plagiarism

Plagiarism is a serious business for professional authors and for you. It is both illegal and unethical, resulting in an expensive lawsuit or disqualification from an exam. Although it may be quicker to cut and paste chunks of information from online sources, this is plagiarism. On this spread we give you some guidance.

> Plagiarism is the publication of someone else's words, thoughts and ideas without permission and due credit. You can use someone else's words but you must indicate this by using quotation marks and identifying the source. This includes copying another student's EPQ.
>
> Acts of plagiarism are illegal and, from the point of view of an EPQ, risk disqualification.

Rewriting

Make it your own

The real challenge when selecting and synthesising sources for your EPQ is to demonstrate the relationship between your ideas and the reading you have done in journals, books and also on the Internet. An over-reliance on what others say will prevent you developing your own ideas. The purpose of the EPQ is to show your own thinking, not to create a patchwork of borrowed ideas.

However, you may still include quotes from expert sources to support your arguments.

Rewrite, don't cut and paste

When making notes you should not cut and paste from the Internet, as you may get confused about what was your own writing and plagiarise accidentally. If you do cut and paste, make sure you note the source so that later you either rewrite the text or place it in quotes.

Paraphrasing and summarising

If an argument or a factual account from one of your sources is particularly relevant to your EPQ topic but does not deserve to be quoted verbatim, consider:

- Paraphrasing the passage if you wish to convey the points in the passage at roughly the same level of detail as in the original.

- Summarising the relevant passage if you wish to sketch only the key points in the passage.

Using quotes

Credit the source

If you need to quote a memorable phrase then place it in quotation marks and give the name of the person who wrote it plus the date of publication. The full details of where it was written will be listed in your references (see pages 90–91) so you should also keep a record of the title of the book/article and publisher/website.

You can use single or double quotation marks – either is acceptable but be consistent. Throughout this book we have included quotes from key authors, so you can see how it is done. A few examples are shown below.

Credit ideas as well as words

Plagiarism can apply to taking ideas from someone else as well as their actual words. Reference every source you use, citing the reference as soon as you have mentioned the idea you are using.

What about general knowledge?

General knowledge refers to facts easily found in standard reference books such as the date of the assassination of Martin Luther King or the present population of China. Well-known facts do not need to be acknowledged but if the facts you refer to might be disputed within your discipline such as newly published data, you will need to establish their credibility by demonstrating that the source of the facts is authoritative. Check with your supervisor if you're in doubt whether a specific point is considered general knowledge in your field.

A famous case of plagiarism

Plagiarism can also exist in areas other than academic circles. In a famous case former Beatle George Harrison was accused by Bright Tunes Music of plagiarising the melody for his worldwide smash hit, 'My Sweet Lord' from a hit single from 1963 called 'He's So Fine' by the Chiffons.

You can read more about the case at http://abbeyrd.best.vwh.net/mysweet.htm

You can also listen to both songs on YouTube and see if you consider them to be similar.

> `If I did what has already been done, I would be a plagiarist and would consider myself unworthy; so I do something different and people call me a scoundrel. I'd rather be a scoundrel than a plagiarist!'
>
> Paul Gauguin (1870)

> **Further information on plagiarism**
>
> You can find further detailed advice on plagiarism at www.plagiarismadvice.org
>
> A guide to plagiarism and using sources aimed at college and school students can be found at: www.ofqual.gov.uk/files/2009-12-24-plagiarism-students.pdf

EXAMPLES OF HOW TO QUOTE

Credit ideas

Mennell (1994) suggests that the notions of identity and habitus are closely linked, the former being at a more conscious level, the latter residing more in the subconscious.

Credit quotations

Mennell describes the multi-layered habitus as 'more inclusive layers of identity, suggesting development is related to changing balances between different layers of habitus and identity' (1994, p.179).

or

The multi-layered habitus is described as 'more inclusive layers of identity, suggesting development is related to changing balances between different layers of habitus and identity' (Mennell 1994, p.179).

Plagiarism is a form of theft

How will anyone know?

You may think that your supervisor or the moderator will not be able to detect that your text is copied. But often copied text stands out because the writing style changes. Your supervisor or moderator can paste the sentence into Google and the original source will be identified.

There are also specialist software packages that detect plagiarism such as *Turnitin*. Your whole document is uploaded and analysed. A score is produced and chunks that have been copied are identified.

How much should I quote?

The focus of your essay should be on *your* understanding of the topic. If you include too many quotations in your essay, it will obscure your own ideas.

On the other hand, if you do not quote enough then there is very little theoretical underpinning in your work. Even an artefact should be accompanied by a 1000-word REPORT containing references to relevant sources.

Consider quoting a passage from one of your sources if it meets one of the following criteria:

- The language of the passage is particularly elegant, powerful or memorable.
- An authority on the topic can add strength to your argument.
- The passage provides a useful point for discussion.
- You wish to argue with someone else's position in considerable detail.

Using long quotations

If possible you should avoid using very long quotations of 10 lines or more. Select some memorable phrases instead of the whole quotation and try to paraphrase the rest. Try to emphasise the key points that are relevant to your own argument. Even if you are not using the exact original words, you are using the ideas and therefore should credit the source.

Can I cut and paste a diagram or a map from the Internet?

Images may still be copyright material and you should check for this. Assume that any images you use are copyright and give credit to the source. Even if you have reorganised a table of data, or redrawn a figure, you should still acknowledge its source.

How much is too much?

Many students may think that if they over reference then they will lose marks because the work is not their own idea. This is far from the truth! The rationale behind documenting sources is to demonstrate that you know what is going on in your field of study. It shows respect to the original author and it is also a courtesy to the moderator and your supervisor because it helps them consult the material that you have found. This is especially important for Internet sources. By quoting experts in the field this adds to your credibility because it shows that you have used resources sensibly and selectively.

EXERCISE 3.15
Identifying plagiarism

Consider the following opening paragraph to an EPQ project entitled *'To what extent can Jane Eyre be considered the ultimate heroine?'*

> One of the earliest representations of an individualistic, passionate and complex female character, Jane Eyre knocks our socks off. Though she suffers greatly, she always relies on herself to get back on her feet — no wilting damsel in distress here.

The language in this paragraph is both sophisticated and unusual which will alert the moderator that it may have been plagiarised.

Try typing the first few lines into Google and you will find that this passage has been cut and pasted from flavorwire.com/265847/10-of-the-most-powerful-female-characters-in-literature.

Rewrite the first sentence in your own words.

WORDS TO USE

Stating a point

McAdam (2001) states that 'Woman belong …' (or suggests, says, comments)

Arguing a point

Brown (1994) argues that experiments are useless…' (or asserts, insists).

Different introductory phrases

In the words of Brown 'Reflections from history …' (or according to …)

OTHER ISSUES

More than one author

Where there are two authors both surnames are given.

Where there are more than two authors write as Thomas et al. or Thomas and colleagues.

Introducing a long quotation

Always write a full sentence explaining how the quotation fits into your arguments. If your quotation is longer than four lines place it in a separate indented block and do not use quotation marks.

If you need to alter a quotation

If a quotation does not fit in your sentence use square brackets, for example:

Davies writes that '[boys] are troubled by …' (The actual quotation said 'they' because 'boys' had been mentioned earlier.)

If you remove some text from a quotation

Replace it with three dots:

In Postscript Heaney comments 'Useless to think you'll park or capture it … You are neither here nor there.'

Crediting the source of a picture or diagram:

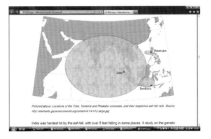

Figure 1 pictured above: Locations of the Toba, Tambora and Pinatubo volcanoes and their respective ash fall radii. Source http://elements.geoscienceworld.org/content/4/1/41/F2.large.jpg.

Chapter 4

Develop and realise

This chapter is focused on the AO3 component of your project, described on the facing page.

The most important element of AO3 is the production of your final REPORT and this chapter mainly focuses on that.

`Writing is thinking. To write well is to think clearly. That's why it's so hard.'

David McCullough (2002)

One size doesn't fit all

This chapter provides some general principles for presenting your REPORT – but the actual organisation and divisions will vary depending on your personal preferences and on the kind of project you have done. Remember THERE ARE NO RULES, moderators are looking for your individual thoughts and work not a product where someone has followed a set of rules.

The structure of your report

The EPQ REPORT does not have a set structure but the sections outlined on the left are commonly used. Whether you use all of these sections will depend on the kind of project you have done.

For all projects the written REPORT is likely to contain:

- A literature review, or other background research.
- Details of the design, knowledge, understanding and skills used.
- A conclusion to include an evaluation of the outcomes.
- References to sources and information accessed.

Artefact

You will be writing a short REPORT of about 1000 words. You still need to ensure fluency and organisation. Your REPORT might include a short summary, introduction, literature review, a discussion of your method and findings and their implications, a conclusion and references. An example of an artefact REPORT can be seen in Appendix I (pages 108–110).

EPQ using secondary data only

You will be writing a full REPORT of 5000 words. As you will not be collecting your own data you do not need a method section and probably not a findings section. Your REPORT may involve repeating the sections – so you might deal with one topic (for example, literature review, discussion, conclusion) and then another topic (for example, literature review, discussion, conclusion) and so on. It helps to start with an overview (abstract) and you should end with a final conclusion. An example can be seen in Appendix II (see pages 111–116).

EPQ with primary and secondary data

Your REPORT should be the full 5000 words and should be in the form of a scientific REPORT, which includes all the sections listed on the left. An example of a REPORT based on primary and secondary data can be seen in Appendix III (pages 117–122).

What's in this chapter

Assessment objective 3

The third skill in the mark scheme, called AO3, is 'develop and realise'. This will account for 40% of your final mark.

The AQA mark scheme states the following objectives:
- Problem solving
- Decision making
- Creative thinking
- To achieve planned outcomes.

What the moderator is looking for

The AO3 objectives, like all the other AOs, are not located in just one part of your EPQ.

When determining your AO3 mark the moderator is considering:	Where this is usually demonstrated
Has appropriate data been collected and thoroughly analysed?	The final PRODUCT (report or artefact with report) can demonstrate this through your presentation of data and also thoroughly examining the data you have collected.
	Your PRODUCTION LOG can also document the data that you plan to collect in the PLANNING REVIEW, MID-PROJECT REVIEW and PROJECT PRODUCT REVIEW.
Is the project plan fully implemented? Is the outcome fully realised to a high standard and consistent with a candidate's finally agreed plan?	The PRODUCTION LOG, in particular the PROJECT PRODUCT REVIEW (see Chapter 3) shows well-evidenced conclusions in relation to the title. The EPQ title has been addressed.
	The final PRODUCT (report or artefact with report) can show the moderator that you have achieved your objectives (this is covered in this chapter).
	Your PRESENTATION can also provide clear evidence that you have fully implemented your project plan (see Chapter 5).
Is there evidence of autonomy? (Or has your supervisor taken too many decisions for you?)	The issue of autonomy is assessed under decision making. The moderator needs evidence that you have made your own decisions rather than being over directed by the supervisor or relying on the supervisor to make the decisions for you.
	The PRODUCTION LOG (see Chapter 3) shows your responses to your supervisor's advice in the PLANNING REVIEW, MID-PROJECT REVIEW AND PROJECT PRODUCT REVIEW.
Is there evidence of creative thinking?	This can be shown both in the PRODUCT and in the PRODUCTION LOG where you generate ideas which show imagination and originality.
	The ideas and rationale for selecting a topic is evidenced in the PRODUCTION LOG and the original idea is then followed through into the PRODUCT.
Is there clear evidence of appropriate changes to, or development of, the initial project plan or title or aims and objectives, with clear and appropriate reasons for any changes?	The PRODUCTION LOG can document changes to your project plan. The evidence of these changes can be documented in the INITIAL IDEAS, PLANNING REVIEW, MID-PROJECT REVIEW and PROJECT PRODUCT REVIEW (see Chapter 3).
	You may use management tools to aid development, such as the diary of progress, as evidence of development.
Has information been synthesised from a variety of sources?	You will show the ability to integrate material from the sources you have used into a coherent REPORT.
	Also your references or bibliography will show that you have used a variety of sources.
Is the research report well written, fluent and academic in style? Are the findings communicated fluently in an appropriate format, and presented within a logical and coherent structure that addresses closely the nature of the task?	Assessed in the final PRODUCT, which should be in an appropriate format, logically organised with coherent paragraphs, and include an evaluation of sources. This is covered in this chapter.

Where do I begin?

It is a daunting prospect starting to write down the results of all your reading and research.

We call this **BLANK PAGE SYNDROME.**

Below are a number of ways to overcome this problem.

What should I write?

Just get something down on paper, it is a start.

Make a large flow chart or diagram to summarise what you have read so far.

Write the ending first, what do you want your reader to know, what do you want to achieve?

Don't write your abstract or summary yet, wait until your project has evolved.

Think out loud as if you were explaining your ideas to a friend.

Go through your notes and see if you can sort these into piles. These could form the structure of your project.

Start with the bit you feel most comfortable writing.

Try to give each section a working title or subheadings.

Look at the exemplar projects in the appendix of this book to see how they are written and structured.

'Either write something worth reading or do something worth writing.'

Benjamin Franklin (1774)

Change location – head out to a coffee shop, library or anywhere new. We associate places where frustration occurs with the frustration itself – change your place, change the frustration.

Set achievable objectives

A lot of times we worry about how long it will take us to finish and how much there is to do. This may prevent us from starting in the first place.

So try this: set a timer for three minutes, and see how much you can write in those three minutes. Write gibberish if you must but, if you can, stay focused and know that you can stop in three minutes.

Or try writing just five sentences.

Each day set yourself achievable goals.

By giving yourself achievable goals that you can quickly accomplish, this will act as a motivator. A lot of times, you will write something even in those few minutes and be able to keep on going until you have made an impressive start.

Overcoming the blank page syndrome

The blank page syndrome is the same thing as authors often refer to as 'writer's block'. Some writers find themselves staring at a blank page and wondering where to start. Although genuine writer's block is more than just getting beyond the blank page, many writers often find themselves staring at a blank page and wondering where to start.

Here are some examples of how students overcame their writer's block.

Exemplars

EPQ project 1: **The impact of the French Revolution on British politics 1789–1848.**

The history of political thought is intriguing in particular the impact of the French Revolution on British Politics. I found a wide research base that was quite overwhelming and really didn't know where to start. So I placed all of my notes into a pile and started to sort through these. I wrote down some possible subheadings for my essay. I then created an essay plan and a structural flow chart that helped me to organise the task of writing.

EPQ project 2: **To create a sculpture based on the history of the Warsaw ghetto.**

I wanted my EPQ to combine architecture and history. When I stumbled across the story of the peculiar reconstruction of the Warsaw Jewish Ghetto I was fascinated to see how closely architecture and history are linked. I was struggling to come up with an idea for a possible model to symbolise the poverty and struggle of living in the ghetto. However, my eagerness to make the artefact symbolic as well as visually appealing blocked my creativity. I was able to overcome this by breaking down the planning process into visuals, functions and historical relations and by giving each section a working title and by doing this I could focus on one aspect at a time.

EPQ project 3: **How far can it be proved that immigration from central and eastern Europe has benefitted the economy?**

I tracked my progress by having an EPQ diary that proved a useful tool in helping me by setting myself achievable goals.

EPQ project 5: **To what extent does England need new laws to be able to deal with defamation, abuse and contempt of court in relation to social media and the Internet?**

I overestimated the amount of data available. I kept looking at my notes but got more and more confused about how to write the opening paragraph. I wanted something to capture the reader's attention to draw them in. I just stared at a blank page and just didn't know what to write. I was so frustrated and so I went for a run. When I came back I just started to write the opening paragraph that contained something I felt comfortable writing about.

EPQ project 6: **Design a range of costumes for the witches in Macbeth with the aim of making the most effective design into a costume.**

I had to think first about what I wanted to achieve, the bigger picture was to create an effective costume for one of the witches in Macbeth. As I have to write a report to accompany my artefact I need to properly record the physical process of creating my final design. I will therefore place the process in chronological order in my portfolio starting with the sketches of the images the process of creating the costume, fabric, etc., and then take a photograph of the model wearing the costume.

EPQ project 4: **Why were all the assassination attempts on Hitler's life in the period 1921–1945 failures?**

I have read quite a few books some of which were not entirely helpful. In order to help me in my research I drew up a large flow chart to summarise what I had read. I then divided the information up into categories such as the Valkyrie attack, Hitler's security team and so on. I think this will prove useful when I begin to write my final essay because it will be easy to distinguish what falls into each paragraph. So the flow chart could be structured as Valkyrie, other similar assassination attempts and minor assassination attempts.

EXERCISE 4.1 Blank page syndrome

Consider how each of the students above has overcome the blank page syndrome.

Project	Way(s) of overcoming the blank page syndrome
1	
2	
3	
4	
5	
6	

Suggested answers on page 124.

Writing fluently and critically

A key aspect of your AO3 mark is the ability to communicate 'fluently in an appropriate format' (AQA specification, assessment objectives for AO3).

An EPQ that is well-structured, easy to follow, logical, and coherent, will be a joy to read. On this spread we consider ways to improve the quality of your descriptive and critical writing.

'The moment we want to believe something, we suddenly see all the arguments for it, and become blind to the arguments against it.'

George Bernard Shaw (1928)

Think of the moderator

The moderator who reads and marks your EPQ deserves your consideration. Make their job easy for them. They will be reading and marking many EPQs. If you make your argument hard to follow, they will need to re-read a paragraph (or more) to try to make sense of what you have written. You are at risk of irritating them because it makes their job slower and harder. It is your task to present your arguments in a way that your moderator can follow. It is not their job to detect the points you are trying to make.

You are not expected to produce a unique, perfect or revolutionary piece of work. Instead the moderator will be happy to read a reasonably well-planned, well-argued and well-written essay. They will mark positively not negatively.

Clear line of argument

What you write should tell a story. One piece of information should logically follow from the previous piece of information so that the reader can make sense of the whole. In some cases it may be better to remove some items because, even though they are impressive, it confuses the 'story' you are telling.

Well-structured paragraphs

It is vital to separate the points you are making into separate paragraphs so that the reader understands where one line of thought finishes and another begins.

Paragraphs can also provide a clear separation between descriptive writing and critical analysis, by switching to a new paragraph when you move from description to critical writing, and vice versa.

Points are based on evidence

You need to support your opinion with evidence from academic sources. It should be an objective position presented as a logical argument. The quality of your evidence will determine the strength of your argument. The challenge is to convince the reader of the validity of your opinion through a well-documented piece of writing.

Both description and critical analysis

It is important that you focus mainly on critical analysis in order to access the high mark bands. It is likely that in the early parts of your report a certain amount of descriptive writing is needed. Beyond that, however, there is a danger that too much descriptive writing will use up valuable words from your word limit, and reduce the space you have for the all important critical analysis of your topic, critical writing that will enable you to access higher mark bands.

Critical writing includes:

- Explaining what the evidence means. A useful habit to get into is to make sure that, if you describe some evidence relevant to your arguments, you need then to explain to the reader why it is relevant.

- Explaining the relevance of the evidence. Do not assume that the moderator is following the same logic as you, or will just work out the relevance of the quote or data you have described. You must explain it.

- A recognition of the limitations (or strengths) of any evidence. You may challenge the conclusions reached by others by criticising their evidence.

- Drawing conclusions from your evidence.

Making your point – writing a *POWERFUL* paragraph

ALISTAIR'S EPQ ON NEW LAWS

There is a knack to constructing effective descriptive or critical points. Let us have a look at an EPQ exemplar:

EPQ title: **To what extent does England need new laws to be able to deal effectively with defamation, abuse and contempt of court in relation to social media and the Internet?**

There is a significant argument that suggests that the Communications Act of 2003 goes too far in limiting free speech. This is an opinion shared by Kier Starmer, QC, Director of Public Prosecutions (DPP) and head of the Crown Prosecution Service. Starmer suggested, in an interview for BBC News on 11/10/12, that we should divide communications that are grossly offensive from those which are a campaign for harassment. However, it is also true that teenagers need to be protected from malicious communications that cause serious harm, as demonstrated by the number of teenagers who have committed suicide as a result of cyber bullying campaigns. So we can see that there are certain issues relating to social media that need to be addressed.

Deconstructing the paragraph on the left

Such a structure may not work with every point or paragraph you write but is a useful structure to aim for.

Identify the point	There is a significant argument that suggests that the Communications Act of 2003 goes too far in limiting free speech.
Justify the point	This is an opinion shared by Kier Starmer, QC, Director of Public Prosecutions (DPP) and head of the Crown Prosecution Service.
Elaborate upon it	Starmer suggested, in an interview for BBC News on 11/10/12, that we should divide communications that are grossly offensive from those which are a campaign for harassment.
Further elaboration (e.g. a counterpoint)	However, it is also true that teenagers need to be protected from malicious communications that cause serious harm, as demonstrated by the number of teenagers who have committed suicide as a result of cyber bullying campaigns.
Conclusion	So we can see that there are certain issues relating to social media which need to be addressed.

Avoid personal opinion

In academic writing it is not desirable to express your own opinions. Let the facts do the arguing for you.

For example, if you are writing a project on the arguments for and against animal experimentation in medical research you shouldn't write: 'In my opinion I consider animal experimentation to be cruel and unnecessary and instead we should use prisoners or people with incurable illness as they are of little use to society.'

Apart from being subjective this is a very unhelpful opinion. State the arguments and keep your opinions to yourself!

Use precise language

Avoid vague expressions that are not specific enough for the reader to derive their exact meaning. For example, using terms such as:

- 'They' or 'we' – who does this refer to?
- 'People' – which people?
- 'The organisation' – what organisation?

Avoid abbreviations and contractions

Avoid using i.e. and e.g. – spell it out as 'in other words' and 'for example'.

Avoid words such as isn't and can't – spell it out as 'is not' and 'cannot'.

Use of quotations

Both short and long quotations can be used as an effective way to explain your point. The way to introduce and use these is explained on page 71.

It is important, however, to remember that you also need to interpret the quotes for the reader, and to explain their relevance, discuss their validity, and show how they relate to other evidence as exemplified below.

> *According to Recinos (1405), a medieval woman '[was] taught to look up to female saints as role models'. Recinos's view is supported by the academic concept of the Mary and Eve dichotomy that suggests that medieval women were placed into one of two stereotypes by leading church figures; either Mary, chaste and virtuous, or more commonly Eve, a woman drawn to sin and a leading figure in tempting men away from a virtuous life.*

Here are some useful phrases for creating a critical commentary:

This suggests that …

So we can see that …

This would imply …

One consequence would be …

One advantage of this is …

An alternative explanation …

Therefore …

This is challenged by …

In comparison …

In contrast …

However …

The passage below uses some of these phrases to create a critical commentary (useful phrases are highlighted).

EPQ title: What are the costs of alcohol?

Alcohol has played a prominent role in British life for many years and can be traced back to the Roman Conquest. Alcohol is a psychoactive drug and it is a central nervous system depressant that brings advantages and disadvantages when taken in excess. One consequence is the cost to the NHS. Around 40% of admissions to Accident and Emergency Departments are diagnosed with alcohol-related injuries or illnesses. Between midnight and 5am this figure rises to 70%. So we can see that alcohol has some major disadvantages. Therefore, this suggests that alcohol-related emergencies are of prominent concern to the NHS.

However, despite the fact that alcohol consumption seems to be falling over the past 2–3 years (according to the annual survey from the Office for National Statistics), in comparison there are still 10 million people drinking over the government's recommended daily levels and 1.6 million dependent drinkers. This would imply that binge drinking is still an issue in Britain.

EXERCISE 4.2 Powerful paragraphs

Look at your work so far and try to write one point using the structure of a powerful paragraph

Identify the point	
Justify the point	
Elaborate upon it	
Further elaboration (e.g. a counterpoint)	
Conclusion	

EXERCISE 4.3 Useful phrases

Use the phrases at the top of the page to make the following paragraph more critical.

In 2010 there were 160,181 prescription items for drugs for the treatment of alcohol dependency. This is an increase of 6% on the 2009 figure of 150,445 and a 56% increase on the 2003 figure of 102,741. Alcohol misuse, in the form of binge drinking, is common among young people and seems to be a characteristic of the British drinking culture. In the recent past the government has reformed licensing laws and implemented strategies aimed at reducing alcohol harm. Experts and critics of the current licensing laws have debated whether the government should have greater control over the younger generation. Binge bashes can take to the street and in most cases cause serious violence, antisocial behaviour, crime and injury. Restrictive controls may result in an increase in the production of illicit liquor, difficulties of law enforcement, loss of tax revenues and a reduction of personal and social enjoyment.

Suggested answers on page 124.

Optional content for projects involving just the collection of secondary data or an artefact. Required content for projects involving primary data.

The abstract

An abstract is a succinct summary of a piece of research used at the beginning of articles in academic journals to give a quick summary of the report. It should provide the reader with a clear understanding of the aim, background research, conclusions and the implications of the findings. Method and findings should be included where primary data has been collected, and the method will be relevant in projects involving an artefact.

Word count

The intention is to give a very brief overview – so keep this brief. Probably about 150–250 words.

There is a good example in the Appendix, Exemplar III page 117.

Guidelines for the abstract

There should be no subheadings in an abstract and it is usually one or two paragraphs long.

The succinct nature of the abstract is quite a challenge so we will look at how other EPQ students have managed it in the examples on the facing page.

First or last?

The abstract appears at the beginning of the REPORT but it is often wise to leave its preparation to last so you know what has gone into each of these elements.

Alternatively, it can be useful to write the abstract earlier on, as an aid to identifying the crucial main thread of your research, its purpose, and its findings, which could then guide the structure of the EPQ.

A planner for your abstract

HARRY'S EPQ ON CANNABIS USE

You can use this grid to write your own abstract – but remember not to include the subheadings in your final draft.

Aim and/or hypothesis	The abstract should begin with what you intend to research.
	This can be stated as an aim, for example 'In this project I aim to…investigate the impact of cannabis usage on young people'.
	Or you may state a hypothesis, for example 'There is correlation between age and cannabis use'.
Relevant background literature	Present a very brief overview of how your topic relates to previous research in the field.
	For example 'Research suggests that cannabis use in teenagers can have long-term effects on the mind and body' (Zhang *et al.* 1999). Might be good to give an example as well in a project that is just secondary sources (i.e. no research study).
Method	Describe the method you will use to investigate your topic.
	If you are using secondary data you might say 'My research used a variety of materials such as books and journal articles and official statistics'.
	If you are using primary data you might say 'I also collected primary data from an opportunity sample of sixth formers to investigate whether teenagers understood the risks associated with cannabis use'.
Findings	Provide the results of your investigation, if appropriate.
	If descriptive statistics are used you might say 'The graphs indicate that more young adults aged 24–29 are using cannabis on a regular basis than any other age group'.
	If inferential statistics have been used state whether results were significant (see page 84). For example, 'A test of correlation showed that there was a significant negative correlation between age and cannabis use (p=0.449)'.
Conclusion (relate to background research)	It is important that you relate your conclusions to the background research you have discussed in your introduction. Does it support or challenge it?
	For example, 'From a literature review it is rational to conclude that cannabis has a large impact on the health and well being of young people if taken in excess'.
Implications (relate to findings)	Finally you need to provide a brief statement of what your results mean beyond this study. Do the findings have any real world implications?
	For example, 'This study shows that existing drug awareness campaigns are not getting the message across to all teenagers about the risks of cannabis and different strategies need to be employed. This suggests that current campaigns are not working'.

JENNY'S EPQ ON YELLOWSTONE

EPQ title: **Will the Yellowstone Caldera erupt in our lifetime and, if so, what are the consequences?**

Abstract

The project examines whether the Yellowstone Caldera is likely to erupt in our lifetime and what the impacts of such an eruption would be on the planet. I hope to examine previous eruptions and analyse their effects on civilisation at the time. I will use secondary research and data to collect information, such as peer-reviewed articles, and also websites, such as the USGS or the Geographical Society.

The findings that the Huckleberry Ridge Tuff was created over two or three eruptions separated by around 6000 years leads me to conclude that the possible impact of the eruption of Yellowstone is likely to be less dramatic than eruption of Toba 74,000 years ago. The discovery that there are also less quantities of sulphurous gases in the magma encased beneath Yellowstone also helps me to determine that the prediction of a global cooling and dimming of the Earth for a period of several years will not be as severe as once predicted. Although there would be major losses and devastation to agriculture and the civilisation of the United States, the eruption will most likely not produce a major population bottleneck or extinction as the technological advances of the human race allow planning to be undertaken to mitigate the effects of such an eruption.

Moderator comments

A concise abstract of about 200 words that provides the aim and method in brief. The findings could have been more detailed. The implications/inclusions are also extensive.

Moderator comments

Abstract of 133 words. The aim is clear and the methods and findings are given but no inferential statistics are presented which would be useful.

JUSTIN'S EPQ ON ATTRACTIVENESS

EPQ title: **To what extent do we seek partners of the same levels of attractiveness?**

Abstract

The matching hypothesis states that people are attracted to members of the opposite sex who are similar in terms of physical attractiveness rather than seeking the most physically attractive mate. This study aims to test this hypothesis by selecting a set of photographs of married couples and asking participants to rate the attractiveness of each of the partners (females rate male photos and males rate female photos). Forty-eight participants from the sixth form at our school took part (24 girls and 24 boys) and were asked to rate the physical attractiveness on a scale of 1 to 10 (10 = highly attractive). The correlation was not significant ($p = 0.05$, critical value = 0.65, observed value = 0.44, null hypothesis accepted). This suggests that, when looking for a partner, people do not try to match their own physical attractiveness; they may be influenced by a variety of other factors.

Moderator comments

A succinct and well-written abstract of 145 words. Aims and hypothesis are given but no reference to past research. The method is clear and the inferential statistics are reported along with a conclusion but no implications.

COURTNEY'S EPQ ON ADVERTS

EPQ title: **Do children's adverts use traditional gender stereotypes?**

Abstract

This project reports the results of a content analysis of 167 commercials broadcast during children's films which aimed to investigate whether these adverts portrayed traditional gendered expectations of males and females.

Partially replicating the research by Smith (2003) the characters were coded for gender, role within the commercial (major or minor), product type (toys, games, food) and location of the character (home, work, or outdoors).

The findings show that males are more likely to be shown in a major role advertising toys and in a work setting.

Advertisers are continuing to use traditional gender portrayals in adverts aimed at children and are thus perpetuating gendered stereotypes. More pressure needs to be exerted on the media to change the images they use to sell products to children to show real-world sex-typed behaviours.

EXERCISE 4.4 Identifying the sections

Read the following abstract and highlight the aim and/or hypothesis, background research, method, results, conclusions with different colours.

The aim of this EPQ was to investigate cultural differences in spider phobia. According to research one of the most common phobias in Western cultures is fear of spiders (Costello 1982). In studies conducted on adult populations in the United Kingdom and the Netherlands, the spider was one of the top five most feared animals (Bennett-Levy and Marteau 1984). According to Davey (1994) there may be evolutionary reasons for this fear but the fact that spider phobia is not universal suggests that there may be cultural reasons why spiders are feared. For instance, spider phobia may well be the result of the negative portrayal of spiders in a variety of media, including popular children's stories and modern horror and thriller films such as the US movie *Arachnophobia*.

It was hypothesised that there would be a significant difference in fear ratings, namely the Indian sample would have higher fear ratings overall due to the types of spiders in India being larger and more prone to biting (e.g. jumping, orb). Two groups of participants were selected by means of opportunity sampling. There was one group of 20 UK participants and one group of Indian participants living in India. Both groups were asked to complete a Spider Phobia Questionnaire (SPQ) (Klorman *et al.* 1974). The SPQ is a 31-item self-report instrument that measures fear of spiders. Scores ranged from 0 to 31 with higher scores indicating greater fear. The results of the Mann Whitney U were supported $p<0.05$. The calculated value of Mann Whitney U = 92, critical value of U = 138. It was concluded that spider phobia is a result of cultural differences supporting earlier work by Davey (1994). This has implications for how spiders are portrayed in different cultures.

Suggested answers on page 124.

EXERCISE 4.5 Abstracts

Read the following abstract and state what is missing:

A laboratory experiment was carried out to investigate if there was a difference in recall rates of neutral and emotional words. This was based on Levinger and Clark's (1961) classic study on the role of emotion.

The investigation used an opportunity sample of 15 participants and a repeated measures design was used. This is because participants were given both the emotional and neutral words and then immediately asked to recall them. The alternative hypothesis predicted that more neutral words would be recalled than emotional words. A Wilcoxon Signed Ranks test was performed to establish a statistically significant difference.

Suggested answers on page 124.

The introduction

The introduction is a key element in your REPORT. This is where you present your background research/reading and your analysis of that material.

We have subdivided the introduction into:

- An overview
- A literature review.

Word count

For projects with secondary data the introduction may be as much as 4000 words. However, there is no hard and fast rule about how much should be introduction (a literature review) and how much should be discussion (considering the value of the evidence). In Exemplar II (page 111) the introduction is just 1000 words.

An overview

The purpose of the overview is to signpost the reader to the content of your EPQ. This part of your introduction is a statement of what is to come – an overview of the argument you are presenting. A good overview will show that you are going to answer your EPQ title and that you understand the issues and themes.

Like an abstract it may be better to leave the writing of the overview until you have written the literature review. The reason for this is you may not know until the end what you are summarising.

One of the challenges of writing a good overview is to be brief and stay focused. Aim to write three or four paragraphs describing what is to come. If your overview is overly long it will not create a good first impression.

Here are some helpful suggestions:

- A **starting point** and a definition of the topic being discussed, make a statement of your objectives.

- A **brief outline** of what you intend to cover.

- Establish the **research territory** by showing that the general research area is important, central, interesting and/or problematic.

- Establish a **niche** for your project by indicating a gap in the previous research or by suggesting how you will be extending previous knowledge in some way.

- **Background**, a mention of previous work on the subject, keep this brief as the literature review will be discussed next.

- A statement of the **scope of the work** – if you are researching a large topic such as eating disorders you may be only looking at obesity as an example of an eating disorder. Explain that other eating disorders are beyond the scope of this research.

(Adapted from Trzeciak and Mackay1994, Swales and Feak 2004.)

How do you start the overview?

You can either start with a topic sentence that uses very similar words to those contained in your title, for example:

> This project will examine whether the recent badger cull has been effective in limiting the spread of bovine TB.

> This project will investigate whether we are in reach of establishing a base on Mars in which people could live permanently.

Or you could use an attention grabbing statement for the same topics above:

> 'Badger culls were cruel and ineffective' says an independent panel.

> 'Single planet species don't survive, just look at the dinosaurs' says former astronaut John Grunsfield.

A literature review

On page 16 we explained how to carry out a preliminary literature review. You did this to help develop your topic idea.

We have also discussed literature review on pages 64–65 when considering how to use and synthesise multiple sources. This material will now form the bulk of your introduction.

This intensive literature review should:

- Relate directly to your topic. The research context could be theoretical (looking at different theories on a particular topic), methodological (looking at how researchers carried out research into a particular issue) or historical (looking at research through a period of time or a certain decade).

- Identify any areas of controversy in the field. For example, if you are writing about whether Churchill was a good leader, you may wish to look at evidence for and against this view. If you are looking at the nature–nurture debate you may wish to summarise arguments for nature and for nurture and for an interaction between the two.

- Present a summary of what is currently known about your specific topic.

- Provide a clear statement of the research question(s) or problem(s) you will be addressing.

Narrow down to the aims and hypothesis

Remember, your literature review is like a funnel. It begins quite wide – you may use a few paragraphs to discuss the general area of study. Then narrow down to the specific area of your topic and review expert evidence that is relevant. The review should lead logically to your aims. State the aims of the project and, in the case of a research study, also state the hypothesis.

What order? You may organise the material

- **Chronologically** – You could write about the sources according to the order in which they were published starting with the earliest first, or you might write about sources in the historical order that the events occurred. For example, if you were investigating an 'Analysis of Afghan women under the Taliban and how this has changed since their downfall' you would look at the educational and political progress of Afghan women before and after the fall of the Taliban.

- **Thematically** – This will organise your sources around a topic rather than the passage of time. Although you may still organise your events chronologically, you may shift between different time periods and your focus is more on the theme. For example, when looking at the importance of the European Union in British politics the focus is more on different areas of British politics rather than the history of the EU.

JACOB'S EPQ
ON MARS

An exemplar overview

EPQ title: **How feasible is the prospect of establishing places of permanent habitation on Mars?**

This project will investigate whether we are in reach of establishing a base on Mars in which people could live permanently. This would be useful for humanity as any number of apocalyptic disasters could destroy civilisation in its current state; having a backup could preserve the knowledge we've amassed over the millennia. 'Single planet species don't survive, just look at the dinosaurs' says former astronaut John Grunsfield.

I will review the research to date which has focussed on various obstacles to establishing a base on Mars such as radiation and microgravity. Technology is currently being developed in order to minimise the risks to potential astronauts during their journey to Mars. The radiation the astronauts will be exposed to varies throughout the solar cycle so good timing of a mission will be paramount; with this in mind the radiation exposure level could be within safe levels.

Muscle and bone atrophy also stand to be major health problems. The fitness regime that the astronaut will have to maintain is laborious and time consuming to keep muscle and bone density at levels similar to those initially. On Mars the gravity is less than on Earth so atrophy will still affect the astronauts on arrival; however, their bone and muscle density will maintain itself at a level at which strength is comparable to that on Earth so preventative measures seem to be taken only if a return journey is planned.

When on Mars, a base will have to be established which would be able to support the colonists' needs. As most of these needs essentially are energy and infrastructure concerns, a solution is sending multiple spacecraft carrying nuclear generators and the infrastructure needed. This would be incredibly difficult as mission success rates to Mars are relatively low, so a solution will be needed to ensure the colonists receive the equipment they need. It will take years of effort and work to even get close to a point where its implementation could even be considered. However, there is currently a lot of work being done to study the intricacies and hopefully all the challenges posed can be overcome as technology develops.

Moderator comments

This overview has established a research territory in the first paragraph by showing how important the topic is. The quotation is also thought provoking.

In the second paragraph there is a brief mention of background research that will be further discussed in the literature review.

In the third paragraph relevant themes and issues are identified.

In the final paragraph there is mention of differing viewpoints on the topic.

Word count: 328

EXERCISE 4.6   Overview

Examine the overview below. Use coloured pens to identify the relevant subheadings from the list below:

starting point, brief outline, research territory, niche, background, statement of the scope of the work

Boys will be boys. A critical discussion of whether 'lads' mags' are sexist, harmful or harmless fun

Lads' mags such as *Nuts'* and *Loaded* are a popular mass-produced and publicly shared media form. It is not uncommon for lads' mags to get a bad press. These lifestyle magazines aimed at young men feature women in sexualised poses and are viewed as 'poor quality dross for the undiscerning masses' (Kehily 1999). Furthermore, they are argued to fuel a culture of laddism and gender stereotyping. Lifestyle magazines aimed at males are relatively new and *Loaded* was introduced in 1994.

Research has shown that boys who are exposed to a high diet of sexualised media images of women are likely to perceive women to be sex objects (Peter and Valkenburg 2007). It is important to focus on the impact of lads' mags for several reasons. First, lads' mags may serve as a powerful tool in the mainstreaming of sexist images and ideals. The second reason is the impact of lads' mags on readers has attracted media commentary and become a focus of debate for politicians. For example, former Labour MP Claire Curtis-Thomas presented a Bill to Parliament in 2006 attempting to restrict their

display in shops, and Prime Minister David Cameron has expressed concern over lads' mags fuelling a culture of youth violence. In contrast, a 2007 Ofsted report suggested that 'while at times lads' mags may reinforce sexual attitudes they also provide a positive source of information for young people'.

The role of lads' mags in popular culture is therefore complex where the direction of causality is knotty. For example, do males already predisposed to sexism read the magazines as a way of confirming their existing attitudes or do the magazines encourage sexist attitudes towards women? However, there is a need for research to explore how lads' mags affect readers' perceptions of, and attitudes towards, women, sex and sexuality. The key question that will be addressed is what image of women do readers of lads' mags hold? This will be explored by looking at contemporary research in the field and a small-scale survey of male sixth form students at a comprehensive school.

Suggested answers on page 124.

Optional content for projects involving the collection of secondary data. Required content for artefacts and projects involving primary data.

The method

If you have collected primary data then the method section is very important.

The method section may also be important for an artefact or other kind of report because you may wish to describe what you actually did.

When collecting primary data you must be very precise with your method section. The overriding principle is that you must describe what you did in sufficient detail for someone to able to replicate (i.e. repeat exactly) what you have done.

> **Word count**
>
> *About 500–600 words.*
>
> *This may be shorter or longer depending on the complexity of the procedures.*
>
> *See Exemplar III on page 118–119.*

> **Appropriate scientific style**
>
> In general it is expected that the method should be written in the past tense.
>
> For example, 'an experiment was carried out to investigate …' rather than 'an experiment will be carried out to investigate …'.
>
> It is also customary to refer to yourself as the researcher not 'I' or 'me'.
>
> For example, 'the questionnaire was designed by the researcher' instead of 'I designed the questionnaire'.

KEY WORDS

Debriefing A post-research interview designed to inform the participants of the true nature of the study and to restore them to the same state they were in at the start of the study. It may also be used to gain useful feedback about the procedures in the study.

Pilot study A trial run of a research study, involving only a few participants who are representative of the *target population*. It is conducted to test any aspects of the research design, with a view to making improvements before conducting the full research study.

Sampling A method of selecting participants from the target population being studied and intended to be representative of that population.

Standardised instructions A set of instructions that are the same for all participants. If instructions differ this might explain why participants responded differently to the task.

Structure of this section of your report

The method section usually contains the following subsections:

1. Design

State the design used, such as an experiment using an independent group design or a case study or a correlational analysis or a questionnaire or a case study using a questionnaire.

Explain why this design was chosen.

Explain any design decision, such as the type of questions used or controls in an experiment.

In an experiment or correlation describe the variables in your study. Provide clear measurable (operational) definitions. For example, in an investigation of whether type of music affects levels of concentration: The independent variable was the type of music, classical (Elgar's Nimrod) or rock (The Prodigy Firestarter). The dependent variable was concentration, operationalised as the number of correctly identified words in a word search in the space of three minutes.

2. Participants

If live participants were used, describe the target population from which they were drawn, what sampling method was used and how they were allocated to conditions (see pages 52–53). Do not use names; instead use pseudonyms or numbers.

3. Materials/apparatus

All equipment must be referred to in order to allow replication. Describe the quantitative aspects the masses, volumes, incubation times, concentrations, etc., that another researcher needs in order to replicate your study.

Copies of any questionnaires, tests, etc., should be placed in the appendix where you might show one blank copy of any questionnaire and one completed copy. Don't place every answered questionnaire in the appendices as it will make your project very bulky.

Standardised instructions, consent and debriefing forms should also be placed in the appendix.

4. Date(s) and location

For field studies you should give full details of where the field study was conducted, including the date of the study and the precise location. If you are a geography student you will know the rationale for this! Don't write 'Saltwells Nature Reserve, near Dudley West Midlands'. Instead give the latitude and longitude of the site.

Maps and plans should be included in the appendix.

5. Ethical considerations

Where research involves live participants, a discussion of how ethical issues were dealt with should be included (see pages 48–51). Examples of any consent forms should be placed in the appendix.

6. Procedure

In this subsection you will describe in as much detail as possible how you carried out your study. This may include information about:

- A pilot study (see page 56).
- Standardised instructions given to participants (full details can be given in the appendix).
- Precisely what participants were required to do. (Get someone else to read this to check you really have explained everything.)
- Controls that were used.

Reporting your method is like writing a recipe for a cake. You need to provide every detail so that someone else could do the same thing, i.e. replicate your study.

It is not just a matter of whether someone could do a similar study but whether they could do the exact same study. If another researcher changes small details, such as the kind of participants, this may explain why they get different findings. So replication must be identical as far as possible in order to validate the original findings.

Try writing a description of something you know well – such as how you get to school/college every morning or how you prepare your favourite meal.

EXERCISE 4.7 Writing a concise procedure

Writing lots of information is not required when trying to record precise details.

Problematic example 1: This is a very long and wordy description of a simple procedure in microbiology. Read and highlight the unnecessary detail:

The researcher came into the room, took off their school blazer and placed on their lab coat as this complied with the health and safety rules. They asked the technician for the key to the cupboard where the petri dishes were kept. They then placed the petri dish on the table and raised the lid ever so slightly. They used an inoculating loop to transfer the E coli culture to the agar surface. In order to spread the culture they moved the inoculating loop backwards and forwards several times with a few gentle strokes. The next step was to incubate which means to put in a special apparatus at a fixed temperature (usually 37°C, human body temperature, for possible pathogens, or 25°C for bacteria from the environment). The period of incubation was 24 hours at 37°C.

How would you improve this example? Try to give all of the important information in one concise paragraph.

Problematic example 2: This is a very long and wordy description of a simple procedure to investigate if rust is dependent on the presence of moisture.

The researcher asked the lab technician if they could have a desiccator which is a special container that has two 'layers' separated by wire gauze. Different substances can be placed in it without mixing the two while still allowing them to 'interact' since they can both be exposed to the air that is circulating within this container. Alternatively the researcher could use two test tubes. The first test tube could have iron nails placed in it and a piece of cotton wool preventing air getting in then calcium chloride crystals and cotton wool again. Calcium chloride crystals are used to absorb any moisture present in air. The second test tube can simply have some moistened iron nails placed in it, exposed to air. The researcher also had to ensure that the rust did not come into contact with any open wounds as this may cause infection. Several clean dry iron nails were placed above the wire gauze of the desiccator. The calcium chloride crystals were placed in the lower layer base of the desiccator. A few more nails were dipped in water and hung outside the desiccator. This was then left for three weeks.

How would you improve this example? Try to give all of the important information in one short paragraph.

Suggested answers on page 124.

Optional content for projects involving the collection of secondary data. Required content for projects involving primary data.

The findings

The findings section is where you present the outcome of your primary data collection in a logical sequence. You should not discuss or provide an interpretation of the findings at this stage.

Word count

About 500–600 words.

This number of words will depend on whether there are lots of tables rather than just narrative descriptions that require more words.

See Exemplar III on pages 119–120.

Appropriate scientific style

In general it is expected that the findings should be reported in the past tense.

For the appropriate style for your EPQ topic it is essential to have a look at a few journal articles on similar topics to see what reporting conventions are used.

Negative findings should also be reported

This is called the 'file-drawer problem' (see page 69). If researchers only report positive findings we fail to get a real picture of the phenomenon being studied.

The absence of an effect may be highly informative in many situations. In any case, your findings may be of importance to others even though they did not support your hypothesis.

Do not fall into the trap of thinking that findings contrary to what you expected, or findings that do not support your hypothesis, will result in a lower EPQ mark. On the contrary, provided you carried out the work well, you can access the higher mark bands as long as you provide a sound interpretation.

KEY WORDS

Significance A statistical term indicating that the research findings are sufficiently strong to enable a researcher to reject the null hypothesis under test and accept the research hypothesis.

Popper (1959) argued that science should follow a methodology based on falsification. Science cannot prove anything but disproof is possible (rejecting the null hypothesis). Popper used the example of trying to prove there are only white swans – no number of sightings of white swans can prove that all swans are white whereas the sighting of just one black one will disprove it. This led to the realisation that the only way to *prove* a theory correct was actually to seek disproof.

Null hypothesis A statement of no difference or no correlation.

Structure of this section of your report

1. Descriptive statistics

The findings section usually begins with text, outlining the key results. Provide as much information as possible about the nature of differences or relationships you have found. For example, if you are testing for differences among groups, and you find a significant difference, it is not enough to simply report that 'groups A and B were significantly different'. Instead say how they were different. It is much more informative to say something like, '...when using the Spider Phobia Questionnaire the group of participants from India had significantly higher scores than those from the UK'.

2. Summarise

You may have quantitative and/or qualitative data. In the findings section you should summarise these and provide any raw data in the appendix, e.g. details of all soil samples collected or participants' scores on a psychological test.

Quantitative data: Tables and graphs

Use descriptive statistics to summarise your data.

This includes measures of central tendency (averages) such as the mean, median or mode, as well as measures of dispersion such as the range, interquartile range and/or standard deviation (see details on page 47).

Do not use every descriptive statistic; select the one that is best for your data. Graphs permit the reader to 'eyeball' the data and at a glance get a sense of the findings. A graph should have a title and both axes should be clearly labelled. Tables should have clear headings and would never contain raw data.

Qualitative data

If you are summarising qualitative data you could present it as a series of selected quotations. For example, you might use quotes from students in response to a particular question.

You may also wish to convert qualitative to quantitative data by summarising responses into categories or themes – as in example 1 on the facing page.

See page 47 for advice on analysing qualitative data.

3. Inferential statistics where appropriate

If you have posed a testable hypothesis then you should use inferential statistics to determine whether the hypothesis is supported.

The mathematical calculations for any inferential test belong in the appendix. In the body of the REPORT explain what test was used and justify this choice. State the calculated statistic and whether this is significant. State whether the null hypothesis can be rejected.

If you are doing an inferential test you will need appropriate guidance from an expert to decide which test to use, how to calculate the observed value of your statistic and how to determine significance.

We recommend the following books to help you with inferential statistics:

- Coolican, H. (2014). *Research methods and statistics in psychology* (6th edition). London: Hodder and Stoughton.

- Flanagan, C. (2012) *The research methods companion for A-Level Psychology.* Oxford: Oxford University Press.

How to present tables and figures

When you have analysed all of the data, arrange the figures and tables in the sequence that presents your findings in a logical way. Simple rules to follow related to tables and figures:

- Assign numbers to tables and figures.

- The first table you refer to is Table 1, the next Table 2 and so forth.

- Similarly, the first graph is Figure 1, the next Figure 2, etc.

- For each table and graph/figure include a brief description (but not interpretation) of the findings in the body of your text.

- For a table the usual reporting convention is for the title to go at the top (tables are read from top to bottom).

- For a graph/figure the usual reporting convention is for the title to go at the top as shown in exemplar 1.

RACHEL'S EPQ ON COMPETENCE

Exemplar 1

EPQ title: **A recipe for success: To what extent do study skills contribute to academic competence?**

All the findings are summarised in Figure 1. The most common resource used by the students was their textbook (all students said they had used this in the last half term), followed by creating revision notes (21 out of 22 students said they had done this).

Another common resource used was practising past exam papers for homework (18 out of 22 students said they had done this).

None of the students had accessed lunchtime or after school support nor had any students ticked 'use ICT'.

Figure1: Type of resources used by students in the past half term.

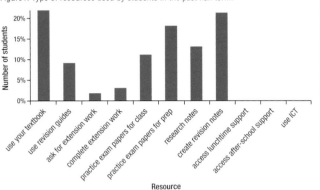

Moderator comments

This example highlights the trends that the student wants the reader to focus on.

Moderator comments

In contrast, this example strays into the realms of interpretation by going beyond the data presented ('This shows that …'). Leave interpretation to the discussion.

Exemplar 2

The findings shown in Figure 2 were fairly surprising as they indicated that the majority of students did not know their target grade even though they had recently received their termly grades. This shows that termly grades may not be an effective means of communicating target grades, as the students had clearly not made the connections between the two.

Figure 2: Pie chart to indicate whether students know their target grade.

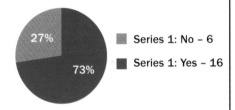

EXERCISE 4.8 Interpreting data

Describe what each of these bar charts shows – i.e. highlight the trends shown in the bar charts. Give a summary of what is there and then draw a conclusion.

Figure 1 How students rated the written and verbal feedback given by their teacher in the last term.

Figure 2 The percentages of pupils who were drunk on one or more days in the week preceding the survey (Schools and Students Health Education Unit (SHEU) 2006).

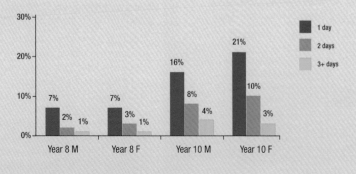

Suggested answers on page 124.

The discussion

The discussion section is concerned with interpreting the meaning of your research.

You should review your own research in relation to the wider context in which the project is located. You can refer back to the rationale that you gave for your research in the literature review, and discuss what your own research has added in this context.

It is important to show that you appreciate the limitations of your research, and how these may affect the validity (meaningfulness) or usefulness of your findings. Given the acknowledged limitations, you can report on the implications of your findings for theory, research, and practice.

Word count

For projects with secondary data the discussion may be the longest part of your REPORT, as much as 3000 or 4000 words with a short introduction plus a conclusion. Or the introduction may be longer and a shorter discussion. In Exemplar II (pages 112–115) the discussion section is about 3000 words.

For projects with primary data, you will have method and findings to report as well so the discussion may be about 1500 words. See Exemplar III on pages 120–121.

For projects with an artefact the report is only 1000 words long and the method section will be as important as the introduction and discussion. See Exemplar I on page 109.

Structure of this section of your report

It may help to structure your discussion as follows (you can include the subheadings if you wish):

1. Explain the findings in relation to the hypothesis

If you worked with a hypothesis then you should begin the discussion by explaining your results in relation to the research hypothesis. Do more than *state* the findings, try to *explain* them. It may help to discuss some particular examples. Relate findings to the aims/hypothesis. You can also explain other findings such as comments from participants during debriefing. In the case of a correlational project, be careful to not use causal language to discuss your results; unless you did an experiment you cannot infer causality.

Exemplar

> JUSTIN'S EPQ ON ATTRACTIVENESS

EPQ title: **To what extent do we seek partners of the same levels of attractiveness?**

The results from the study do support the directional hypothesis because 13.2% of women were found to be seeking attractiveness in a partner, whereas 25.2% of men sought physical attractiveness. The hypothesis can therefore be accepted 'Men are more likely than women to seek qualities of attractiveness in a partner of the opposite sex'.

Females were significantly more likely to refer to their own attractiveness than males, with 54.7% referring to their own attractiveness as opposed to 40.8% of males. This supports the sociobiological theory, as females see their attractiveness as being a significant factor when successfully acquiring a mate. This compared well with research carried out by Harrison and Saeed (1977), who found that men seek physically attractive women who are younger than them. So women make more reference to their physical attractiveness. Similarly the present study related to the research carried out by Waynforth and Dunbar (1995) who found that 68% of women referred to their physical attractiveness while only 51% of men referred to their physical attractiveness.

2. Explain the findings in relation to previous research (literature review)

It is important to carefully consider all possible explanations for your project's results. Consider how the findings/conclusions from other research and/or experts may be combined with yours to derive a new or perhaps better-substantiated understanding of the problem.

Questions and issues raised by previous research may have been the driving force behind your EPQ. So you will need to discuss how your research supports the results of previous studies.

It is also important to indicate the points of departure between your research and previous research.

Exemplar

> KYLE'S EPQ ON CHARITY

EPQ title: **An analysis of whether the perceived controllability of the 'victim' is a factor in willingness to donate to charities**

The study found that participants were more willing to donate to charities that they considered to be deserving than those considered non-deserving. The research found that the MacMillan cancer support charity was rated as the charity participants would most likely make a donation to. However, addiction charities such as Action on Addiction were also rated highly. The results departed from previous research such as Weiner's (1992) attribution theory, which states that the determining factor of whether to help someone is the perceived controllability of their predicament. If a victim was perceived as responsible for their plight they would not receive help compared to a victim whose plight was out of their control. This can explain why cancer charities received more sympathy from respondents than addiction charities according to Weiner. This research challenges this as some respondents believed than although addicts may not be blameless this did not mean that they were unworthy of help. Also cultural changes between 1992 and 2014 may have been responsible for a change in perceived controllability.

Moderator comments

There is a comprehensive discussion of the findings in relation to the hypothesis and also the sociobiological theory which underpinned the study. Furthermore, the student has discussed the findings in relation to previous research (e.g. Harrison and Saeed).

The purpose of the discussion is to consider previously mentioned research in relation to your own research. Therefore it is not expected that you will introduce new research here.

Moderator comments

This gives a clear statement of the results and relates the results to a published theory. There is also important further material in the form of a brief alternative explanation.

An exemplar of strengths and limitations

EPQ title: **What are the religious issues involved in school-based PE for Muslim students?**

Potential limitations include the possibility of bias, uncritical insider positioning, loss of detachment and objectivity in scientific research. According to Benn et al. (2010) 'all researchers have value positions and face similar dangers. Scientific approaches depend on world-view and can be complementary' (p.10).

A further limitation is that, because of the age of the Muslim girls in the sample, they often had difficulties in verbalising their broader understanding of PE. Furthermore, they often found difficulty in articulating their experiences in PE. As with the findings of Nugent and Faucette (1995), others had difficulties in expressing their opinions in a consistent way.

A strength of this work is the quality of relationships sustained with the respondents. Without their open and honest accounts, willingness to participate (and for the teachers sample) to find time in their busy schedules, this research would not have been possible. The depth of interview responses with the Muslim sample increased with time. The advantage of having a small sample of girls was that all of the pupils in this year group were interviewed and I did not have to rely on the teachers to select a representative sample for me. Only one pupil declined the opportunity to take part.

GRACE'S EPQ ON IDENTITY

Moderator comments

Insider status has been discussed successfully as a limitation of the research. Grace also gives a candid account of other limitations of her research. She will not lose marks by pointing these limitations out but instead she will gain marks for the reflection on the limitations. She has also considered one strength, to her credit, as it is often harder to think of strengths.

3. Strengths and limitations of your project

All studies have limitations. Even the best studies in the most prestigious journals have limitations. The limitations can be linked to your methodology or the type of participants used or the design you used. For example, you might consider why the type of participants would affect the conclusions of the study or you might consider why participants did not answer the questions honestly. Avoid simplistic criticisms such as saying the sample was too small.

You can also point out the strengths of your project. For instance, you might mention the extensive piloting that was done to improve the design of the study and avoid certain problems.

The box at the top of this page gives an example of how Grace wrote her strengths and limitations.

4. Implications

Although your EPQ may have provided the answer to your research questions, there may still be some questions left unanswered. You need to briefly mention further investigations that could be done to clarify your working hypotheses.

You might, for example, suggest that a further study could collect qualitative data to provide insights into why participants behaved as they did, or you might suggest using focus groups to provide further data.

For example, here is an implication from Grace's EPQ:

EPQ title: **What are the religious issues involved in school-based PE for Muslim students?**

It would seem imperative that teachers are encouraged to expand their understanding of Muslim girls' attitudes towards and experiences of physical activity to one that includes physical culture. This would entail exploring the meanings that girls attach to sports, activities, clothes, friendship groups, music and the media and the ways in which they relate to the physical culture (Macdonald 2002).

Moreover, Initial Teacher Training and subsequent CPD may be the very context through which to develop these wider understandings of the needs of teenage Muslim girls. There is evidence to suggest that teacher education programmes have not given sufficient attention to critical issues of culture and diversity (Goodwin 2007) and subjective experiences are often side-lined (Flintoff 1993, Rich 2001).

Here is an implication from Kyle's EPQ on Charity:

EPQ title: **An analysis of whether the perceived controllability of the 'victim' is a factor in willingness to donate to charities**

There is a need to address what charities can do to increase their chance of donations especially amongst causes that are thought to be less deserving. Breaking down any barriers to giving, especially perceptions that donors might have about the worthiness of causes is therefore a key issue. By appropriately framing the cause and by supporting the development of empathy for the cause should maximise donations.

EXERCISE 4.9 Good discussion

Four elements that should be in the discussion section are listed on this spread.

Read the following example of part of a discussion section from a study that has looked at drinking preferences. Identify the elements of the discussion you find in each sentence of the text.

① The results from the investigation supported the alternative hypothesis that predicted that that female Sixth form students overestimate the amount of alcohol male peers want a typical 18-year-old female to drink. ② These findings support those of Labrie *et al.* (2009) but contrast to those of Lewis and Neighbors (2004), who did not find a mismatch between male and female perceptions of drinking. ③ The results show that women's motivations for drinking may relate to a motivation to develop and maintain social relationships (Eagly 1978, Gilligan 1982, Gleason 1994). ④ A further explanation is that it supports research that suggests that men find it attractive and sexually appealing when a woman can drink as much as a man does (Young *et al.* 2005). ⑤ This study shows that males prefer their sexual partners to drink less and one of the main reasons for this might be that males may have an awareness of the dangers of alcohol and related health risks and also fears of infidelity from heavy drinking partners as drinking may be a precursor to sexual encounters. Hence if their partner drinks heavily there may be a risk of infidelity. ⑥ If females mistakenly believe that males want them to drink more this makes them more likely to drink to risky levels. ⑦ The present investigation had several limitations. An opportunity sample of 20 Sixth form male and 20 female students was selected from only one school. This is unlikely to represent the views of the target population. Also as students were only 18 they may have limited experiences of drinking alcohol and so further research could investigate undergraduates where drinking is more culturally ingrained into University life. ⑧ A more diverse sample may increase the validity of the findings. ⑨ Self-report data is also an area of concern with issues of social desirability although answers were confidential which may increase validity. ⑩ The questions were also forced choice and closed and participants were not able to expand on their answers. A future study could include both closed and open questions to establish why males do not want their sexual partners to engage in heavy drinking. ⑪ The findings have implications for health promotion aimed at females to correct errors in the perceived preferences of opposite-sex peers. These interventions may correct not only the misconceptions but also encourage safer levels of drinking in females.

Suggested answers on page 124.

The conclusion

The conclusion is a valuable tool. The aim of the conclusion is to leave the moderator satisfied that you have realised what you set out to do (AO3) and it also is credited under the AO4 Review criteria.

The conclusion is not just a summary of your work but an *analysis* of what has been reported, providing some generalisations that can be made.

In some academic journals the conclusions section is a paragraph or subsection at the end of the discussion, whereas other journals require a separate conclusions section.

'What is your 'take-home message' ... what do you want the reader to remember from your study?'

Dean R. Hess (2004, p

Word count

About 300 words.

Focus on analysis.

See Exemplar II (page 115) and Exemplar III (page 121).

What is a take-home message?

A 'take-home message' requires you to think about and focus on what it is you want people to remember most after they have finished reading your 5000 words. You need to make sure that you make the point, and make it clearly. Often an EPQ project will leave the moderator wondering what the point was, or which of many points they are supposed to take most seriously.

Write down the point you want to make in plain English. Be blunt, imagine you are on a soapbox telling a particularly obtuse listener the message you want them to understand. Wag your finger at them!

Some BLUNT examples, just giving the take-home message in plain English:

Once you have written down your take-home message in non-academic 'blunt' terms – you then need to make a convincing case for it in your conclusion. You need to turn this blunt message into something more academic that resonates.

You may need to look back to the start of your EPQ and consider the line of argument from there to the end of your project. Make sure the moderator can follow this line of argument to the inevitable conclusion.

Remember the *writer* must do as much as possible to make sure that the *reader* finishes the paper knowing what they are meant to take away from it.

Here are some take-home messages that RESONATE, using more academic terms:

FELIX'S EPQ ON FRACKING

EPQ title: **Do the benefits of hydraulic fracturing supersede the environmental threat it poses?**

There are arguments for and against fracking and an honest debate is needed to address these arguments.

Opponents of fracking argue that extraction causes environmental destruction. Supporters see it as global revolution we cannot afford to ignore. We either need to re-engineer our society to require less energy or look for new sources of energy. An honest debate on these issues is required.

ROHAN'S EPQ ON MARRIAGE

EPQ title: **A consideration of the arguments for and against the legalisation of same-sex marriage.**

There are loads of reasons why same-sex marriage should be legalised but the one main reason is to do with basic morals.

The single best reason to legalise same-sex marriage is not because it is inevitable, or because it is what our legal history demands of us, or because it is more conducive to family life. It is because legalising same-sex marriage is the kind thing to do and kindness is a basic moral value.

AILISH'S EPQ ON ADHERENCE

EPQ title: **What are the consequences of poor adherence to long-term therapies for chronic diseases?**

There are serious consequences involved when people don't follow advice and stick to therapies for chronic disorders. This can have real knock-on effects and affect the health of the nation.

The consequences of poor adherence to long-term therapies are poor health outcomes and increased health care costs. Poor adherence to long-term therapies severely compromises the effectiveness of treatment, making this a critical issue in population health both from the perspective of quality of life and of health economics.

DON'T...

Your conclusion should not:

- End with a lengthy quotation.
- Just 'sum up' up what you've written so far.
- Focus merely on a minor point in your argument.

Avoid using the following phrases in your conclusion:

- In conclusion ...
- In summary ...
- In closing ...

Although these phrases can work well in speeches, they can come across as wooden and trite in writing.

Also avoid:

- Stating your proposition (thesis) for the very first time in the conclusion.
- Introducing a new idea or subtopic in your conclusion.
- Ending with a rephrased thesis statement without any substantive changes.
- Making sentimental, emotional appeals (out of character with the rest of an analytical paper).
- Including evidence (quotations, statistics, etc.) that should be in the body of the thesis.

Structure of this section of your report

A generic structure that you may find useful is:

- Brief recap of what you have covered in relation to the essay title.
- Reference to the larger issue.
- Highlight the most important aspects.
- Evaluate the main arguments.
- Take-home message.

See page 104 for a detailed explanation of these. Here is an exemplar conclusion:

EPQ title: How does Geoffrey Chaucer present women in *The Canterbury Tales*?

Brief recap	This essay has looked at the debate surrounding the way in which Chaucer presents the role of women in his work.
Reference to the larger issue	In Chaucer's 'Canterbury Tales', female narrators and characters function as a focus to explore women's gender roles and their struggle for maistre (sovereignty). Even though Chaucer is a man writing about women, he experiments with the feminine voice, thus he uses his tales to disseminate his knowledge of women's unfair oppression, perhaps hoping to spark a discussion on women's subjugation.
Highlight the most important aspects	Chaucer wrote in a misogynistic era where women were seen as either pure or sinful, known as the Mary and Eve dichotomy. Yet many of his tales challenge this medieval stereotype of women. According to Martin (1990) Chaucer's female narrators cannot be judged by today's standards of feminism; however, when they are examined from the medieval point of view, 'the undertone of feminism in their behaviour and tales emerges. They are concerned with bettering the conditions for women, they challenge the authorities in their tales'.
Evaluate the main arguments	In the 'Clerk's Tale', I have highlighted Griselde's qualities of weakness and virtue that comply with the medieval Mary stereotype but consider the alternative view that in her pursuit of virtue Griselde abandons motherly compassion. Concerning the Merchant's Tale, May's ability to deceive conforms to the Eve stereotype but alternatively as a peasant woman who overpowers her socially superior husband she is arguably a Marxist feminist figure of interest. In the 'Wife of Bath's Tale' the protagonist can be seen as both a pro- and anti-feminist model. Finally, Chaucer finds a middle ground between the chaste and pure women by presenting Dorigen in the 'Franklin's Tale' as her husband's equal in marriage but also as a woman striving to maintain her reputation and faithfulness. She is unafraid to assert her opinion and this is what leads to success in marriage.
Take-home message	Chaucer's varied portrayal of female characters suggests that he completely rejects the accepted medieval female stereotypes, opting to portray that there existed not just one single medieval woman but some who conformed to the medieval ideal while others did not.

YASEF'S EPQ ON CHAUCER

Appendices

Items that can usefully go in the appendices are those that a reader would want to see, but which would take up too much space and disrupt the flow if placed within the main text. Make sure you reference the appendices within the main text where necessary (i.e. 'see Appendix I').

Headings

Each appendix should be identified by a Roman numeral in sequence, i.e. Appendix I, Appendix II, etc. Each appendix should contain different material.

Don't go overboard and produce masses of extra material – it won't win the respect of a moderator who then has to wade through masses of material. Make sure you include the essentials from this list:

- Standardised instructions.
- Raw data, e.g. test scores for each participant.
- Consent forms.
- Debriefing scripts.
- Explanation of formulas for data analysis.
- Specialised computer programs for a particular procedure.
- Full generic names of chemicals or compounds that you have referred to in somewhat abbreviated fashion or by some common name in the text of your paper.
- Diagrams of specialised apparatus.
- Copies of questionnaires (one blank and one completed with names removed).

Figures and tables in appendices

Figures, graphs and tables are often found in an appendix. These should be formatted as discussed previously (see page 85) but are numbered in a separate sequence from those found in the body of the paper. So, the first figure in the appendix would be Figure 1, the first table would be Table 1, etc.

Conclusion words

Writing a conclusion can be challenging but it need not be. Here are some words that will help you to write the conclusion to your EPQ. Most of the time, using the word or phrase in the middle of a sentence is better than making it the first word of the conclusion.

in fact	for these reasons
in effect	as a result of
indeed	altogether
clearly	surely
overall	truly
all in all	due to
obviously	definitely
ultimately	thus
consequently	

EXERCISE 4.10 Conclusions

Highlight the conclusion words used in the text below and identify the take-home message.

Whether 'medical marijuana' (*Cannabis sativa* used to treat a wide variety of pathologic states) should be accorded the status of a legitimate pharmaceutical agent has long been a contentious issue. In effect the decision whether to legalise the medical use of marijuana should be based on a dispassionate scientific analysis. Indeed, a number of such investigations have recently been published in the peer-reviewed literature. Data from these studies suggest that medical marijuana has demonstrated safety and efficacy in treating several devastating human pathologies. Some individuals as a result may believe that this documentation now warrants marijuana's approval for use as a legitimate therapeutic agent. Others may think that additional scientific scrutiny is necessary. So should marijuana be approved as a bona fide medication? In conclusion, this essay was not intended to provide an answer, instead it has strongly argued in favour of the concept that scientific data and methodology, rather than political and ideological considerations, ultimately should lead to a rational decision. Whether the data derived from current and future scientific investigations will justify the approval or disapproval of medical marijuana remains a challenging issue for the future.

See suggested answers on page 124.

Referencing your sources

Previously we discussed how to credit your sources in the text (see page 71) by supplying an author's surname and the date of their work. The full details of the publication must be supplied in alphabetical order in a bibliography (often simply called 'references') at the end of your piece of work. This is called *referencing*, i.e. providing the full reference so that someone else can access the source if they want to follow the topic up.

See Exemplar II (page 115) and Exemplar III (page 122) to see how other students have referenced their work.

Formats for referencing

There are many different referencing conventions in common use. Each subject will have its own preferred format, and every journal or book editor has a set of 'house rules'. Although no particular system of referencing is required for the EPQ, consistent use of one referencing system will be expected if you are to access the higher marks for AO2.

The general principles of referencing will be explained here by giving details of the most commonly used format, known as the Harvard system. Once you have understood the principles common to all referencing systems you should be able to apply the specific rules used by your subject. One way to find this out is to look at books and journals in your specialist area.

Whatever system you choose to use – be consistent.

Getting the details

The details required for the full reference can be found from the source itself or you can often obtain these by typing some of the information into Google.

Book references must include:

- The surnames and forenames or initials of all authors.
- The date of publication.
- The book title.
- The place of publication.
- The name of the publisher.

For example:

Offer, D., Ostrov, E. and Howard, K. (1981). *The Adolescent – a psychological self-portrait.* New York: Basic Books.

The title of the book should be in italics to distinguish it from the other details. I the example above the title is italicised, but it could be in bold, underlined or in inverted commas. When multi-authored works have been quoted, it is importan to include the names of all the authors, even when the text reference used was *et a*

Papers or articles within an edited book should in addition include

- The author(s) of the article, the date and title of the piece.
- The editor of the book.
- Title of the book and the place and name of the publisher.
- The first and last page numbers of the article or paper.

For example:

Milner, D. (1970). Ethnic identity and preference in minority-group children. In: H. Tajfel, (1981) *Human groups and social categories.* Cambridge: Cambridge University Press, pp.329-356.

Journal articles must also include:

- The name of the journal.
- The volume and issue number of the journal.
- The first and last page numbers of the article.

The publisher and place of publication are not normally required for journals.

For example:

MacKay, G. (2002). The disappearance of disability? Thoughts on a changing culture. *British Journal of Special Education*, 29 (4), 159–163.

Note that in the last two references above, it is the book title and the journal nam that are italicised, not the title of the paper or article.

Endnotes and footnotes

Some humanities and science disciplines prefer the use of endnotes or footnotes rather than name + date referencing as described above. A number is placed in the text where you would normally put (Milner 1970). Such numbers do not interrupt the flow of the text as much as names and dates.

Endnotes – The full references are provided at the end of the chapter.

Footnotes – The full references are provided at the bottom of the page.

Endnote or footnote markers are usually a sequential series of numbers either in brackets or slightly above the line of writing (superscript).

Word processors such as MS Word allow you to insert footnotes and convert to endnotes if you wish.

Exemplar using footnotes

EPQ title: **Who wants to live forever?**

MICHAEL'S EPQ ON LIVING FOREVER

It is also important to consider whether it would in fact be beneficial to the human race to live much longer than we already do. Leon Kass[1] said that 'simply to covert a prolonged life span to ourselves is both a sign and a cause of failure to open ourselves to procreation and any higher purpose'. Elsewhere he has written '[to] desire to prolong youthfulness is not only a childish desire to eat one's life and keep it; it is also an expression of a childish and narcissistic wish incompatile with devotion to posterity.'[2]

---

[1] Kass, L. R. (1985). *Toward a more natural science: biology and human affairs.* New York City: Free Press. p.316

[2] Kass, L. R. (2001) *Claim and its limits: Why not immortality?* [online] http://www.firstthings.com/article/2007/01/claim-and-its-limits-why-not-immortality-36 [accessed 15 February 2013]

Internet pages

As information on the Internet changes rapidly and Internet pages move it can be difficult to find the source you used. Therefore, it is useful to make a note of the Internet address at the outset. The final reference should include:

- Author of the information (this may be an individual, group or organisation).
- Optional: The date the page was posted on the Internet (most Internet pages have a date at the bottom of the page).
- The title of the article.
- The http:// address.
- The date you accessed the Internet page (in case the information has been subsequently modified).

For example:

Jackson, R. (2004). *Inclusion: A flawed Vision.* GSSPL [online]. Available at: www. gssp1.org.uk/html/inclusion_aflawed-vision [Accessed January 2014]

Other types of publications

You may also wish to refer to other types of publications, including PhD dissertations, lectures, translated works, newspaper articles, dictionary or encyclopedia entries or legal or historical texts. The same general principles apply to the referencing of all published sources. Here are some examples:

Goodwin, L.J. (2007). The inclusion of children with physical disabilities in physical education. Rhetoric or reality? Unpublished Ph.D. Thesis University of Surrey.

Smith, J. (14th November 2013). The benefits of the Extended Project, Lecture 1. University of Somewhere.

Guardian (2007). I felt more welcome in the Bible belt. Friday 20th April 2007, page 14.

Please note that in contrast to the format used for the published sources, the formatting of references for unpublished sources does not include italics, as there is no publication title to highlight.

Personal communication

If the idea or information that you wish to cite has been told to you personally, perhaps in a discussion with a teacher or an email from a specialist in the field whom you have interviewed, the point can be referenced as shown in the example below:

Robertson, M. (2012) personal communication.

Same author same year

If one author has written a number of things in the same year the letters a, b, c, etc., are used in the text and bibliography. For example:

TEXT

It would be wrong to assume that there is any kind of homogeneity in what is placed under the broad and crude heading of SEBD (Cooper, 1999a).

Children and young people with SEBD experience notable difficulties in learning (Cooper, 1999b)

BIBLIOGRAPHY

Cooper, P. (1999a). Changing perceptions of EBD: maladjustment, EBD and beyond. *Emotional and Behavioural Difficulties, 4* (1)**,** 3–11.

Cooper, P. (1999b). Educating children with emotional and behavioural difficulties; The evolution of current thinking and provision. *In:* Cooper, P. (ed.) *Understanding and Supporting Children with Emotional and Behavioural Difficulties.* London, Jessica Kingsley.

EXERCISE 4.11 Referencing

Spot the mistake! Identify what is missing from the following references:

Example 1

Jackson, R. Inclusion: A flawed vision. GSSPL [online]. Available at: www.gssp1.org.uk/html/inclusion_aflawed-vision

Example 2

Ang, I. (2001). *On not speaking Chinese: Living between Asia and the West.*

Example 3

Bennett-Levy and Marteau (1984). Fear of animals: What is prepared? *British Journal of Psychology,*

Example 4

Waynforth, D. and Dunbar, R.I.M. (1995). Conditional mate choice strategies in humans: Evidence from "Lonely hearts" advertisements. *132,* 755-779.

Suggested answers on page 124.

When you are convinced that you have finished your EPQ, you need to take a break from your REPORT so that you can return to it with fresh eyes for the final editing. The checklist below will help you to decide whether you need to make any further changes.

> 'When you write...you spend day after day scanning and identifying the trees. When you're done you have to step back and look at the forest.'
>
> Stephen King (2000)

EXERCISE 4.12
Checking academic style

Examine the extract from a PRODUCTION LOG below to identify any typographical or spelling errors, examples of colloquialism or informal vocabulary.

EPQ title: **An evaluation of the contributing factors leading to the start of the Syrian civil war, and its continuation today**

Over this project I have found many differnet reasons for both the initiation and the continuation today. Many of these facters cannot be singled out and it was part and parcel of the combination of several different internal and external reasons that created the war we see today. I feel that unknowingly it was the american aid in supporting the first military coup that started the ball rolling for the escalation; this is due to the beginnings of the political system the people were fighting against. There is no way we cannot conclude fully this was down to America as many other factors may have been involved in this politicl system, but it was the creating of a dictatorial system that created the need for reform.

Suggested answers on page 124.

Checklist – am I done?

This is not a list to just tick things off. You need to go back to your REPORT and consider the issues carefully. For example, really look through your REPORT to see if you have divided the text into paragraphs.

Literature review	
Have I included at least five sources to support/ challenge my arguments?	Yes/No/Not applicable
Have I provided a full reference for every quotation I have included (author, date and page number)?	Yes/No/Not applicable
Have I taken out any irrelevant material?	Yes/No/Not applicable
Have I removed any sweeping or emotive statements that are not supported by evidence?	Yes/No/Not applicable
Have I included a complete list of references listing all my sources?	Yes/No/Not applicable
Have all illustrations and figures that have been taken from someone else's work been cited correctly and acknowledged as a reference?	Yes/No/Not applicable
Have I used plenty of paragraphs? Can I divide the text further?	Yes/No/Not applicable
Are the paragraphs clearly structured? • Start paragraph with clear sentence stating the point to be discussed.	Yes/No/Not applicable
• Other sentences which provide evidence/elaborate the point.	Yes/No/Not applicable
• A final sentence to conclude.	Yes/No/Not applicable
• One main idea for each paragraph.	Yes/No/Not applicable
Does the literature review show how my EPQ relates to other studies that *support* my perspective?	Yes/No/Not applicable
Does the literature review show how my EPQ relates to other studies that are *contrary* to my perspective?	Yes/No/Not applicable
Research question	
Have I included the research question or my aims and objectives?	Yes/No/Not applicable
Methodology	
Have I provided a justification for my choice of method?	Yes/No/Not applicable
Is my description of the methods I have adopted clear enough for another researcher to replicate?	Yes/No/Not applicable
Have I included relevant subsections for the practical report?	Yes/No/Not applicable
Are relevant materials such as copies of questionnaires, standardised instructions, and raw data in the appendices?	Yes/No/Not applicable

'My EPQ has been one of the best academic decisions I have made throughout my time in education. It has allowed me to do research and study into an area that otherwise I wouldn't have had the opportunity to do. It has allowed me to expand my knowledge about a period of history that I find simply fascinating and to be recognised and credited at the end is a huge bonus. However, my extended project journey hasn't been easy. Writing a 5000-word report is just the beginning as the research and presentation of the materials is a project in itself.

The EPQ is unique and valuable as it allows students like myself to assess themselves outside the exam hall in an environment that they may not be used to.

The knowledge that I have gained from undertaking an EPQ is unquestionable. The Civil Rights Movement in the USA is a topic that I now feel confident about and enjoy taking up discussions about it regularly.'

Henry, EPQ student

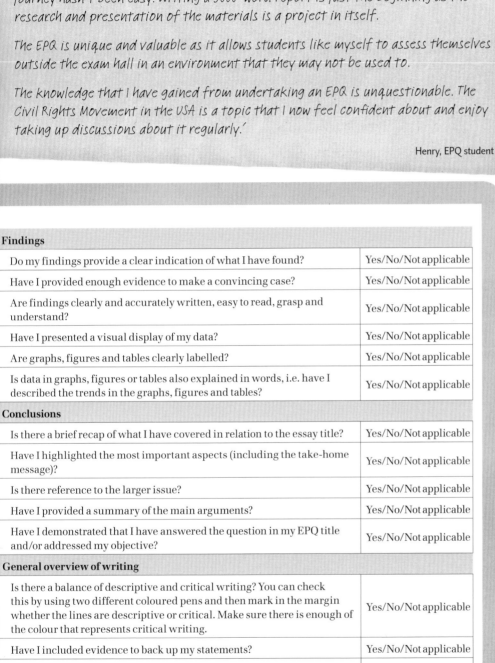

Findings

Do my findings provide a clear indication of what I have found?	Yes/No/Not applicable
Have I provided enough evidence to make a convincing case?	Yes/No/Not applicable
Are findings clearly and accurately written, easy to read, grasp and understand?	Yes/No/Not applicable
Have I presented a visual display of my data?	Yes/No/Not applicable
Are graphs, figures and tables clearly labelled?	Yes/No/Not applicable
Is data in graphs, figures or tables also explained in words, i.e. have I described the trends in the graphs, figures and tables?	Yes/No/Not applicable

Conclusions

Is there a brief recap of what I have covered in relation to the essay title?	Yes/No/Not applicable
Have I highlighted the most important aspects (including the take-home message)?	Yes/No/Not applicable
Is there reference to the larger issue?	Yes/No/Not applicable
Have I provided a summary of the main arguments?	Yes/No/Not applicable
Have I demonstrated that I have answered the question in my EPQ title and/or addressed my objective?	Yes/No/Not applicable

General overview of writing

Is there a balance of descriptive and critical writing? You can check this by using two different coloured pens and then mark in the margin whether the lines are descriptive or critical. Make sure there is enough of the colour that represents critical writing.	Yes/No/Not applicable
Have I included evidence to back up my statements?	Yes/No/Not applicable
Have I included formal vocabulary and avoided colloquialism (e.g. easier said than done, part and parcel) and personal language (e.g. I think, in my opinion)?	Yes/No/Not applicable
Have I explained any technical terms or abbreviations (a glossary may be a useful idea)?	Yes/No/Not applicable
Have I proofread my EPQ for grammatical/spelling errors? (In Word these are clearly identified for me with green or red underscoring yes but some students still hand in with errors!!!)	Yes/No/Not applicable
Is the word count appropriate?	Yes/No/Not applicable

You have finished the report!

If you have completed your checklist you should be able to take it to the final review meeting with your supervisor. At this meeting the checklist can serve as an agenda to guide your discussion and help you decide your priorities for the final review stages of the EPQ process, covered in Chapter 5.

Chapter 5
Review

EVALUATE

EXAMINE

ASSESS

MEASURE

REVIEW

This chapter is focused on the AO4 component of your project, which is concerned with evidence of outcomes and an evaluation of your learning.

The PRESENTATION will also provide evidence of outcomes and allows you to show your learning points.

In addition there is evidence in the MID-PROJECT and PROJECT PRODUCT REVIEW, where you review the successes and failures as you follow your plan.

The AO4 evidence will be in your SUMMARY AND REFLECTION in the PRODUCTION LOG where you provide a short review of your findings in 50–150 words, and a reflection on your EPQ journey including learning points for the future.

AO4

Assessment objective 4

The final skill in the mark scheme will account for 20% of your final mark.

The AO4 objectives include:

- Evidence of communication skills.
- Ability to convey and present evidenced outcomes and conclusions.
- Evaluation of own learning and performance.

What the moderator is looking for

Part of the AO4 review skill involves an evaluation of strengths and weaknesses, not only of the completed project but also of your own learning.

You need to be able to stand back and look at the planning and management of your product as well as the final PRODUCT itself.

You need to reflect on your EPQ journey and consider how much have you grown as a result of your journey.

You need to show that you are aware of your successes and failures and strengths and weaknesses.

When determining your AO4 mark the moderator is considering:	Where this is usually demonstrated
Does the candidate provide a detailed and careful evaluation of the strengths and weaknesses of the completed project in relation to the project plan?	Your PRODUCTION LOG shows an outline of your successes and failures as you follow your plan. This applies in particular to the MID-PROJECT and PROJECT PRODUCT REVIEW, PRESENTATION RECORD and SUMMARY AND REFLECTION.
	The PRESENTATION can also provide clear evidence of your EPQ journey not just focus on your final PRODUCT. For example, what successes and failures did you meet along the way?
	The REPORT can also show the moderator that you have communicated your findings and conclusions clearly.
Is the material consistently relevant, well structured and appropriately presented?	The REPORT will provide evidence that you have shown clear links between sources of information and the themes of your project.
	The PRESENTATION is also a vehicle to justify the choice of material in an appropriate format.
Are the conclusions based on evidence?	The REPORT can demonstrate that the conclusions that you have drawn are based on evidence rather than opinion.
	The PRESENTATION is also a useful way to convey your conclusions. Remember to include evidence of your PRESENTATION such as copies of the PowerPoint slides.

What's in this chapter

Planning the presentation

Your PRESENTATION is an essential requirement of the EPQ. You cannot submit your EPQ without it.

It is also a requirement of the EPQ that this PRESENTATION is made to a non-specialist audience.

You will obtain marks for AO1 (planning) if you refer to the management of the project. AO2 marks (use of resources) can be gained if you have referred to your resources. There will also be evidence of AO3 (develop and realise) in the presentation as it showcases the finished PRODUCT and also your evidenced conclusions.

Different types of visual aids

Select a visual aid that you feel comfortable with and which will suit your presentation.

Microsoft PowerPoint

Microsoft PowerPoint is probably the most commonly used form of visual aid but Prezi, Google presentations, Keynote and Beamer are also worth a look.

Do	Do not
Make your title clear.	Make up a new snappy title.
Refer to the EPQ journey.	Outline the key facts you have covered in the project.
Use a font size large enough to enable your audience to read it (minimum 20pt).	Use too much text on each slide.
Keep the background simple.	Overdo the animation or play the music too loud, as it can be distracting.
Keep your images consistent. Use the same font, titles, layout, etc., for each image.	Have endless slides.
Make things visual.	Give your audience too much text or overly complicated diagrams to read as this limits their ability to listen.
Reduce the amount of information on each slide.	Read from the slide.
Make sure your images are of a high quality.	Display slides with spelling and/ or grammatical errors.

Video, DVD or YouTube

Use of film can give you a chance to show stimulating visual information. It can help to bring movement, pictures and sound into your PRESENTATION. Make sure that the clip is directly relevant to your content. The same applies to music.

It may help to introduce the clip by telling your audience what to look for. Avoid showing any more film than you need.

Finally, before you do your PRESENTATION, make sure that the audio-visual equipment is working properly and any link to YouTube is still working.

Interactive white board

You can use an interactive board in three main ways:

- Projecting pre-prepared slides by PowerPoint. These can be words or images either hand written/drawn or produced on a computer.

- Spontaneously produced – you can write on the board as you speak to illustrate your points or to record comments from the audience. Make sure you write legibly.

- A mixture of each – try adding to pre-prepared slides when making your presentation to show movement, highlight change or signal detailed interrelationships.

Non-interactive board

A static non-interactive board can be very useful to help explain the sequence of ideas or routines, particularly in the sciences. It can also demonstrate that you are highly familiar with the material you are presenting, as you are writing 'live', rather than using pre-prepared slides. However, you must be familiar with the material if you choose to use this method.

A static board in addition to PowerPoint can be used to clarify your title or to record your key points as you introduce your PRESENTATION (this will give you a fixed list to help you recap as you go along). Rather than expecting the audience to follow your spoken description of an experiment or process, write each stage on the board, including any complex terminology or precise references to help your audience to keep track of the structure of your presentation.

However, once you have written something on the board you will either have to leave it there or rub it off – both can be distracting to your audience. Check to make sure your audience has read any text/ illustration before rubbing it off. It can be highly frustrating for an audience if you do not give then sufficient time.

If you do need to write 'live', check that your audience can read your writing.

Paper handouts

Handouts can be useful and can be appropriate if your information is too detailed to fit on a slide or if you want your audience to have a full record of your findings.

Consider the merits of passing round your handouts at the beginning, middle and end of a presentation. Given out too early may mean they may prove a distraction. Given too late and your audience may not have time to read them. If you give them out in the middle of the presentation your audience will inevitably read rather than listen.

One way of avoiding these pitfalls is to give out incomplete handouts at key stages during your presentation. You can then highlight the missing details vocally, encouraging your audience to fill in the gaps. This can help to engage your audience and encourage their ownership of the material.

Flip chart

A flip chart is a large pad of paper on a stand. It is a flexible way of recording information during your presentation – you can even use pre-prepared sheets for key points. Record information as you go along, keeping one main idea to each sheet. Flip back through the pad to help you recap your main points. Remember to make your writing clear and readable and your diagrams as simple as possible.

Artefact or props

If you have been on a plane you will probably have seen the safety routine when the cabin crew demonstrate the use of safety equipment – i.e. using artefacts.

If you use an artefact in your PRESENTATION, make sure that it can be seen and be prepared to pass it round a small group or move to different areas of a large room to help your audience view it in detail. Remember that this will take time and that, when an audience is immersed in looking at an object, they will find it hard to listen to your talk.

Conceal large props until you need them, they might distract your audience's attention.

A market place display

If you are a student at a large centre you may be invited to give a market place style presentation. This is where you are invited into a hall to set up a stall similar to an exhibition stand. On the stall you can display various aspects of your work to staff and other students. You could also play a film clip and/or make artefacts available. Paper handouts can be provided.

It is important that the stall should create enough visual impact to enable you to get your main point(s) across to as many people as possible. According to Bourne (2007) 'It is analogous to being in an elevator and having a few seconds to peak someone's interest before they get off'.

It is important you are asked questions concerning your EPQ because your answers can be assessed as part of the presentation assessment.

A poster presentation

Posters offer a different medium from oral presentations. An effective poster 'is not just a standard research paper stuck to a board. An effective poster uses a different, visual grammar' (Hess *et al.* 2009).

The key difference between a poster and an oral presentation is that the poster should do most of the talking. This may sound like an easy option, allowing you to disappear back to the student common room. Wrong! You need to stand by your poster. You will have to answer questions and provide further details. According to Bourne (2007) 'Posters should be considered a snapshot of your work intended to engage colleagues in a dialog about the work'.

Here is a list of what makes an effective poster and what does not.

An effective poster	An ineffective poster
Expresses your points in graphical terms.	Is crammed full of text and the result can often appear messy.
Has elements visible from 4 feet away.	Has text that is too small or has poor graphics.
Displays the essential content – the message – in the title, main headings and graphics.	Is visually chaotic, with many jagged edges or various-sized boards that distract the viewer.
Uses fonts that are easy on the eye, such as Arial.	Uses too many font types that are distracting, especially when they appear in the same sentence.
Indicates the relative importance of elements graphically: each main point is stated in large typeface headings; details are subordinated visually, using smaller typeface.	Lets the viewer hunt for the main message or even worse, invent the message.
Shows only the main findings of the project. (However, do keep other results handy so that you may refer to them when asked.)	Includes extraneous material.
Uses colour to emphasise, differentiate and to add interest.	Uses large swathes of bright garish colours like bright green, pink, orange or lilac.
Uses pastel shades to convey feelings of serenity and calm.	Uses dark bright colours to conjure images of conflict and disharmony.
Diagrams are labelled and should be clear enough so that they are still legible from a distance.	Has spelling mistakes.
Uses clip art to add interest to the display and complement the subject matter.	Doesn't include visual interest.

EXERCISE 5.1 A good presentation

Use the criteria above right to judge the effectiveness of this poster presentation on the crowd factors that encourage potential suicide victims to jump.

Actual dimension of poster A1 size (59.4cm x 84.1cm).

Suggested answers on page 124.

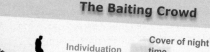

The Baiting Crowd

Individuation

Cover of night time

Large crowd

10 in 21 suicide cases the crowd said "jump"!

Distance between crowd and victim

Presentation skills

The ability to present information clearly and effectively is a key skill to get your message or opinion across. Presentation skills are very important in school or business where you may very well be asked to give a talk to a group of people. Therefore these are useful skills to develop.

Doing a PRESENTATION can be a very daunting prospect, but careful preparation can help to calm your nerves and give you the confidence you need for the all-important EPQ PRESENTATION.

Upspeak and discourse fillers

Avoid using upspeak. This is common among American and Australian speakers of English and entails a rising intonation at the end of any and all utterances. In other words, upspeak (also known as uptalk) turns every sentence into a question.

Peterson (2010) comments on upspeak and other discourse fillers:

> *Linguists have studied upspeak, finding that it occurs most frequently among younger individuals and among women...from Southern California. Linguists have concluded that upspeak serves conversational purposes, discouraging interruption and seeking reassurance.*

> *Be that as it may, upspeak jars me. I spent the past semester listening to my students make presentations, and no matter how brilliant their ideas, their reliance on upspeak distracted me to no end. Along these lines, what about the 'likes', the 'you knows' and the 'whatevers' that intrude into what many of my young students say? Should I call their attention to how annoying these discourse fillers may be, or would that just make them self-conscious and therefore even worse speakers?'*

EXERCISE 5.2   Adding interest

News story: Southampton man hospitalised by Britain's most venomous spider

> A young father was rushed to hospital this weekend after suffering ten painful bites from the UK's most poisonous arachnid, the False Widow spider. The nasty little critter is thought to have been introduced to Britain from the Canary Islands as far back as 1879, probably arriving on a bunch of bananas. In the past 100 years or so the spider has spread across the country and is becoming increasingly common.

> On Saturday 31-year-old Chris Galton was shopping with his wife and baby daughter when he collapsed on the floor of a Toys R Us store in Hampshire feeling hot and queasy. Chris was rushed to Southampton General Hospital where an examination revealed he'd been bitten ten times by the spider; the bites had swollen up to large, red, ugly welts. Chris was given painkillers and sent home.

> From *The Morning Star* 20 Feb 2012

Take four highlighter pens and identify the following elements of this text: dramatic, solemn, places to pause, words or phrases that could be repeated.

Now read the text out to your friends as if you were a newsreader.

Preparation beforehand

Know your material

By the time you have completed your EPQ you will be the expert. You need to demonstrate expertise in your PRESENTATION and you can do this by reading through your project.

Try to anticipate possible questions that your audience will ask.

Use notes to support the style of your presentation

Do not rely too closely on a script, as this can be a sign that you are not familiar with your material. It is better to prepare notes beforehand but don't read these out. Reading from your notes can be a sign that you are unfamiliar with your material. Reading from your notes means you are focusing your thoughts on your notes rather than on your audience. Reading can also reduce your voice to a monotone, removing energy and enthusiasm from your delivery.

The briefer your notes the better. They should just act as triggers to remind you what to say.

The most common form of note making is to use index cards. These can be read at a glance. Use one card for each main idea, including details of the supporting information for each point.

Remember to connect your cards together with a treasury tag so that they remain in the correct order.

Don't overlearn your notes as you might lose a sense of energy and enthusiasm. Always work for a sense of confident spontaneity.

Rehearse

It won't be alright on the night! Steve Jobs was regarded as one of the outstanding presenters of our generation. He would spend days on end rehearsing important presentations.

- Do *several* trial runs.
- Stand up in a room and deliver your presentation to the walls.
- Get used to hearing the sound of your own voice.
- Rehearse in front of a friend and ask them to be honest about whether you have any off-putting mannerisms or phrases. For example do you overuse a phrase such as 'OK', 'like' or 'err'?
- Videotape yourself and watch what your talk looks like.
- Amend your notes after each practice so they remind you of key points.
- Familiarise yourself with the words and phrases in your presentation. Are there any long and tricky words that are at risk of being mispronounced?
- Ask if you can practise in the room where you will give the presentation, as the acoustics will be different. It will also help you relax when doing the actual presentation.

It is no laughing matter

According to Bachorowski and Owren (2001) 'Humour is non-threatening and helps to strengthen social bonds and serves as a social lubricant to communication'. In the context of a presentation only use humour if you know it will work and it is appropriate to do so. Humour needs to be relaxed and confident. If the joke falls flat, or if the humour is in some way offensive it will only heighten senses of awkwardness and anxiety. Use humour if you know you can and if you feel it is appropriate to do so

On the day

Where to start

It is always a good idea to begin your PRESENTATION by acknowledging your audience. You could start by thanking them for their time. Also another good starting point is to ask if everyone can see and hear you, or check that lighting and sound levels on audio-visual equipment are satisfactory.

The glass is always half full

Anxiety can inhibit the flow of saliva and so your throat may get dry causing you to cough. It is a good idea to have a glass of water nearby to quench your thirst if you are speaking for a long time.

Be polite and assertive

Directly addressing your audience will help to engage your audience.

You should be polite and greet your audience. Be natural. Remember that your audience wants to listen to you. They may take a few minutes to settle down so wait before you start speaking and then assert yourself in a confident way.

Do not be afraid to ask politely for them to be quiet if this does not happen in a reasonable amount of time, for example two minutes. It may also be a useful idea to ask the audience to turn off their mobile phones.

Pump up the volume?

Your voice can be used in many different ways. In terms of volume you should ensure that your voice is loud enough for your audience to hear clearly. You may wish to check with your audience, 'Can you hear me at the back?'

- Add volume for emphasis.
- Speak quietly to draw the audience in.
- Vary the volume to avoid sounding monotone.

Pace yourself

To add energy to your PRESENTATION, try changing the pace of your delivery – for example, sometimes talk faster to draw attention to a particular point. But remember, if you speak too quickly your audience will have difficulty following your talk. Too slowly and it can appear dull and lacking in energy.

Mind your language

Use language that is welcoming and involving throughout your PRESENTATION. Avoid using complicated specialist terminology to alienate your audience but also do not patronise them by dumbing down too much. It is about striking a balance.

Don't forget to breathe

If you are anxious about making a presentation your breathing will become fast and shallow. This will affect the quality of your voice and your ability to speak clearly for extended periods of time. Try to take a few deep breaths before you make your PRESENTATION, then make a conscious effort to slow your breathing down and take in more air with each breath. During your PRESENTATION, use pauses after questions or at the end of sections to allow comfortable breathing patterns. Pausing may seem like forever but it is probably just a few seconds and your audience will appreciate a short break.

Non-specialist audience

Remember that your audience must be made up of non-specialists. This means that, for example, if your EPQ relates to History then you should not deliver your presentation to a group of A-Level History students. In other words the audience should not consist of specialists in the field to which your EPQ relates.

Connect with your audience

It is often said that a poor presenter seems to be speaking to an empty room. Connecting and establishing a rapport with your audience helps to maintain interest and will encourage them to believe that you are genuinely interested in talking to them.

You can connect with your audience in various ways:

- **Eye contact** This will help to give the audience a sense of involvement in your PRESENTATION and it will also help you to convey your objectives on a more personal level. Make sure that you share eye contact with all members of a small audience and all areas of a large audience. It is important that you do not just address your supervisor, instead regularly shift your focus around the room.

- **If you prefer not to look directly** at people you may wish to look at their forehead instead. People will just think that you are looking at the row behind.

- **Hands up** You will probably use your hands and arms when you are talking to your friends to convey meaning or to emphasise certain points. Use open gestures to welcome your audience. These are gestures where you move your arms away from your body. Too much movement can be distracting but if you do keep your arms rooted at your side then this can look awkward. You need therefore to make sure that all gestures are controlled and precise and are used to create emphasis to introduce your main points or to indicate an ending.

- **Asking questions** You can show acknowledgement to your audience during your PRESENTATION by asking rhetorical questions which you then answer, such as: 'How do we know this was true?' or 'What does this show?'

- **Encourage involvement** by introducing visual aids by saying 'If *we* look at this slide we can see that ..' or 'This slide shows *us* that…'.

- **Encourage the audience to ask questions** at the end of the PRESENTATION. In fact this is an EPQ requirement and your supervisor should also keep a record of your answers.

Dealing with questions asked

At the end of your PRESENTATION you must invite your audience to ask you questions about your EPQ. Your answers are then assessed as part of the PRESENTATION.

It is important to think beforehand about how you will deal with these questions. You want to try to anticipate the questions you may be asked and if you are asked a difficult question then take time to compose a response.

> 'The power to question is the basis of all human progress.'
>
> Indira Ghandi (1981)

An example of questions asked following a presentation

JACOB'S EPQ ON MARS

EPQ title: **How feasible is the prospect of establishing places of permanent habitation on Mars?**

Questions asked	Response
To be viable how many individuals would you need to set up a colony on Mars?	Initially a few to minimise the cost but the team would have to consist of people capable of working the equipment. The medical profession would also need to be represented.
Should we be funding space travel in the current economic climate?	Some projects are being put on hold but nations who can afford it are still working on the possibility of travelling to Mars.
Also, should we be funding it if the possibility of establishing a colony is so long into the future?	This was beyond the scope of the project but it is primarily an energy issue. I agree it is way off technologically.
What would people eat if a colony were established?	The colony could generate enough power to produce algae. Also they could take an amount of frozen water that could be used for recycling. Plants may also be able to be grown but it would depend on the amount of nitrogen in the soil.
You said that the first set of 'astronauts' should be a mechanised workforce. Why would this be useful?	I thought about this but it would be a problem. A mechanised workforce may be more unreliable and could soon get out of touch.
Could bone atrophy be a problem for those wanting to return to earth?	Their bones would degrade but they would need to get their fitness up. Before they return they would need to maintain a strict exercise regime.
Would lots of materials be needed to sustain energy?	There would be a large colony at first but would need to use nuclear power at first.

What if I don't know the answer to a question from the audience?

Remember that you are in control of the presentation. But you cannot be expected to know everything. It is better to admit that you don't know rather than trying to bluff or make something up. Instead here is one way of politely saying you haven't got a clue!

'Actually I am not familiar with the work of Smith and Jones but it sounds really thought provoking I will be happy to chat about it with you after the presentation.'

EXERCISE 5.3 Preparing answers

In preparation for the questions after your presentation here are a few obvious ones to ask yourself.

You can also prepare some of your own questions. Try to generate as many questions as you possibly can and write down your answers. Also, you can ask your friends to think of the toughest questions they possibly can.

Question	Response
Are there any weaknesses in the current research?	
Are your arguments backed up by evidence?	
Why did you select this topic?	
What is your own opinion on the topic?	

List other possible questions

A re you ready to give your PRESENTATION?

Make sure that you have prepared properly for the important EPQ PRESENTATION using this presentation-planning checklist.

Then you are ready to fill in PRESENTATION RECORD PART A.

PRESENTATION RECORD PARTS A and B

In the PRODUCTION LOG there is a form called PRESENTATION RECORD PART A. Here you will record the planned nature of your PRESENTATION.

PRESENTATION RECORD PART B is filled in by your supervisor (and discussed on the next page).

An exemplar of PRESENTATION RECORD PART A

KIM'S EPQ BORN THIS WAY

Planned format of my presentation
(e.g. timing, audience, use of visual aids, slides, use of notes, etc.).

My presentation is going to last for approximately twenty minutes including time for questions. My audience will be my supervisor, three other members of staff and six Year 12 students. I will use a PowerPoint presentation with 12 slides. I plan on using mainly pictures and key phrases on each slide in order to keep the audience focused, rather than having blocks of texts to read which could become quite tedious. For this reason, I will put together my own script to accompany the slides so I can engage with the audience verbally.

I have considered the structure for my presentation. I will firstly explain the aim of my project and how I went about achieving this aim. I will also explain the EPQ journey as well as describe my product. Following on from this, I plan to briefly describe the terms 'nature' and 'nurture', and then move onto brief discussions of the three categories within each side of the debate. I will then finish by stating my conclusion based on the research I put together.

I will read through the project several times to try to anticipate possible questions.

Planned content of my presentation.

I have considered the structure for my presentation. I will firstly explain the aim of my project and how I went about achieving this aim. I will also explain the EPQ journey as well as describe my product. Following on from this, I plan to briefly describe the terms 'nature' and 'nurture', and then move onto brief discussions of the three categories within each side of the debate. I will then finish by stating my conclusion based on the research I put together.

Modifications I have made as a result of rehearsal and/or discussion with my supervisor.

My supervisor said that I should also focus on my EPQ journey as well as my EPQ report. I thought that I only had to focus on my report and so I am going to add slides which look at the reason for my choice of topic. One slide will look at the sources I have used and justify the choice of books, journals, etc. I will also look at how I managed my project, the successes and failures I faced and also time management. My supervisor said that the presentation provides evidence for all of the assessment objectives.

I will also include a slide where I reflect on my journey and consider how I have developed as a person as a result of my journey.

My supervisor also said that I should then read through my reports and try to anticipate possible questions and so I am going to write a list of possible questions and a response in preparation for my presentation.

	I have:	Tick
Preparation	Checked my facts.	
	Checked the dos and don'ts of good slides on page 96.	
	Included comments on the EPQ journey and what skills I have learned.	
	Secured and numbered my notes in case I lose my place.	
	Prepared any visual aids that I may need.	
	Prepared any handouts that I wish to give out.	
	Saved my PowerPoint presentation onto at least two formats (disc/USB/hard drive/email).	
	Anticipated a list of likely questions that I may be asked.	
Rehearsal	Read through my EPQ report several times.	
	Rehearsed my presentation in front of a mirror.	
	Rehearsed my presentation in front of a friend.	
	Taped/videoed myself and listened back to it.	
	Checked that my presentation runs to the time allotted.	
	Prepared speaker notes or cue cards.	
Venue	Seen the room that I am going to be presenting in.	
	Confirmed that the audio-visual equipment I require will be in the room.	
Audience	Thought about who is going to be in the audience.	
	Thought about how to greet my audience.	
	Thought about any special needs my audience may have.	
	Thought about ways to engage the audience in my presentation.	
You	Considered how to combat my nervousness.	
	Thought about my personal appearance.	
On the day	Brought a bottle of water to drink if my throat gets dry.	
	Turned my mobile phone off.	

Moderator comments

Moderators like to see a presentation designed to illustrate and explain the journey travelled by each candidate from original idea to final product. The skills developed and their potential future uses should be highlighted.

Supervisors and other members of the audience should use questions at the end of the presentation to give candidates opportunities to confirm and develop their evidence.

The questions asked and answers given should be recorded by the supervisor because they are valid only if they are placed in the public domain through accurate records. The onus is on the supervisor to keep an accurate record of questions and answers.

Assessing the presentation

The person who assesses your project (your supervisor) will see your PRESENTATION and assess this. However, the moderator will not have seen your PRESENTATION so the *presentation feedback form* on this page is useful evidence for the moderator to evaluate your PRESENTATION.

You can add this *presentation feedback form* to the PRESENTATION RECORD PART A which is part of the PRODUCTION LOG.

PRESENTATION RECORD PART B

You fill in PRESENTATION RECORD PART A (see previous page). Your supervisor fills in PRESENTATION RECORD PART B, commenting on the following aspects of your PRESENTATION:

- *The nature of the audience (include numbers of staff, students and others present).*
- *The nature of the presentation (include use of notes, use of display items, and use of presentation software).*
- *The content and delivery of the presentation.*
- *The response of the candidate to questions that demonstrated understanding and grasp of the project and/or its production (give examples where appropriate).*
- *Outline the nature of any additional presentation evidence that the candidate might add (e.g. speaker notes, handouts, presentation slides, recording).*

Presentation feedback form

JACOB'S EPQ ON MARS

EPQ title: **How feasible is the prospect of establishing places of permanent habitation on Mars?**

Criteria: 1 = Unacceptable   2 = Acceptable   3 = Good   4 = Very Good   5 = Impressive

	1	2	3	4	5	Comments from supervisor, e.g. particular strengths or suggestions for improvement
Audibility: Can student be heard clearly throughout?				X		*Yes audible throughout.*
Pace: Is the pace of the speech/flow of ideas too fast or too slow?				X		*Good pace, a few hesitations. Long periods of technical talk that slowed pace on occasions.*
Fluency: Does the speech pattern flow, indicating familiarity with the material and rehearsal of delivery?				X		*Obvious knowledge and planning preparation. Fluent and not reliant on reading from PowerPoint notes.*
Tone and energy: Is there sufficient variation in tone? Does the presenter seem enthusiastic?				X		*Enthusiastic and at times humour was used appropriately.*
Eye contact: Is the presenter making eye contact across the audience?					X	*Yes engaging.*
Body language and posture: Is the presenter's posture upright and confident?				X		*Sat down during the presentation, confident posture behind the desk.*
Appropriateness to audience: Is the content and approach relevant interesting and engaging?		X				*Generally knowledgeable, less engaging when too long was spent talking about one slide.*
Structure and cohesion: Was the structure clearly outlined? Was the order logical and easy to follow?				X		*Good clear introduction, too much talking on one image. Very good structure, planning/research evident in the presentation.*
Use of visual aids: Is there a suitable amount? Easy to read?				X		*Very good PowerPoint and excellent visual images, clear and engaging graphics. Spoke quite fluently without the need for notes, did not read from the board.*
Verbal content of talk				X		*Extra information given for each slide demonstrating high level of understanding.* *Also mentioned the EPQ journey in answers, and planning and preparation was evident in the answers.*
Responses to questions: Questions were answered with confidence and demonstrated a familiarity with the material.				X		*Handled questions and answers with audience extremely well. Thought about their answers and used evidence to expand the answers.* *The student demonstrated their familiarity with the material when they were asked questions at the end of their presentation.*

A student EPQ presentation

KAYEIGH'S EPQ ON ANIMAL ETHICS

Slide 1

Arguements against the use of animals in research

Slide 2

Scientific arguments

- Critics argue that animal studie s can neither confirm or refute hypothesis about human physiology or pathology: human clinical investigations are the only way such hypotheses can be tested. At best animal experiments can suggest new hypotheses that might be relevant to humans. However, there are countless other, often superiour, ways to derive new hypotheses.

- Recent surveys of the value of psychological research with animals for clinical psychology suggest that the benefits of such research has been over-stated.

markwersel.com

Slide 3

Ethical arguments

- Some argue that animals have made an important contribution to advances in medicine and clinical psychology. However these contributions have often been at considerable expense in terms of animal suffering. Although a cost-benefit analysis of research projects should ensure that the costs and the benefits are predictable, neither of these are certain prior to the study commencing e.g. during Harlow's original monkey studies no one was able to predict the extent at which the monkeys were traumatised in later life.

- By calculating the benefits to human kind but the cost to animals, we might be committing speciesism.

- Most ethical guidelines are based on a 'cost-benefit' model, where the recipients of costs (i.e the animals) and benefits (i.e. humans) tend to be different. These guidelines ignore the substantive rights of animals in favour of practical considerations.

Slide 4

- Animals have rights by virtue of their 'inherent value'. These include the right to be treated with respect and not harmed.

- The traditional scientific position on animals treats animals as 'renewable resources' rather than as organisms of value.

- However if one was to argue that they do not have rights like the statement above just because they do not fulfil a role within society then infants and the mentally ill must also be denied wrights. (Singer 1976)

Slide 5

- One argument for the use of animals is that evolution has placed human beings 'on top' of the phylogenetic tree, so it is only natural for us to make use of 'lower animals' for our own needs.

- However this is naturalistic fallacy David Hume said that 'what is cannot dictate what ought to be'. Natural history may well have provided us with an understanding of why our morels have evolved into their present form but cannot transcend by our nature. Not using other species for our ends may be seen as the next step in that evolution.

Slide 6

- Another argument for animal research is that a number of less invasive have been developed and are being used in animal researcher.

However, if researchers were not allowed to use animals in research, they would have to develop other techniques to take the place of animal research. CT, PET and MRI scans along with computer modelling are among the modern approaches that are alternatives to animal research.

Slide 7

- There is evidence that animals do feel pain
- Sneddon et al. 2003 did research on fish and found that they did display a pain response.

- The main focus of the utilitarian argument is that what is ethically acceptable produces the greatest pleasure and happiness for the greatest number of people. In this argument, no one person's happiness is more important than any other's. Singer (1990) extends this to include all sentient creatures. His 'principle of equality' holds that all such creatures have an equal interest in avoiding pain and suffering.

Slide 8

The end

EXERCISE 5.4 A good presentation

Just take a minute to think about what makes a good presentation and what makes a bad presentation. It may help you to think of examples of presentations which you have seen – teachers talking in class or assembly, speakers at a conference, politicians and so on.

Good presentation	Bad presentation

On page 98 there is a list of dos and don'ts for presentations.

How has Kayleigh fared?

Has she made clear what her title is?

The title slide is clear but it does not match their original EPQ title and 'arguments' is misspelt, this does not create a good first impression.

Has she referred to her EPQ journey?

There is no reference to sources used, planning or any details of the EPQ journey. The presentation only contains the arguments against the use of animals.

Is the font size large enough to enable the audience to read it?

Although the font size is larger than 20, slide 3 has quite a lot of text and could be reduced.

Is the background simple?

The audience may focus too much on the background images rather than on the text and so time should be allowed for the audience to read the slides.

Are the images consistent?

Although the images and fonts are consistent the background is distracting.

Is the content appropriate to the audience?

There is a lack of jargon although the terms phylogenetic and speciesism may need a clearer explanation.

Harlow's monkey study may need explanation.

Abbreviations have been used which should be written in full (CT, PET and MRI).

Errors identified

A lot of misspelling, such as 'studie s', 'experiments' and 'superiour' on slide 2.

On slide 5 the quote from David Hume does not have a date.

Is suitable academic style used?

Sneddon et al. 2003 should be presented as Sneddon et al. (2003).

There is no conclusion.

Improvements could include:

The use of more images to illustrate ideas that do not form part of the background of the slide.

More care should be taken when checking spelling and grammar.

The summary

The SUMMARY is part of the SUMMARY AND REFLECTION in the PRODUCTION LOG. On this page in the PRODUCTION LOG you are asked to record 'your summary, reflection and evaluation when you have completed your project product and given your presentation'.

You should not write your SUMMARY AND REFLECTION until after your presentation.

For the SUMMARY:
1. You can simply use your abstract (if you have done one) as a summary (see pages 78–79), or
2. You can turn your conclusion (pages 88–89) into a summary as illustrated on this spread.

These are the divisions also recommended on page 89 for writing a conclusion. There is no requirement that says you have to include all five elements in your summary, or in a specific order – but it helps.

Writing a good summary

A summary should be focused on the goal of conveying to the reader that you have succeeded in answering your research questions or title.

The SUMMARY can follow the same guidelines as for a conclusion:

1. Brief recap of what you have covered in relation to the essay title

A brief recap of your argument is important because it shows the moderator that you have constructed a cohesive argument that is evident in your work from start to finish. The SUMMARY will emphasise 'I have kept on track and here is the evidence to support or challenge my research question(s)'.

2. Reference to the larger issue

Emphasise the importance of your subject by placing it in a larger context.

3. Highlight the important aspects

Quotes, anecdotes or examples can allow you to develop your essay in a way that not only gets your main point across but also is stylistically effective.

4. Evaluate the main arguments

Base your criticisms (positive and negative) on evidence and come to a balanced verdict.

5. The take-home message

What it is you want people to remember most after they have finished reading your 5000 words. You should leave the moderator with a clear idea of what points they should take seriously.

JACOB'S EPQ ON MARS

Turning a conclusion into a summary

EPQ title: **How feasible is the prospect of establishing places of permanent habitation on Mars?**

	Conclusion	Summary
Brief recap	Throughout my project I have only brushed upon the myriad of problems and considerations regarding a colonisation project on Mars.	Throughout my project I have considered the myriad problems regarding colonising Mars.
Reference to the larger issue	It must be a unified effort between all the national and continental space programmes in order to achieve this colossal goal, which is in the best interest of our species as a whole.	To achieve this colossal goal is in the best interest of our species as a whole.
Highlight the important aspects	*'Single-planet species don't survive'*, says former astronaut John Grunsfeld (2013), who still works at NASA. *'That's a pretty sound theorem – just look at the dinosaurs. But we don't want to prove it.'* Although there are still many questions that need answers, many technological, scientific, financial and psychological hurdles to cross establishing a permanent, sustainable outpost on the Red Planet may be our civilisation's only chance of long-term continuity.	'Single-planet species don't survive' (Grunsfeld 2013). Our best hope for the future is to establish a permanent, sustainable outpost on the Red Planet. This may be our civilisation's only chance of long-term continuity.
Evaluate the main arguments	There are many factors which have the potential to cause harm to the humans who would be sent on this mission, from the radiation levels to which they'd be exposed to the possibility of their mission failing in its descent on to the Martian surface. Even after getting to Mars the process of establishing a viable colony would take tremendous amounts of work and years of planning. The challenges faced scientifically could be overcome and amazing new fields of research have opened up in the last few years which could make the mission a lot easier and safer for the astronauts involved.	There would be great dangers for humans sent on a mission to Mars, such as radiation levels. Establishing a viable colony would take years of planning. However, new fields of research have opened up in the last few years that could make the mission easier and safer.
The take-home message	There is still a lot of work to be done, and there are still major challenges to be addressed. The process of colonising Mars won't be an easy feat and it may take us years to fully invest in and develop a substantial plan. However, after researching all the innovations to overcome challenges faced I feel assured that colonisation of the Red Planet will happen sometime in the future. It must be a unified effort between all the national and continental space programmes.	There remain big challenges but I feel assured that colonisation of the Red Planet will happen sometime in the future. 127 words

DON'T...

Don't bring in new material – it is one thing to generalise or place your argument in a broader academic context, but it is quite another to introduce a whole new idea that you do not have room to develop. If you find yourself mentioning additional ideas in the SUMMARY, you may need to add an additional paragraph in the main body of the report.

Don't leave the moderator to draw their own conclusions. According to Stott (2001) *'The main aim of a summary is to conclude it in such a way that the reader feels all questions have been addressed.... Your goal is to create a self-contained argument within the essay, not leave the reader waiting for a sequel.'*

Word count

The recommended length for the summary is 50–150 words. Students who write a very long summary will be penalised in their AO4 mark.

Exemplar summaries

JOSHUA'S EPQ ON LIBERTY

EPQ title: **Security versus liberty: To what extent can it be justified to set aside Civil Liberties and basic rights for the sake of security in the UK?**

Since the 9/11 terrorist attacks on the USA by Al Qaeda, the UK government has introduced a multitude of new security measures and legislation that impinges on personal freedoms. These measures include the extension of the surveillance state, the proposed introduction of identity cards and the increase in police powers, allowing terrorist suspects to be detained without trial for up to 30 days. Critics argue it is wrong to discard these freedoms so readily, that it is unnecessary and dangerous to hand so much power over to the state, but proponents instead argue that if we do not act appropriately to combat the threat of terrorism then the lives of British citizens will be put at risk and also emphasise the benefits of the increased efficiency that would ensue should the state receive more power. Ultimately can a balance be struck between the two?

144 words

Moderator comments

This summary briefly recaps what the EPQ is about, namely whether liberty should be sacrificed for the sake of security. There is reference to the larger issue of the increased security measures that may impinge on liberty and the counterarguments are presented. However, the summary ends on a question. It would have been preferable for the candidate to include a sentence that provides an answer to the question. The take-home message is missing.

MARIA'S EPQ ON ADHD

EPQ title: **Has society's perception of ADHD changed in the past 20 years?**

My project is about ADHD and society's perception of this over the past 20 years. My final product is my dissertation, which clearly explains what ADHD is (including the symptoms, treatment, diagnosis) and the advancement of the acceptance culture surrounding ADHD. My conclusion is that there has been a change over the past 20 years in perception of disabilities such as ADHD and the acceptance of ADHD as a disability has increased.

My project has helped me to overcome potential problems as they arise and helped me to manage my time more effectively. It has taught me the importance of keeping to strict deadlines and the impact that not doing so can have on the subject and the research in question.

120 words

Moderator comments

A brief summary that begins with a short recap of what she has covered. The take-home message could be more explicit as it seems to suggest that the acceptance of ADHD has increased but it could have been expressed more clearly. It would also be helpful to have reference to the larger issue and evaluation of the main arguments and the most important aspects. The final section includes a consideration of learning points, which belongs in the REFLECTION not the summary.

BELLA'S EPQ ON DRINKING

EPQ title: **Should the Government take measures to discourage the amount of binge drinking which occurs in Britain today?**

The extent of damage caused by binge drinking is well documented. In contrast with the Mediterranean, binge drinking is a problem in the UK. Furthermore public ambivalence towards the culture of binge drinking has led to many young people being intoxicated in city centres on Friday and Saturday nights. Access and promotion are also issues. There are various impacts of binge drinking including physical and social. I am dismissive of the age limit, all promoted strongly by the beverage alcohol industry. I advocate the opinion of scientists and medics.

In conclusion, to curb binge drinking and promote a sensible attitude towards alcohol, it is vital for the government to intervene and the best method they can use is with taxation.

120 words

Moderator comments

An effective summary containing the key elements described on the facing page. The opening two sentences provide a brief recap and refer to the larger issue respectively. The main arguments from scientists and the beverage industry are briefly presented. The take-home message appears in the final sentence so that the reader is left in no doubt that the government should discourage binge drinking through taxation.

EXERCISE 5.5   Annotate a summary statement

Look at text written below. Try to decide which is an example of each of the five features of a summary (see facing page). Place the appropriate number (from list on facing page) in the box at the start of each paragraph.

EPQ title: **What are consequences of the stigma of schizophrenia?**

☐ The concept of the 'interpersonal' relates to concealment such as a refusal to share the problem or refusing support. Damaged self-esteem seems to be the main intrapersonal consequence which can lead to withdrawal and changed behaviour, therefore stepping into the expectations others have of the problem caused by the stigma in the first place.

☐ Consequences to the mental health services in relation to the medical model affect the way that everyone with schizophrenia is treated by professionals, the advice they are given and the help they receive.

☐ I aimed to look at three consequences of schizophrenia: interpersonal, intrapersonal and consequences for the mental health service.

☐ The stigma of schizophrenia is a complex issue. There are many awareness schemes out there trying to dispel misconceptions. A greater tolerance and understanding is required. In the words of Elyn Saks 'Please hear this: There are not "schizophrenics". There are people with schizophrenia.'

☐ According to Hocking (2003), 'Schizophrenia has a long history of stigma which may prevent people with schizophrenia from accessing the type of support they need to manage their illness and lead to feelings of social isolation and loneliness'. Acton (2013) found that while mental illness has achieved acceptance in the wider community as being treatable. He also found that there was still a misconception that people with illnesses such as schizophrenia and bipolar disorder were not fit for positions of authority or personal relationships.

Suggested answers on page 124.

Writing a reflection

The process of reflection involves 'the analysis of an event, thoughts, experiences, or insights into the impact of an experience or projected goals for the future' (Danielson 1996, p.53).

Your REFLECTION is recorded as part of the SUMMARY AND REFLECTION in the PRODUCTION LOG. This will enable you to evaluate your personal experience of the EPQ process. Not only what you have learned from the EPQ journey but also a reflection on your planning, changes you would make if you did the EPQ again and advice to others starting the project.

You should not write your SUMMARY AND REFLECTION until after your presentation.

The REFLECTION can provide a brief summary of six aspects of your EPQ:

1. What have you learned from completing this project?

Brockbank and McGill (1998) suggest that reflection is when someone is 'learning about their learning'. Learning can fall into two categories:

- Learning about the whole EPQ experience, e.g. 'I gained more knowledge about the subject'.

- Learning about yourself. Be honest with yourself about your previous ignorance and any new learning. You may have found the experience challenging, absorbing, stimulating, worthwhile … and may have become more proficient, methodical, self-reliant, industrious, enthusiastic, organised ….

2. What new knowledge or expertise have you enjoyed or found valuable?

This is the opportunity to consider the project management skills you have learned.

3. What are the strengths and weaknesses of your project (including planning and organisation)?

You can comment on your time management and whether your project plan enabled you to proceed in an organised fashion. You can consider whether your targets were realistic. You can be positive ('I managed to keep to the deadlines in my Gantt chart') as well as negative. You may comment on the sources you used and whether you had issues with data collection.

4. What skills have you improved?

This can include a number of key, transferable skills that will assist you in the future such as working to deadlines, analysis of the reliability of sources, presentation skills, and writing in an analytical way.

5. What changes would you make if you undertook such work again?

Many students refer to time management issues, wishing they had started their literature review or data collection earlier. They also wish they had kept a list of references as they went along, had selected a better title, and were more organised when meeting their supervisor.

6. What advice would you give to others undertaking such a project?

Would you recommend the EPQ to other students? What particular advice would you give to them to get the most out of their project? You might suggest ideas about the kind of project or title that works best.

Word count

You should write about 400–500 words.

You should not include the subheadings provided on this spread – they are there to help you think what to write.

CONOR'S EPQ ON DIABETES

Reflection – Exemplar 1

EPQ title: **What is the most significant cause of the recent increase in diabetes mellitu**

1. What have you learned from completing this project?	Firstly, from doing the EPQ, I gained more knowledge and a deeper understandi a topic I'm interested in. I found it satisfying to complete such a multifaceted piec work. From my research I found out completely new things and also found out mo about things I had come across in lessons. I really enjoyed this and also found th this increased understanding helped me in lessons and the Biology Olympiad I to part in.
	I found that the EPQ really helped me with interviews for university too. In one inter I discussed my EPQ at length and it gave me an opportunity to show my enthusi for my subject, the breadth and depth of my knowledge and my organisation.
2. What new knowledge or expertise have you enjoyed or found valuable?	I also hadn't done an essay subject since GCSE so writing the EPQ helped me re some of the skills that I had not used in a while, this will be very useful at univers where I will have to write reports and essays. Furthermore, I have a greater clari and understanding of the most significant increases in diabetes mellitus.
3. What are the strengths and weaknesses of your project (including planning and organisation)?	I believe that my project contains a number of strengths. One strength is I have u a variety of sources that I hadn't used before including web pages, peer-reviewed literature and research studies. I believe that I have successfully synthesised this information to form a coherent argument. A further strength that I feel my projec contains is its focus upon the question that I set – 'What is the most significant cause of the recent increase in diabetes mellitus?' I feel that I have maintained an analytical focus and referenced directly back to the question throughout my exte document. Also, I removed bias that may occur by focusing upon objective data collected from reliable sources (such as peer-reviewed literature) rather than inclu opinion based views from potentially unreliable sources.
	A weakness is it took me too long to formulate an analytical title. Furthermore, I quite slow getting started; sitting and looking at a blank document knowing I had write 5,000 words was quite a daunting prospect and I spent quite a great deal time procrastinating rather than just getting some ideas down on paper.
4. What skills have you improved?	The skills I have gained from doing the EPQ will be invaluable at university in term of time management and effective planning to ensure everything I wanted to do w finished by an appropriate date. I think how I set deadlines for myself, such as the time I wanted to have finished researching by or when I wanted to have finished ea section, helped me to stay organised and on track and wasn't rushing to finish it.
5. What changes would you make if you undertook such work again?	If I could do the project again, I would spend more time researching and reading widely before focusing the topic down as I found I could write the report quite quic once I had all the information and so factored in too much time for the writing par the project. Although I am happy with the amount of information I found and includ in the project, I did find some more theories after I completed the project that it ma have been interesting to include.
6. What advice would you give to others undertaking such a project?	Overall, I really enjoyed doing the EPQ and would recommend it to anyone who wanted to increase their knowledge in a subject they enjoy as I really feel that it has benefitted me and taught me skills which will be very valuable.

Moderat commen

An honest reflect that gives a deta insight into stren weaknesses and learning points.

A total of 572 wo

Alice's assumptions about the world in Lewis Carroll's *Alice Through the Looking Glass* were challenged as she became increasingly aware of a new perspective. The looking glass provided a reflection on the world for her to explore. Like Alice, you may find your assumptions challenged as you reflect on your EPQ.

EXERCISE 5.6 Reflection

Look at the REFLECTION below.

Use the six headings suggested on this spread to consider what is missing.

EPQ title: **Is cutting funding for the treatment of self-inflicted diseases the right way to go about NHS cuts?**

After finishing my project I feel it has been very rewarding despite being challenging at times. I knew it would be a very difficult question to answer, due to all the different subjects it covers; ethics, economics, politics and health. With all the people involved, it was always going to be difficult to come to a conclusion that meant everyone was happy. I have thoroughly enjoyed researching my EPQ title, as it was something I was very interested in. I now have a more open-minded view of all three self-inflicted diseases I have studied. My original opinion had been severely influenced by the media. I also enjoyed learning about things I do not study at A-Level, and in some ways it gave me a break from my three subjects. I have never been particularly interested in Psychology or Politics, but feel I now have a better understanding, and will keep up to date with news in these areas. I also learned to write essays and references. I had not written essays since GCSE, and this is the biggest piece of written work I have done, I believe this will help me at university as I know dissertations and essays play a big part. I also learned about literature reviews and the Harvard Referencing System, something I had never come across before. Again, I believe this will help me at university. At points I struggled to manage my time especially at the start of the school year due to university applications and later mock examinations. However, I think this project will help me in the future and in the upcoming exams. I believe my organisation has been good, and keeping a log of issues and a progress log were very helpful in doing so. They gave me targets to meet. I have improved my skills of essay writing and an awareness of evidence-based conclusions rather than taking social media and tabloid media reports on the NHS at face value. If I were to do the project again, I think I would have looked more into binge drinking and also looked into the psychological areas of each of the self-inflicted diseases. Perhaps, in the future I could have kept with my penultimate title idea of 'Should the NHS fund self-inflicted diseases?' as there is an ever growing amount of evidence for each argument. I also would start my EPQ title earlier in the summer.

Suggested answers on page 124.

Reflection – Exemplar 2

SOPHIE'S EPQ ON LAMINITIS

EPQ title: **An investigation into the causes of the disease laminitis in horse hooves.**

1. What have you learned from completing this project?	By doing this project I certainly feel that I have learned a lot, not only how to create and write a well-written report but I have learned about my topic in more detail.
2. What new knowledge or expertise have you enjoyed or found valuable?	I also learned how to search the Internet to find out information on the topic I was completing my project on. I also learned how to analyse and cross-reference the sources I found. I have enjoyed researching deeply into my topic and finding out more about the technologies available.
3. What are the strengths and weaknesses of your project (including planning and organisation)?	The strengths of my project are that I feel that I organised my time to complete this project reasonably well as I was able to complete the essay and log in sufficient time. I also feel I planned my work out well because I created headings for the information I wanted to find.
4. What skills have you improved?	I feel that I have developed my presentation skills via undertaking my project. I have developed my knowledge of the technical aspects associated with presenting, like projecting the voice and incorporating techniques to encourage the audience to engage with the speaker.
5. What changes would you make if you undertook such work again?	The changes I would make if I did the project again would be to find a wider range of sources such as book sources. I would also try and find quotes from people in sport to back up my points I stated and improve my project.
6. What advice would you give to others undertaking such a project?	If I were to give advice to someone starting an EPQ it would be to make sure that they know exactly what they are going to do before they start and that time management is very important. It is a good idea to organise your time by having specific deadlines that you have to meet such as the mid-project review and other project deadlines.

Moderator comments

The candidate gives a consideration of research and writing skills gained from completing the EPQ.

Moderator comments

The candidate is aware of some knowledge or expertise but does not elaborate sufficiently and covers these issues in a superficial way.

Moderator comments

The strengths focus on planning but the candidate has not focused on weaknesses.

Moderator comments

Narrow focus on just presentation skills.

Narrow range of changes identified for question 5.

Moderator comments

In general this REFLECTION is superficial and lacking much expression of the higher-level skills. Material is relevant but lacking in breadth.

286 words

Congratulations You're done!

Appendix I
Exemplar EPQ – An artefact

If you are producing an artefact for your EPQ you will need to accompany it with a 1000-word REPORT. Although this is much shorter than the 5000 words needed if you opt for the long written report, it will still need to be academic in nature. The report also has to closely relate to the artefact. Only the REPORT and ARTEFACT are shown her A PRODUCTION LOG (with SUMMARY AND REFLECTION were also handed in.

EPQ title: **To produce a poem for children in the style of Dr Seuss**

'I like nonsense, it wakes up the brain cells. Fantasy is a necessary ingredient in living.'
(Dr Seuss)

I have been inspired to write a poem about spiders by my pet tarantula called 'Gordon'. He is really friendly but I know not everyone would share this view. Popular culture has given the humble spider a bad reputation, but according to Jose 'much of the ire toward them is undeserved. While some spiders can be dangerous to humans, they play an important part in almost every ecosystem. Spiders are not only the romantic and dangerous figures they are made out to be in folklore, but like all creatures, they struggle to survive and take care of their young.'[1]

Spiders have been around for a long time and many millions of years. Spiders are ancient animals with a history going back many millions of years. Many people think that spiders are insects. Although spiders belong to the same group of animals (arthropods).[2]

But they aren't insects. Spiders are arachnids. Spiders have received a bad press in children's stories. If we look at some examples:

- Little Miss Muffet was frightened by a spider while she was eating her curds and whey.
- J.R.R. Tolkein, in the *Hobbit* (1937) included giant spiders. They roamed Mirkwood and would sometimes attack the other characters.
- In the *Lord of the Rings* the spider Shelob is a menacing character. Tolkien gave them some attributes not seen in real spiders (apart from the obvious size issues), including compound eyes, beaks and spinning of black webs.
- J K Rowling, in *Harry Potter and the Chamber of Secrets*, had the giant spider Aragog.
- The 1952 children's novel *Charlotte's Web* by E. B White portrays the spider in a positive way as a heroine rather than an object of fear or horror.
- The poem *The Spider and the Fly* is a cautionary tale of seduction and betrayal. The poem inspired a film made in 1949 and a song by the rock band The Rolling Stones in 1965.

'Will you walk into my parlour?' said the Spider to the Fly,
'Tis the prettiest little parlour that ever you did spy;
The way into my parlour is up a winding stair,
And I've a many curious things to show when you are there.'
'Oh no, no,' said the little Fly, 'to ask me is in vain,
For who goes up your winding stair can ne'er come down again.'

The poet Walt Whitman wrote a poem about spider in 1868 called *A Noiseless Patient Spider*. So a more positive poem about spiders.

I mark'd where on a little promontory it stood isolated;
Mark'd how to explore the vacant vast surrounding,
It launch'd forth filament, filament, filament, out of itself;
Ever unreeling them – ever tirelessly speeding them.

And you O my soul where you stand,
Surrounded, detached, in measureless oceans of space,
Ceaselessly musing, venturing, throwing – seeking the spheres to connect them;
Till the bridge you will need be form'd, till the ductile anchor hold;
Till the gossamer thread you fling catch somewhere, O my soul.

In graphic novels the spider is portrayed as a superhero or villain, for example one of the most well-known characters in comic book history has taken his identity from the spider, the Marvel comic book hero Spiderman.

With these images in mind I decided to do a survey with primary school children, and find out two things:

- What makes a good poem for children?
- Why didn't they like spiders?

---

[1] http://indian-spiders.blogspot.co.uk/ accessed 12/4/13

[2] (Ancient Greek: arthro = joint, podos = footed) – animals with hard external skeletons and jointed limbs

---

Moderator comments

No attempt made to explain how and why the quote is relevant to the artefact.

The opening line is written in a naïve style and does not set an appropriate academic tone from the outset. There is some academic referencing here using footnotes. The quote from Jose is more than four lines so should be set apart and indented. The word 'ire' may not have been the best to choose to illustrate public perception of spiders. Rather than creating anger spiders tend to create a sense of fear.

The third paragraph ('But they aren't insects …') lacks an element of clarity. A clearer definition and some examples of arachnids and arthropods would be helpful in addition to the Greek derivative.

The candidate could have provided a smoother transition from talking about spiders to the introduction of children's literature.

Although the list of examples is useful, it is not chronological and the format is inconsistent. Dates are not always included and Charlotte's Web *could have been listed separately, as a positive portrayal of spiders in contrast to the negative ones listed.*

What images are in mind? A brief summary to synthesise evidence would be helpful here.

Survey of poems

I am aiming to find out what makes a good poem and also why you don't like spiders.

Please answer the questions below. Thank you for your time.

1. What children's stories do you like to read?

2. What is your favourite children's poem?

3. What makes a good poem?
   - Pictures
   - It is funny
   - It has nonsense words
   - It rhymes
   - It is scary
   - It is realistic
   - It is fantasy

4. Why don't you like spiders?
   - They bite
   - They look ugly
   - They run fast
   - They are dirty

Thanks you for your help. Any questions?

I wanted to write a poem for children in the style of Dr Seuss. I have been inspired to write this because of 'Gordon' (my tarantula) and I am a great fan of Dr Seuss. My ambition is to write poems for children and illustrate them and for them to be instantly recognisable like Dr Seuss.

Dr Seuss (real name Theodor Seuss Geisel) published over 60 children's books over the course of his long career. In 2000, when *Publishers Weekly* compiled their list of the best selling children's books of all time 16 of the top 100 hardcover books were written by Geisel,

> *Green Eggs and Ham (Number 4)*
> *The Cat in the Hat (Number 9)*
> *One Fish Two Red Fish Blue (Number 13)*

Seuss was a well-known author but many have also speculated on Seuss as a social commentator. Seuss was also described by *Relevant Magazine* as 'progressive and a moralist'. The magazine also said that Seuss 'expressed his views in his books through the use of ridicule, satire, wordplay, nonsense words, and wild drawings to take aim at bullies, hypocrites, and demagogues'.[3]

Dr Seuss's books made reading fun but also helped children to learn. Consider this line from *I Can Read with My Eyes Shut* (1978): 'The more that you read, the more things you'll know. The more that you learn the more places you'll go'. Seuss did not claim to write his books with political or moral messages in mind but 'the creator of Thing 1 and Thing 2, with their hair coloured blue, had more than just wacky words up his sleeve … he had an agenda, too'. (*Relevant Magazine* March 7th 2012)[4]. Here are some of the messages in Dr Seuss's well-known books:

- *The Lorax* – Deals with ecosystems and how humans are destroying nature. The impact of humans on our planet is told from a simplistic yet environmentally accurate viewpoint, and shows how manmade production can have an impact on natural resources.

- *The Grinch* – Anti-commercialism, it shows we don't need lots of presents to celebrate Christmas.

- *The Cat in the Hat* – Pretty simple, and it used 225 words. According to H. Burdorff in *Subversive Seuss*, Seuss continued to champion progressive ideals in the sequel to The *Cat in the Hat*, titled *The Cat in the Hat Comes Back*, in which the Cat may be a symbol of colonial or absolute dictatorial power. The Cat tries to clean up a mess he made with a dress that was not his, but ends up making things worse. When the Cat realises that he can't do it all by himself, he brings in helpers, Thing 1 and Thing 2. Burdorff suggests they may represent the working public, the underclass, or the democratic citizenry. When the Cat recognises the potential of the working people, he sees the need for democracy.[5]

Dr Seuss actually said Yertle was a representation of Hitler.

With these messages in mind I decided to write a poem for children about spiders. The message in the poem is be nice to them. As Dr Seuss said 'A person's a person, no matter how small'. (1954)

---

[3] http://en.wikipedia.org/wiki/Political_messages_of_Dr._Seuss

[4] http://www.relevantmagazine.com/culture/books/features/28468-what-dr-seuss-was-really-up-to accessed 14/3/13

[5] Burdorff, H. (2012). Subversive Seuss: Global North–South Relations in *The Cat in the Hat Comes Back*. Interdisciplinary Humanities, 29(1), 77–84.

1200 words

THE ARTEFACT

Spiders are arachnids not insects or bugs
We aren't cute and cuddly you can't give us hugs
Spiders have been on earth for a very long time
So give us a chance and listen to my rhyme
Some humans don't like spiders and move out of our way.
But I hope that humans will grow to love us one day
Lots of humans are so scared of spiders it's true
So they hoover us up or we're flushed down the loo
These are such horrible, cruel, and wicked things to do!
So the next time you break our webs, or crush us with your feet
Remember cobwebs are our homes, filled with lots of bugs to eat.
Spiders are good and just want a nice quiet life.
They don't want to annoy you or cause trouble and strife
So please read my poem and please be good and kind
The story I will tell you will hopefully change your mind

Two legs good eight legs better

Sammy a hairy large black spider lived in a house.
He wasn't any trouble he was a quiet like a mouse
But a little boy called Alfie didn't like Sammy at all
He broke his webs, he chased him, tried to pull him off the wall
Alfie said, "two legs are good and 8 legs are so dumb
So stop building cobwebs or I'll go and tell my Mum!"

Now Sammy, the hairy Spider was as good as gold
A well-behaved Spider he wasn't very bold
Sammy did not bite like the naughty False Widow.
Sammy slept in his web not under your pillow
All night long his sticky cobweb he would spin
So lots of bugs and insects would fall in

Sammy would weave a sticky web so delicate and neat
He wove it with great pride to capture lots of bugs to eat
Sammy was nice to have around to weave his web so fine
On which to string the drops of dew which shone in bright sunshine

I will impress Alfie, thought Sammy, he will be my friend one day
So Sammy began to spin his web and started straight away
One night Sammy spun a silver web, he spun with all his might
The web was shaped with silver thread, which caught the pale moonlight
By morning the web hung with morning dew, the drops hung one by one
With colours changing from yellow to gold in the early morning sun.

Sammy's sticky silver web looked like a work of art
Alfie will be impressed with this he will think I am really smart
But Alfie broke Sammy's web again which made Sammy really sad
He thought I will go far away because my webs make Alfie mad
So Sammy packed his web away and sent Alfie a goodbye letter
His final words were, "two legs good but eight legs are even better!"

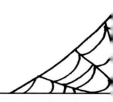

Moderator comments on the artefact

Why and how does the poem in this artefact link to Seuss's style of writing and illustration? Robert has illustrated the poem himself but does not discuss how his drawings resemble those of Seuss.

The message of the poem, which is reasonably entertaining, seems to be – be nice to spiders. It is quite overt whereas Seuss's messages tended to be more subtle/ambiguous. The Cat in The Hat, for instance, has various interpretations.

There is also an Orwellian reference from the book Animal Farm, 'Four legs good, two legs' (which has been adapted). It would have been useful to see reference to this quote in the accompanying report.

It may be seen that this spider project should not have been approved. It was approved by Robert's supervisor and centre coordinator because Robert had a clear aim at the planning stage and the project did have the potential to meet the various assessment objectives. However, these objectives were not fully realised.

ACTIVITY APPENDIX
Improving Robert's project

- What recommendations would you make to improve Robert's project?
- Consider each assessment objective discussed on the previous page.

Suggested answers on page 124.

A project that consists solely of written work should be approximately 5000 words (excluding references and appendices). Such projects may involve the analysis and synthesis of secondary data only – considering the research and comments from reliable secondary sources in order to answer a question. A PRODUCTION LOG (with SUMMARY AND RELECTION) was also handed in.

KIM'S EPQ ON BORN THIS WAY

EPQ title: BORN THIS WAY – are biological factors the primary basis for sexual orientation?

Abstract

In this research, I aim to investigate and evaluate how biological and psychological factors affect the development of sexual orientation (homosexuality), thus addressing the widespread debate of nature versus nurture. 'Nature' is the view espoused by nativists. Nature refers not simply to abilities present at birth but to any ability determined by genes, including those appearing through maturation. 'Nurture' is the view of empiricists, the view that everything is learned through interactions with the environment, the physical and social world, more widely referred to as 'experience'. Nativism versus empiricism, nature versus nurture, refers to the debate over the relative influence of each on any particular behaviour; in this case I am looking at homosexual behaviour. This project will be split into two, with each section devoted to each side of the argument. Within nature, I will explore genetics, neurology and hormonal factors. Within nurture, I will explore parenting, learning and social learning. Some research has already been done into the potential reasons behind homosexuality, but in this project I plan on clarifying and focusing on the three subcategories mentioned within each side of the debate. I hope to achieve these aims by using secondary research such as published, peer-reviewed articles on the Internet, as well as my own primary research involving a small survey. As there is much to learn about the factors contributing to sexual orientation, this project will focus on the contributions of 'nature and nurture' and what influence they both have in relation to homosexual behaviour.

Introduction

I decided to base my EPQ on the debate of nature and nurture in relation to the development of homosexual behaviour, giving me the chance to draw on my A-Level knowledge of both Biology and Psychology. I chose this topic for several reasons: primarily because it is an understudied area within the field of Psychology; secondly, as it is an area of personal interest due to past friendships with homosexual individuals; and thirdly, having watched a BBC documentary called 'The Making of Me' with John Barrowman, this immediately led to curiosity about why homosexual behaviour develops. Several scientific experiments were carried out in this documentary, some of which I will discuss in this project having found more in-depth information from various articles and journals online. An additional reason behind this project is the need for such topics to be understood within society as there is still much ignorance surrounding them. The most recent incident, happening in April 2012, involved the broadcasting of 'anti-gay' posters on London buses by an Anglican Christian organisation, with the slogan 'Not gay! Post-gay, ex-gay and proud! Get over it!' These adverts were soon banned as a consequence of the offensive nature of a matter, which is already in public controversy and sensitivity, without having to publicise it. Due to this type of ignorance, it would appear that more research needs to be put together in order to allow societies to be informed and educated on something which is so commonly misunderstood and consequently discriminated against.

Sexual orientation is defined as 'a person's sexual identity in relation to the gender to which they are attracted', with one aspect of sexual orientation being homosexuality which this project will focus on. In order to assess what affects and causes homosexual behaviour in people, it is necessary to provide a brief overview of the behaviour, its history and also homosexuality as an 'illness'. According to the Oxford Dictionary, the term homosexuality was derived in the late 19th century – 'homo' meaning 'the same' attached to the word 'sexual'. It is defined as 'involving sexual attraction between people of the same sex'. Societal attitudes towards same-sex relationships have varied over time and place, through acceptance, to seeing the practice as a minor sin. Early in the twentieth century, Ellis (1901) argued that homosexuality was inborn and not a disease, therefore not immoral.

Freud's (1905) basic theory of human sexuality was different from that of Ellis. He believed all human beings were innately bisexual, and that they become heterosexual or homosexual as a result of their experiences with parents and others. Freud agreed with Ellis that a homosexual orientation should not be viewed as a form of pathology. In a now-famous letter to an American mother in 1935, Freud wrote:

> Homosexuality is assuredly no advantage, but it is nothing to be ashamed of, no vice, no degradation, it cannot be classified as an illness; we consider it to be a variation of the sexual function produced by a certain arrest of sexual development... It is a great injustice to persecute homosexuality as a crime, and cruelty too... If [your son] is unhappy, neurotic, torn by conflicts, inhibited in his social life, analysis may bring him harmony, peace of mind, full efficiency whether he remains a homosexual or gets changed...

Rado (1940, 1949) rejected Freud's assumption of inherent bisexuality, arguing instead that heterosexuality is natural and that homosexuality is a 'reparative' attempt to achieve sexual pleasure when the normal heterosexual outlet proves too threatening. Other analysts later argued that homosexuality resulted from pathological family relationships during the Oedipal period (around 4–5 years of age) and claimed that they observed these patterns in their homosexual patients (Bieber et al. 1962).

Homosexuality was deemed to be a psychiatric disorder for many years, although the studies this theory was based on were later determined to be flawed. In a review of published studies comparing homosexual and heterosexual samples on psychological tests, Gonsiorek (1982) found that, although some differences have been observed in test results between homosexuals and heterosexuals, both groups consistently score within the normal range. Gonsiorek concluded that 'Homosexuality in and of itself is unrelated to psychological disturbance or maladjustment. Homosexuals as a group are not more psychologically disturbed on account of their homosexuality.' Some psychologists and psychiatrists still hold negative personal attitudes towards homosexuality. However, empirical evidence and professional norms do not support the idea that homosexuality is a form of mental illness or is inherently linked to psychopathology (Herek 2012).

There are numerous speculations that fall under one of the two subheadings 'Nature' or 'Nurture' – the debate centres on the relative contributions of genetic inheritance and environmental factors to human development. To investigate these assumptions linked to homosexuality, I carried out some basic primary research based on a question asking what people believe are the causes of homosexuality; however, due to the potentially sensitive nature of the topic, I have decided to concentrate on peer-reviewed research articles which involves the assessment of scientific work by others who are experts in the same field. The intention of peer reviewing is to ensure that any research conducted and published is of a high quality, thus allowing a means of establishing the validity of scientific research. Nevertheless, my initial primary research did help to formulate the aims of this project and so, I will now examine a number of suggested theories and their influence on a person's sexual orientation based on the peer-reviewed evidence I have found.

Discussion

Nature

Recent laboratory studies indicate that genes and brain development play a significant role in the development of sexual orientation; the specific influence, however, is not yet known. The search for biological roots of sexual orientation has run along two broad lines. The first draws on observations for physical differences between brain structures of heterosexual men, homosexual men and women's. The second approach is the identification of genes by studying the patterns in which homosexuality occurs in families and by directly examining genetic material, DNA. Researchers have long sought within the human brain some manifestation of the most obvious classes into which we are divided – male and female. Such sex differentiation of the brain's structure, called sexual dimorphism, has proved hard to establish. On average, a man's brain has a slightly larger size, matching with his larger body; other than that, casual inspection does not reveal any obvious dissimilarity between the sexes. Even under a microscope, the architecture of men's and women's brains is very similar.

The first significant observations of sexual dimorphism were made in laboratory animals. Gorski (1978) inspected rats' hypothalamuses, a region at the base of its brain that is involved in instinctive behaviours and the regulation of metabolism. He found that one group of cells near the front of the hypothalamus is several times larger in male than in female rats. Although this cell group is very small, less than a millimetre across even in males, the difference between the sexes is quite visible in appropriately stained slices of tissue, even without the aid of a microscope. Gorski's finding was especially interesting because the general region of the hypothalamus in which this cell group occurs, known as the medial preoptic area, has been implicated in the generation of sexual behaviour – in particular, behaviours typically displayed by males. Although this study appears to successfully show a link between sexual dimorphism and sexual behaviour, the use of rats immediately raises the issue of animal research ethics. Many experiments on animals have made important contributions to advances in psychology that have brought major improvements in the health and well-being of human beings; as a result, it is believed that it would be morally wrong not to make use of animals in research, however, these contributions have often been accomplished at considerable expense in terms of animal suffering. Researchers have said that a number of less-invasive procedures have been developed to minimise animal suffering and provide moral justification for animal research, but if researchers were not allowed to use animals in the first place, they would have to develop other techniques to take their place. So, if a model were adopted based on animal 'rights', animals would have the right not to be used by humans for research regardless of how 'non-invasive' the research procedures or how potentially beneficial the consequences for humans. As a backlash and main dispute regarding animal research, it is argued that human life has greater intrinsic value than animal life. Human rights arise because of implicit contracts between members of society and imply duties and responsibilities; animals have no such responsibilities, cannot reciprocate and therefore are deemed as having no rights. The traditional scientific position treats animals as 'renewable resources' rather than organisms of value whose rights must be respected. The problem with this is failing to recognise the rights of other species means violating the principle of respect for all sentient creatures. Since scientific experiments involving animals began, people have expressed concern that the animals may suffer or are somehow sacrificed in the name of science. Due to the many moral arguments and counterarguments for animal research, the concerns raised by animal rights activists will probably always be ongoing until the use of animals for research is ceased. For now, however, researchers remain firm that the kinds of advances and benefits from animal research that have been made would have been impossible without the use of animals. In a survey of psychologists and their relationship with animal research, more than three-quarters of respondents said that they believe the use of animals is critical to the scientific advancement (Plous 1996).

Moving away from the use of animals, Gorski et al. (1989) did find dimorphic structures in the human brain. A cell group named INAH3 (derived from the 'third interstitial nucleus of the anterior hypothalamus') in the medial preoptic region of the hypothalamus is about three times larger in men than in women. LeVay (1991) examined the hypothalamus in autopsy specimens from 19 homosexual men, all of whom had died of complications of AIDS, and 16 heterosexual men, six of whom had also died of AIDS. LeVay also included specimens from six women whose sexual orientation was unknown. LeVay observed that INAH3 was more than twice as large in the men as in the women; INAH3 was between two and three times larger in the straight men than in the gay men; and there was no significant difference between volumes of INAH3 in the gay men and in the women. In some gay men the cell group was altogether absent. The investigation suggested a dimorphism related to male sexual orientation about as great as that related to sex. A primary concern in such a study is whether the observed structural differences are caused by some variable other than the one of interest. A major suspect here was AIDS. The AIDS virus itself, as well as other infectious agents that take advantage of a weakened immune system, can cause serious damage to brain cells thus provoking the question of whether this was the reason for the small size of INAH3 in the gay men, all of whom had died of AIDS. Several lines of evidence indicate otherwise. First, the heterosexual men who died of AIDS had INAH3 volumes no different from those who died of other causes. Second, the AIDS victims with small INAH3s did not have case histories distinct from those with large INAH3s; for instance, they had not been ill longer before they died. Third, the other three cell groups in the medial preoptic area – INAH1, INAH2 and INAH4 – turned out to be no smaller in the AIDS victims. If the disease were having a nonspecific destructive effect, one would have suspected otherwise. After completing the main study, LeVay obtained the hypothalamus of one gay man who had died of non-AIDS causes. This specimen confirmed the main study: the volume of INAH3 in the gay man was less than half that of INAH3 in the heterosexual men.

From this research, the question of what might lie behind these apparent correlations between sexual orientation and brain structure arises. Logically, three possibilities exist. One is that the structural differences were present early in life – perhaps even before birth – and helped to establish the men's sexual orientation. The second is that the differences arose in adult life as a result of the men's sexual feelings or behaviour. The third possibility is that there is no causal connection, but sexual orientation and the brain structures in question are linked to, for example, a developmental event during uterine or early postnatal life. None of these possibilities have been decided on with any certainty, however on the basis of animal research, the second scenario, that the structural differences came about in adulthood, is unlikely. In rats, for example, the sexually dimorphic cell group in the medial preoptic area appears plastic in its response to androgens during early brain development but later is largely resistant to change. The first possibility, that the structural differences arose during the period of brain development and consequently contributed to sexual behaviour, is favoured because the medial preoptic region of the hypothalamus is implicated in sexual behaviour in monkeys. The size of INAH3 in men may indeed influence sexual orientation, but such a causal connection is speculative at this point. The third possibility, stating that some other variable contributes to sexual orientation, has been supported by the research done into hormonal factors and influences.

A study by Gorski et al. (1978) found that androgens – typical male hormones – play a key role in bringing about dimorphism during development. Neurons within the cell group are rich in receptors for sex hormones, both for androgens – testosterone being the main representative – and for female hormones known as oestrogens. Although male and female rats initially have about the same numbers of neurons in the medial preoptic area, a surge of testosterone secreted by the testes of male foetuses around the time of birth acts to stabilise their neuronal population. In females the lack of such a surge allows many neurons in this cell group to die, leading to the typically smaller structure. Interestingly, it is only for a few days before and after birth that the medial preoptic neurons are sensitive to androgen; removing androgens in an adult rat by castration does not cause the neurons to die. In relation to humans, with increased understanding of the endocrine system early in the 20th century, hormonal influences on sexual orientation began to be explored. Manning (2003) examined the androgen-sensitive pattern of finger lengths, with his hypothesis being that, in women, the index finger (2D, second digit) is almost the same length as the fourth digit (4D), although it may be slightly longer or shorter; in men, the index finger is more often shorter than the fourth.

In an anonymous survey, 720 adults who were attending public street fairs in the San Francisco area were asked their gender, age, sexual orientation, handedness, and the number and gender of children their mother had carried before them. As expected, men had significantly longer fingers than women, and it was confirmed that the 2D:4D ratio is greater in women than it is in men. This sex difference in 2D:4D is greater on the right hand than on the left, indicating that the right-hand 2D:4D is more sensitive to foetal androgens than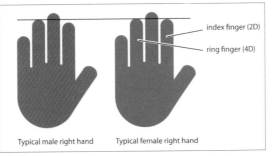

Typical male right hand   Typical female right hand

index finger (2D)
ring finger (4D)

the left-hand ratio. It has been found that the right-hand 2D:4D ratio of homosexual women was significantly more masculine (that is, smaller) than that of heterosexual women, and did not differ significantly from that of heterosexual men. Thus finger ratios suggest that at least some homosexual women were exposed to greater levels of foetal androgen than heterosexual women hence supporting Manning's hypothesis relating to androgen influenced finger lengths and corresponding sexual orientation. The nature of this study, however, is gynocentric due to sample bias – the results cannot be applied to male finger patterns. Furthermore, although the population validity may be criticised, the 'Universal Man' argument would state that it does not matter where such a thing is studied as our five digits and finger lengths are a universal phenomenon.

An additional biological cause suspected to influence sexual orientation is the notion of genetics and heredity. The pooled data for men show that about 57 percent of identical twins, 24 percent of fraternal twins and 13 percent of brothers of gay men are also gay. For women, approximately 50 percent of identical twins, 16 percent of fraternal twins and 13 percent of sisters of lesbians are also lesbian. When these data are compared with baseline rates of homosexuality, a good amount of family clustering of sexual orientation becomes evident for both sexes. Bailey and Pillard (1991) estimated that the overall heritability of sexual orientation is about 53 percent for men and 52 percent for women. (The family clustering is most obvious for relatives of the same sex, less so for male-female pairs.)

It may seem perplexing to even contemplate a 'gay gene' as questions relating to the Darwinian screening for reproductive fitness and parental background of gay men and lesbians arise, but studies have in fact provided some evidence for hereditary influence. Although no research has ever been able to prove genes swayed that homosexuality, Hamer (1993) offered the most convincing evidence to date that sexual orientation was genetically influenced. The lineages of gay men were traced back in order to find signs of homosexuality in all branches of their family tree. Far more gay individuals were found on the mother's side of the families than on the father's side, a pattern consistent with a special type of inheritance called sex linkage. The expression comes from the fact that the relevant gene is on one of the two sex chromosomes,

Moderator comments

The findings of the study are discussed in detail and three possible explanations for the results of the studies are proposed.

Kim writes in an appropriate academic style and she communicate her findings fluently in an appropriate format, synthesising information from a variety of sources and presenting them within a logical and coherent structure which closely addresses the nature of the task.

Kim brings the commentary to life by including relevant images, which are clearly annotated and referenced.

The findings of Manning's study on finger length are linked back to the hypothesis and also the limitations of the study are considered demonstrating the ability to analyse sources.

Additional biological causes are then considered.

in this case the X chromosome. The second part of the study involved inspection of a DNA strand. Using an approach called DNA linkage analysis, a small region of the X chromosome (Xq28) appeared to be the same in an unexpectedly high proportion of gay brothers. This finding provided the first concrete evidence that 'gay genes' really do exist.

As with all research into sensitive topics, Hamer's 'gay gene' study prompted ethical, medical and economic issues to be raised. Might parents decide to screen the foetus for homosexuality, just as they do now for Down syndrome and other genetic defects? Would some doctors regard homosexuality as a genetic defect that should be 'cured' or weeded out of society? Would insurance companies charge men with the 'gay gene' more for coverage or refuse to serve them, knowing the high risk of AIDS faced by gay men? According to Hamer, 'making sure the results of (the) study were used ethically and responsibly (was) at least as difficult as conducting the research itself'. Work into the biology of sexual orientation was concluded by stating:

> Our research has attracted an extraordinary degree of public attention, not so much because of any conceptual breakthrough – the idea that genes and the brain are involved in human behaviour is hardly new – but because it touches on a deep conflict in contemporary society. We believe scientific research can help dispel some of the myths about homosexuality that in the past have clouded the image of lesbians and gay men. We also recognise, however, that increasing knowledge of biology may eventually bring with it the power to infringe on the natural rights of individuals and to impoverish the world of its human diversity. It is important that our society expand discussions of how new scientific information should be used to benefit the human race in its entirety. (LeVay and Hamer 1994)

Of course, biological study of sexual orientation is not without its inaccuracies. Despite the extensive published research on the difference in biology between homosexual and heterosexual individuals, it has been criticised in the scientific world for reducing such a complex subject to simplistic matters of basic biology.

So far I have considered hereditary, neurological and hormonal factors; due to the reductionist nature of biological causes, it seems necessary to consider the nurture of homosexuality – an individual's environment (e.g. upbringing and early social life) – in order to investigate any further reasons that could explain their sexual orientation.

Nurture

Freud (1905, 1953) argued that homosexuality reflected a premature fixation of one's psychosexual development. Although he did not dismiss hereditary factors altogether, Freud thought that fixated psychosexual development was typically due to the presence of a domineering mother and/or absent father. The 'distant father' theory states that homosexuality in males is caused by an unavailability of fatherly affection and attention during a young boy's childhood. Because the father was emotionally unavailable or incompetent in forming bonds with his son, the son would develop a yearning for closeness with a man to compensate for the lack of fatherly love, and this would result in homosexual feelings in the son. Most contemporary psychoanalytic explanations continue to emphasise the theme of a romantic triad including a dominant mother, a weak father, and the mother's favourite son (Bieber and Bieber 1979, Socarides 1968). Research supporting the psychoanalytic explanation primarily consists of evidence that male homosexuals have been reared by unusually protective mothers and/or detached and unloving fathers, although other interpretations of these findings are possible.

Various theorists shared with Freud the idea that homosexuality is an immature stage of psychosexual development, but focused much more broadly than Freud did on many aspects of family life, arguing that psychosexual development can be arrested in the homosexual stage by many factors, including unhappy and broken homes, inadequate parental and same-sex role models, as well as by dominant mothers and/or affectionless and weak fathers (Friedman and Stern 1980). The positive side of this psychodynamic approach points to the fact that it is unique in recognising the complexity of human motives and the irrationality of much human behaviour. Freud's theory was derived from extensive interviews with patients, therefore a rich source of data, however it was biased – his patients were almost entirely middle-class neurotic individuals from Vienna, mainly women. Due to this, Freud's theory of 'normal' development was based on recollections of childhood from abnormal individuals belonging to a distinct cultural group and also to a particular historical period. The fact that Freud worked during a time of great sexual repression may explain the highly sexual nature of his interpretations – people would have been less able to express sexual issues and this may have led to hysteria. Freud himself may have been influenced by the attitudes of his time and this may explain why his interpretations are so highly sexual. Although Freud imposed a meaning on each recollection and provided sound reasoning, they were simply his interpretations; there may be other equally valid explanations. Nevertheless, even if Freud's theories are questioned, his contribution to psychology is unarguable. Many of Freud's insights – for example, the importance of childhood, or the idea that unconscious processes influence us – remain very influential even after most of his theoretical concepts have been rejected by the mainstream.

Another theory, again without dismissing genetic involvement, was proposed by East (1946) who attributed most homosexuality to confusion during the time one learns appropriate sex roles. East contended that if a person's appearance or mannerisms happen to resemble those of the opposite sex, especially if such traits are accompanied by an early homosexual seduction, the individual may elicit incorrect, or at least confusing, social reinforcement for his or her sex role behaviour and thereby become a prime candidate for lifelong homosexuality. East's views were later elaborated by Kagan (1964), although Kagan also invoked the concept of self-labelling as both a response to and a reinforcement of others' impressions of the appropriateness of a person's sex role behaviour. A recent variant of this social learning explanation postulated a homosexual-heterosexual labelling concept (Robertson 1977, Sagarin 1975). According to this view, persons whose sexual experience happened to be with a member of the same sex would be inclined to label themselves as homosexual. Thereafter, the impression would most likely persist unless sufficient heterosexual experiences compensated for the homosexual label.

A further social environmental explanation focused outside the home was proposed by Kardiner (1963), who attributed male homosexuality to excessive societal demands on boys to be 'masculine'. Boys who felt inadequate in complying with those demands were believed to seek refuge in female roles. Reinforcement learning principles inspired other learning explanations in which psychologists argued that homosexuality frequently resulted from the reinforcing nature of same-sex sexual encounters that happened to precede opposite-sex sexual encounters. Similarly, Gagnon and Simon (1973) maintained that sexual orientation was learned through varying schedules of reward and punishment. Assuming that homosexual experiences are fairly common during childhood and early adolescence, Gagnon and Simon reasoned that if these experiences were pleasurable and/or heterosexual encounters were distasteful (for whatever reason), a homosexual orientation was likely to become the dominant preference in adulthood due to this vicarious reinforcement.

The most recent social learning explanation relied more on classical than operant conditioning principles. Working from evidence that male homosexuals reach sexual maturity somewhat earlier than male heterosexuals, Storms (1981) and Wasserman and Storms (1984) argued that early-maturing males are more likely to reach sexual maturity at a time when males are still largely interacting with one another, whereas later-maturing males are more likely to experience their first sexual interests at a time when societal forces have begun to encourage increased heterosexual contacts. Thus early-maturing males are more likely than later-maturing males to pair sexual awakening with males than with females.

An additional, somewhat controversial, theory of homosexuality holds that a possible root of homosexuality is sexual abuse in an individual's childhood. For instance, a young boy sexually abused by an adult male could grow to doubt his own sexuality and might eventually come to the conclusion that he was in fact a homosexual. Such confusion over sexuality has been expressed by male survivors of childhood sexual abuse. However, there are at least two flaws with this chain of argument. Firstly, it cannot explain the incidence of homosexuality in individuals who were not subjected to sexual abuse during their childhoods. Secondly, although confusion over sexuality has been expressed by male survivors, another reaction to this confusion has been open hostility towards other homosexuals. In other words, confusion over sexuality stemming from the abuse is also likely to result in homophobia instead of homosexuality.

An overall weakness of this nurture argument is that it cannot explain why not all homosexuals have observed homosexual behaviour as a child – what of the homosexuals who have never observed such behaviour prior to the personal experience of homosexual feelings? Regarding the claim that an individual would make a choice to adopt this lifestyle, one may wonder at who would choose to live a life which would probably include discrimination aimed at him. Indeed, Nobel Peace Prize recipient Archbishop Desmond Tutu stated, regarding sexual orientation being a choice, that 'the homosexual persons must be the craziest coots around to choose a way of life that exposes them to so much hostility, discrimination, loss and suffering'.

Conclusion

There is still much to know about the development of sexual orientation and why it occurs. The importance in knowing why lies in the impact it will have on society at large as discrimination is still a problem.

In presenting some of the theories which support the view that homosexuality is either a biologically or socially derived phenomenon, it is clear to see that these theories are inadequate as an all-encompassing theory for homosexuality; however, they do have some merit as shown by supporting research and are likely to hold some truth.

Most scientists now agree that the very wording of the question 'nature or nurture?' represents a false single-minded assumption – the relative contributions and precise nature of these factors remain a matter of considerable speculation and debate, largely because of the lack of tools to dissect them. It would seem that the most likely cause of homosexuality is not exclusively biological or social, that factors from both interact and influence to eventually find a middle ground to explain homosexuality, and that neither nature nor nurture can cause homosexuality in the absence of the other. What is known is that both biology and the environment play some role in virtually all human behaviours; what is yet to be discovered fully is which – nature or nurture – plays the dominant role.

References

Books & journals

Ellis, L. and Ames, M.A. (1987) *Neurohormonal Functioning and Sexual Orientation: A Theory of Homosexuality-Heterosexuality.*

Hamer, D. (1994) *Science of Desire: The Gay Gene and the Biology of Behaviour.*

Plous, S. (1996) Attitudes toward the use of animals in psychological research and education: Results from a national survey of psychologists. *American Psychologist*, 51, 1167-1180.

Websites

http://philosophy.illinoisstate.edu/chorvath/PHI202Su10/LeVayHamer%20copy.pdf

    Gorski, R. (1978) Brain Research

    Gorski, R. & Allan, S. University of California, Los Angeles

    LeVay, S. (1991) Science

    LeVay, S. & Hamer, D. (1994) Scientific American

http://www.unl.edu/rhames/courses/readings/homofinger/homo_finger.html

    Manning, J. (2003) Evolution and Human Behaviour, Volume 24, Issue 6, Pages 399-405

Television programmes

BBC One 'The Making of Me' - John Barrowman. Broadcast 24/07/2008. Available at: http://www.bbc.co.uk/programmes/b00cr1ht

Moderator comments

It is unlikely that this is the most recent social learning explanation as it was conducted in the 1980s. It is better to avoid overstating points.

Very useful evaluation of the hypothesis that childhood abuse can lead to homosexuality.

The overall weakness of the nurture argument is considered and a carefully selected quote provides a helpful and thought-provoking conclusion to this section.

The conclusion could have provided a more effective brief recap of what has been covered. It is too brief (just over 200 words) It would have been a useful idea to relate back to the 'anti-gay' posters on London buses by an Anglican Christian organisation in April 2012.

The take-home message is clear as Kim concludes both biology and the environment play some role, and does provide an answer to the original question.

Book references are not fully complete, the publisher details are missing.

Presentation details are shown on the next page to illustrate Kim's planning. The presentation was based on a summary of the EPQ report. Kim missed the opportunity to communicate the journey taken from idea to product, including the decisions made, skills developed and the significance of her conclusions.

Presentation planning

SLIDE 1: Project title

SLIDE 2: The aim of my project and how I went about achieving this aim.

SLIDE 3: Why I chose to investigate the biological and psychology causes (nature versus nurture) of homosexuality – prevention of discrimination, educating society; personal curiosity having watched the BBC documentary 'The Making of Me'.

SLIDE 4: Operationalising definitions of 'nature' and 'nurture'.

SLIDE 5: The three subcategories within each side of the debate: nature – genetics, neurology, hormonal factors; nurture – parenting, learning, social learning.

SLIDE 6: Neurology. Gorski's 1978 study of rats' hypothalamuses; Gorski's 1989 autopsy study of dimorphic structures in the human brain (INAH3).

SLIDE 7: Evaluation of Gorski's 1989 study, focusing on the potential variable of AIDS; a firm piece of evidence to confirm Gorski's hypothesis.

SLIDE 8: Hormones. Gorski's findings relating to the influence of androgens (1978); Manning's 2003 study relating to androgen influenced finger lengths and corresponding sexual orientation, hence supporting Gorski's finding.

SLIDE 9: Genetics: 'gay gene'. Hamer's 1993 study of homosexuality in all branches of gay men's family trees; the identification of Xq28; the ethical, medical and economic issues.

SLIDE 10: Freud's (1905, 1953) 'distant father' theory and the various elaborations from other researchers, including East (1946) and Kagan (1964); Kardiner's (1963) view on societal demands for boys to be 'masculine'; Gagnon and Simon's (1973) view on distasteful heterosexual experiences and pleasing homosexual experiences - reward and punishment; potential male child abuse which caused confusion in early life, however also the possibility of becoming homophobic due to past abusive experience.

SLIDE 11: Archbishop Desmond Tutu's view of why someone would want to choose a lifestyle, which subjects them to discrimination.

SLIDE 12: Conclusion: both biological and environmental factors contribute but which is dominant?

5000 words

Appendix III
Exemplar EPQ — Primary data

A project that involves the collection of primary data should be approximately 5000 words (excluding references and appendices), for example a research report of an investigation. It is important that such reports follow the conventions outlined in Chapter 4 of this book.

A PRODUCTION LOG (with SUMMARY AND REFLECTION) were also handed in with this project.

EPQ title: Out of my league; To what extent is physical attractiveness important in romantic relationships? A look at the matching hypothesis.

PHILIPPA'S EPQ ON ATTRACTION

Abstract

The matching hypothesis states that people are attracted to members of the opposite sex who are similar in terms of physical attractiveness, rather than seeking the most physically attractive mate. This study aims to test this hypothesis by selecting a set of photographs of married couples and asking participants to rate the attractiveness of each of the partners (females rate male photos and males rate female photos). Forty-eight participants from the sixth form at our school took part (24 girls and 24 boys) and were asked to rate the physical attractiveness on a scale of 1 to 10 (10 = highly attractive). The correlation was not significant ($p = 0.05$, critical value = 0.65, observed value = 0.44, null hypothesis accepted). This suggests that, when looking for a partner, people do not try to match their own physical attractiveness; they may be influenced by a variety of other factors.

Introduction

'Love is often nothing but a favourable exchange between two people who get the most of what they can expect, considering their value on the personality market' (Fromm 1955).

If we glance around any public setting we will often observe that people tend to pair up with those who are similar in physical attractiveness.

> The handsome man and the gorgeous woman date and marry each other, while their more homely counterparts pair up with their plainer counterparts. Similarity in physical attractiveness also occurs in gay and lesbian couples. In everyday language, this is referred to as dating in 'one's league' (Sprecher and Hatfield 2009, page 108).

Relationships start with interpersonal attraction. Psychologists have proposed various explanations for interpersonal attraction. One view is that we seek partners who are physically attractive, possibly because this is evidence of their good reproductive potential (evolutionary theory). Features that are considered physically attractive, such as a good complexion and white teeth, suggest the possessor is healthy and has good genes. Mating with such an individual will help maximise your own reproductive success.

An alternative view is the matching hypothesis, which suggests that people aspire to something as a result of its desirability and our chances of attaining it. Elaine Hatfield (married name Walster) and her colleagues proposed the original version of the matching hypothesis. Based on Lewin's (1935) level of aspiration theory, the matching hypothesis suggests that we actually seek a partner whose physical attractiveness matches our own physical attractiveness. This is likely because, even though we find physically attractive people most desirable, we go for a compromise when selecting a potential partner in order to avoid rejection. We don't select a partner who is much less physically attractive because this would limit our reproductive success. We can do better and maximise our reproductive success. Walster et al. (1966) suggested that people are attracted to those of a similar level of physical attraction to their own. Furthermore, if a couple are mismatched the less attractive partner may feel insecure and inadequate, thus placing a strain on the relationship.

The matching hypothesis focuses on physical similarity but, as Price and Vandenberg (1979) found, couples can be similar in other ways. Indeed, in terms of social exchange, one partner may have high physical attractiveness that is matched not by similar attractiveness in their partner but by social status. In fact, evolutionary theory predicts that women may be more interested in the social status of their partners than physical attractiveness because social status guarantees important resources that will assist in providing a good home for any offspring.

Buss (1989) studied men and women in 37 different cultures and found that men sought partners with youth and physical attractiveness and valued fertility, whereas women valued ambitiousness and industriousness, both of which are related to resource potential.

So matching may involve more than matching for physical attractiveness alone. Goffman (1961) believed that men had the tendency to choose spouses who were similar in terms of various attributes such as social skills, wealth, power, intelligence, attractiveness and other skills that are valued in society. Similarity, particularly similarity of attitudes, has also been shown to be an important ingredient in initial attraction and the formation of friendships. Newcomb (1961) studied friendships among first-year male undergraduates at the University of Michigan who at the beginning of the study were all strangers to each other. He measured their attitudes to many things over the course of the first term and found that friendships were more likely to form between students who shared similar attitudes. Kerckhoff (1974) observes, for example, that married partners typically come from the same social, economic and religious groups, and have the same intelligence level and educational background.

A word of warning about dual accreditation: This project covers a well-known study in the field of social psychology which investigates the matching hypothesis. Where a subject is very close to a candidate's A-Level studies, supervisors must identify, in Project Proposal Part B, how the proposed study relates to the A-Level course they are doing and where the extension will be.

This was recorded as follows for Philippa:

> Philippa studies A-Level Psychology but her course does not cover the psychology of relationships and so there is no overlap with her studies. This topic represents a genuine extension of her A-Level Psychology.

Alternatively, if the student does not study psychology but wishes to study it at University this will be evident from Project Proposal A and B.

Moderator comments

The abstract is succinct (145 words) and contains the key elements outlined in Chapter 4 (page 78). It includes the aim and hypothesis, a brief reference to background literature, a brief overview of the method, the findings and a conclusion in relation to the hypothesis and background research. It also considers the implications of the findings.

The introduction relates directly to the topic under investigation and begins with relevant quotes from Fromm, and Sprecher and Hatfield (2009).

We can clearly see that the structure is like a funnel (as described on page 80), it begins quite wide, which discusses the general area of the topic: relationships, love and attraction. It briefly looks at opposing theories on mate selection and then it narrows the area down to precisely what the research will focus on.

The key sources are presented chronologically from the classic research in 1966 to more recent studies in 2011. The chronological approach to presenting relevant literature works very well here because the research follows the same theme and the candidate demonstrates the ability to synthesise sources by considering similarities and differences between each study.

Walster *et al.* (1966) tested this hypothesis in a study called the 'Computer Dance experiment'. About 400 students were invited to a freshers' week dance and told they would be paired with a similar partner (in fact they were paired randomly and judges rated each student in terms of physical attractiveness). At the end of the dance students were all given questionnaires including a question about whether they would like to see their partner again. Walster *et al.* found that students were most likely to want to see a physically attractive partner again rather than one who was more of a match. However, this study was criticised because it didn't relate to real-life relationships very well. When Walster and Walster (1969) repeated the study they did find support for the matching hypothesis probably because this time the participants spent time together beforehand and were given a choice of who to partner. This time they did prefer someone who matched their own perceived physical attractiveness. This makes sense as matching is likely to occur if you are seeking a relationship rather than rating someone who you've been paired with. In the latter case there was no opportunity for selection so matching would not have taken place.

Further support for the matching hypothesis has been found in studies of real-life couples. Silverman (1971) conducted an observational study of couples in public places (such as bars and theatres). The couples were between 18 and 22 and unmarried. Observers independently rated the couples on a 5-point scale and found high similarity between members of a couple. The observers also noted that the more similar the attractiveness, the happier the couple were rated in terms of the degree of physical intimacy (e.g. holding hands).

Murstein (1972) asked couples who were engaged or going steady to rate their own and their partners attractiveness on a 5-point scale. Independent judges also rated the participants' attractiveness. The similarity ratings for couples were compared with ratings made of randomly paired couples. Murstein found that real couples were significantly more similar than the randomly paired couples.

Huston (1973) suggested that individuals did not set out to seek those of the same level of attractiveness for the purpose of matching. Instead rather than seeking a match, individuals wanted to avoid rejection and so sought someone of an equal level of physical attractiveness to avoid rejection from someone of a higher level of physical attractiveness to themselves. Huston studied this by showing participants photographs of people who had already indicated that they would accept the participant as a partner. The results indicated that the participant usually chose the person rated as most attractive. This contradicts Huston's hypothesis but the study does have low mundane realism because the participant was told that people in the pictures would accept them as a partner and so the relationship was certain, there was no risk of rejection. This explains why they would select the most attractive. In a real-life situation people would not be certain and so they would still be more likely to select someone of equal attractiveness to avoid possible rejection. Furthermore, Brown (1986) suggested that the matching hypothesis does exist but offered an alternative explanation that argued, rather than fearing rejection, we adjust our expectation of partners in line with what we believe we can offer others.

Garcia and Khersonsky (1996) studied the matching hypothesis and how others view couples who were matched on physical attractiveness and those who were not. Participants were shown photographs of couples who matched or did not match in physical attractiveness. They were then asked to complete a questionnaire which asked them to rate how satisfied the couples appear in their current relationship, their potential marital satisfaction, how likely is it that they will break up and how likely it is that they will be good parents. Results showed that the attractive couples were rated as currently more satisfied than the non-matching couple. This supports the matching hypothesis and earlier studies of Murstein. Although the validity again is questionable as self-report questionnaires are prone to demand characteristics.

As online dating is increasingly common as a way of meeting people Shaw Taylor (2011) conducted a series of studies to investigate whether the matching hypothesis applied to online dating. The attractiveness of 60 males and 60 females was measured. They then looked at the dating intentions of these people. They monitored who they interacted with and who they replied to. The results partially confirmed the matching hypothesis in that people were more likely to contact others who were significantly more attractive than they were. However, it was found that the person was more likely to reply if they were closer to the same level of attractiveness offering some support for matching in terms of attractiveness.

All of these studies support the matching hypothesis in a variety of different settings and in relation to couples in varying stages of a relationship.

Aims

The aim of this study is to replicate Murstein's research, adapting the original design. Instead of actually asking participants to rate their own attractiveness, this study will use photographs of married couples and require participants to rate the attractiveness of the people in the photographs. We would expect couples to be similar (matching) in attractiveness because they have chosen each other. They should go for someone of a similar level of attractiveness rather than someone who is much more or much less physically attractive.

Hypothesis

There is a positive correlation in the attractiveness ratings given to the partners in a long-standing romantic relationship.

Method

Design

This study is a non-experimental design which involved a questionnaire to collect ratings of photographs and used a correlational analysis to assess the data. The two co-variables were the attractiveness ratings of male partners and attractiveness ratings of female partners. Attractiveness was operationalised as:

'Pleasing or appealing to the senses, appealing to look at; sexually alluring, having qualities or features which arouse interest.' (http://www.oxforddictionaries.com/definition/english/attractive [Accessed 9th June 2014])

Attractiveness was measured on a scale of 1 to 10, where 10 was extremely physically attractive.

Participants

An opportunity sample was taken from sixth form students at our school, 24 males and 24 females. Those students who were available at the time of the study were asked to participate. Some individuals declined to take part. The names of participants used in this study were anonymous, to minimise the chance of demand characteristics.

Materials /apparatus

Photographs of ten couples were selected from magazines and photocopied, labelling them A to J. All photographs were selected according to certain criteria: the faces of each partner were about the size of a passport photograph and looking straight at the camera, both partners were aged between 20 and 30 (otherwise age might be a feature of attractiveness rating). Race was also controlled. Only photographs of white, Europeans were used.

The male and female photographs were cut out separately and pasted onto a male sheet of photographs and a female sheet. The photographs were placed randomly on each sheet so they were not in the same order (i.e. photo 1 for females was from couple C whereas photo 1 on the male sheet was from couple J).

An example of the photographs is shown in Appendix I.

Ethics

Partially informed consent was sought – participants were told what the task would involve them doing and that they had the right to withdraw at any time, and that their answers would remain anonymous.

The minor deception (the aim of the study) was dealt with by debriefing participants at the end of the study. Informed consent forms and debriefing are given in Appendix II.

The photographs chosen were all in the public domain and so consent was not required from people in the photographs.

Procedure

One A-Level student collected data.

Each participant was taken to a separate room to complete the task, away from the distractions of other students. The standardised briefing instructions were read to the participant (see Appendix III) and consent was given.

Female participants were shown the male photos and male participants were shown the female photos, and asked to rate each photograph on a scale of 1 to 10, where 10 was extremely physically attractive. Participants wrote their ratings on a piece of paper with spaces for 10 answers (see Appendix IV). No names were asked for.

Afterwards participants were thanked and given the standard debriefing (see Appendix V) advising them that they would be told further details of the study when all participants had been tested.

Controls

Researcher bias was minimised by using standardised instructions and not watching participants as they completed the task to avoid participant reactivity. An independent rater was also used who selected the photographs. This rater was unaware of the aims or hypothesis of the study.

Participant bias was avoided by asking participants to rate members of the opposite sex because, in a pilot study, boys felt uncomfortable rating men in terms of physical attractiveness.

Differences between photographs were minimised because otherwise this would act as a confounding variable (e.g. age or race).

A pilot study was completed beforehand using five participants. The purpose of this pilot study was to ensure that the instructions were clear and the photographs could be easily rated.

A further control was that the photographs were chosen from national sources. This is to minimise the chances of participants recognising the couples if they were from local newspapers.

Photographs of celebrities were not selected as this would have confounded the results.

Findings

Descriptive statistics

Summary tables of the data for female and male participants are shown below and on the next page (Figures 1 and 2). For each photograph the 12 ratings given to the photograph were added together and divided by 12 to give a mean rating. A scatter diagram was used to display these results visually. The raw data are given in Appendix VI.

Figure 1 Tables of findings

Ratings of female photographs	
Photograph	Mean rating
A	4.9
B	4
C	5.8
D	7.3
E	4.4
F	3.2
G	6
H	6.1
I	3.1
J	5.5

Ratings of male photographs	
Photograph	Mean rating
A	5.2
B	5.8
C	7.1
D	7
E	3.1
F	6
G	6.5
H	4.9
I	4.2
J	5.5

Figure 2   Scatter diagram to show correlation ratings of
male and female members of a couple

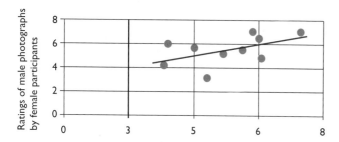

Ratings of female photographs by male participants

Inferential statistics

The scatter diagram indicates a weak positive correlation (the line of best fit was produced by Excel). In order to determine whether this positive correlation is significant I used an inferential statistical test.

I choose to use Spearman's rank correlation test because:

- I need a test of correlation.
- The data used were ratings made by participants which is ordinal data.
- This means we should use a non-parametric test.

The statistical calculations are shown in Appendix VII.

Level of significance: The level of significance selected was 5%, the hypothesis was directional and therefore a one-tailed test is required, n = 10.

The observed value of rho = 0.44.

The critical value of rho = 0.65 (p = 0.05)

As the observed value is less than the critical value we cannot reject the null hypothesis, which is 'There is no correlation in the attractiveness ratings given to the partners in a long-standing romantic relationship'.

Discussion

Explanation of findings related to the hypothesis

The hypothesis predicted a positive correlation between the ratings of physical attractiveness between the male and females members of a couple. The scatter diagram showed a weak positive correlation but this was shown to be nonsignificant at the 5% level when using the inferential test. This means that the results of this study did not support the matching hypothesis. However, some couples did have similar rating and rank positions overall which did support the matching hypothesis. The means for couple J were identical and couples A, D and G were very similar. On the other hand, there were large differences in some other couples such as C and F. Taken altogether this suggests that matching for physical attractiveness is not a general phenomenon when selecting a partner.

Explanation of findings related to previous research

Researchers in the field of social psychology have assumed for several years now that physical attractiveness should play a pivotal role in the formation of romantic relationships. In contrast to these expectations, Murstein's findings 30 years ago found a 'definite tendency' for couples to be of a similar level of attractiveness. The historical period may be significant. It is possible that there were different social norms 30 years ago than now, when conducting this study. Physical attractiveness may have been a more important criteria when selecting a partner then, whereas intelligence may be a more important factor now. A further factor may be that young people did not judge attractiveness in Murstein's study whereas they did here. This may affect the way ratings are given.

Other research has found that couples match in terms of different criteria besides physical attractiveness. For example, Newcomb (1961) found similarity in attitudes was important. Also evolutionary theory predicts that women are more interested in resources than physical attractiveness so they may match physical attractiveness for resources in a male. So if a partner has other attractive qualities, that counts as a way to compensate for a lack of physical attractiveness in their partner. The matching hypothesis states that couples pair together but this was not the case in the present study as the hypothesis was not supported.

Strengths and limitations

There are several strengths of the present study which can enhance confidence in the findings. First, a strength of the research was that a pilot study had been conducted before hand to make sure that any anomalies had been accounted for. Second the two co-variables were well operationalised and controlled. In addition participants were fully debriefed and there were no ethical issues raised by this research. Informed consent was gained and the participants were not harmed in any way either psychologically or physically. Moreover, there were no socially sensitive issues with this research. The study was easy to replicate and so its reliability could be confirmed.

In spite of these key strengths the study was limited in a number of ways. Most importantly the data is correlational and thus cannot support strong causal conclusions. In other words we can't say that physical attractiveness causes relationships to form. The photographs were taken from magazines and it may be that only certain kinds of couples were represented in such photographs. People in magazines may often have done something unusual and therefore may not be typical. One way to deal with this is to get photographs of couples who are known to have more typical relationships. Also we do not know how long the couples had been together or if in fact they were couples or just models posing for the photographs. A future study could just use couples but this may be difficult as we would need to get consent from the couples.

A further problem is that the judges were only 6th formers and they may not see physical attractiveness in the same way as members of a couple do. The homogeneity of the sample limits our ability to generalise these findings to other samples. Also, physical attractiveness may be more important as a factor in the formation of relationships compared to more mature participants and this may have influenced the overall trend of results. This means it may be more appropriate to ask members of a couple to rate themselves and each other in order to see a person as his/her partner sees them. A further limitation relates to the sample of photographs selected – they were all white and heterosexual so these results cannot be generalised to other cultures or same-sex couples. They were all of young couples and so can't be generalised to older couples who may be matched on other qualities rather than attractiveness.

Participant judges may have conferred in their ratings as they were not separated. A future study could address this by seating judges in booths or testing them separately although this would be more time consuming, it would increase validity. Furthermore, the matching hypothesis only looks at relationships in the early stages; factors other than attractiveness may be more important at a later stage. Physical attractiveness is seen immediately, other factors take a while to uncover. On the other hand, it is easier to study physical attractiveness – how would we study compatible needs in a study such as this?

The participant judges could have guessed the aim of the study and so demand characteristics are an issue here. They could have given the answers they thought the researchers wanted or displayed the 'screw you effect' and done the opposite. One way to overcome this would have been to use a double blind procedure where neither the reseacher nor the participants knows the aims of the study.

Implications and suggestions for future research

The implications of these findings are important in evaluating the matching hypothesis, which may only operate in certain circumstances. If it were shown that matching is important in long-term relationships then this could be used by dating agencies to work out the most successful criteria for matching prospective partners.

In contemporary society, matching is sometimes assisted by third parties such as friends, relatives and dating sites whereas the matching hypothesis proposed that people make their own dating and mating choices. Nevertheless families and matching services may also consider physical attractiveness and other desirable traits as they determine who will make suitable matches. Indeed research shows that attractiveness is also important in arranged marriages.

Complex matching could be investigated in a future study. The matching hypothesis proposed that people would pair up with someone as physically attractive as themselves whereas in reality people come to a relationship offering many desirable characteristics. A person may compensate for a lack of physical attractiveness with a charming personality, kindness, status, money, and so forth. The notion that individuals can sometimes compensate for their lack of attractiveness by offering other desirable traits has been termed 'complex matching'. An example of this can be seen when an older wealthy, successful man pairs with a younger, attractive woman. This couple, although not matched on attractiveness, are matched on more complex terms such as fertility and resources.

There are also implications for women as research has shown that women more than men are likely to go for cosmetic surgery to improve their physical attractiveness (Brown *et al.* 2007). This would be an interesting avenue to research to explore whether women are likely to undergo extreme measures to attract and keep a partner.

Further research might be done on comparing couples who have separated with those who have remained together to see if there is closer matching in the couples who stay together. Comparisons could also be made between how older and younger people rate attractiveness in photographs. Also a replication of the study by Shaw Taylor *et al.* (2011) study would give an insight into matching in online dating which is relevant today. Also a replication of the research by Garcia and Khersonsky (1996) could be conducted to see if participants rated matched couples as more satisfied. Additionally as Walster *et al.* (1966) found that when using the matching hypothesis with homosexual couples, physical attractiveness was still a high priority when choosing a partner, but as this study was carried out some time ago more contemporary studies of same-sex couples should also be considered to see whether matching is just a heterosexual phenomenon. Also, according to Jackson (1992) women's attractiveness declines more steeply over time than men's attractiveness. Additionally, it is possible that the sex differences in the importance of physical attractiveness in a long-term relationship partner may change over time.

According to Margolin and White (1987) partner physical attractiveness is indeed more important to men than women in the initial stages of a relationship, what is less certain is whether partner attractiveness is always more important to men than it is to women. Although it is possible that attractiveness may continue to be more important to men than it is to women even among older adults (Thornhill and Gangestad 1999). This could be an interesting avenue for future research.

A final thought is that relationships evolve over time and matching on physical attractiveness may be more important in the early rather than later stages of relationships.

Conclusion

This investigation into the matching hypothesis examined whether people are attracted to members of the opposite sex who are similar in terms of physical attractiveness. The results of the correlation were not significant and so did not support the matching hypothesis. This suggests that, when looking for a partner, people do not try to match their own physical attractiveness; they may be influenced by a variety of other factors. Future research could address these factors. Relationships may therefore be determined by a variety of other issues not just physical attraction. Other theories have suggested that reproductive potential may be one key factor. This study has shown that physical attractiveness may be important but it is by no means the most important factor in mate selection.

Moderator comments

The limitations are relevant although sometimes not well-developed.

Some sweeping generalisations are made such as more mature participants may not value attractiveness as much as younger participants. Where is the evidence for such a point?

This is an interesting point about the focus on early stages of a relationship although it could be elaborated further. What are these other factors which are important in a relationship?

Although this is a valid point about the influence of third parties, the issue could have been expressed more coherently.

An interesting paragraph, although it would have worked better had Phillipa defined 'complex matching' at the outset.

Although some useful suggestions are made, this paragraph is rather list-like and the final sentence lacks evidence to support the statement about more second and third marriages.

This penultimate paragraph needs to be rounded off more effectively because the moderator is left thinking what could be an interesting avenue for further research?

The final sentence could be more profound and thought-provoking.

The conclusion is brief, only consisting of 125 words. There is a brief recap of the investigation. The take-home message (that physical attractiveness is not the most important factor when choosing a mate) is repeated. The brief conclusion will have an impact on the AO4 mark. Many students let themselves down by paying insufficient

References

Brown, R. (1986). *Social psychology, the second edition* (2nd ed.). New York: Free Press.

Brown, A., Furnham, A., Glanville, L. and Swami, V. (2007). Factors that affect the likelihood of undergoing cosmetic surgery. *Aesthetic Surgery Journal, 27*, 501–508.

Fromm, E. (1955). *The Sane Society.* Routledge and Keegan Paul. Oxon.

Garcia, S.D and Khersonsky, D. (1996). 'They make a lovely couple': Perceptions of couple attractiveness. *Journal of Social Behavior and Personality, 11* (4), 667–682.

Goffman, E. (1961). *Encounters: Two Studies in the Sociology of Interaction.* Indianapolis: Bobbs-Merrill.

Huston, T.L. (1973). Ambiguity of acceptance, social desirability, and dating choice. *Journal of Experimental Social Psychology, 9* (1), 32–42.

Jackson, L.A. (1992). *Physical appearance and gender: Sociobiological and sociocultural perspectives.* Albany: State University of New York Press.

Kerckhoff, A.C. (1974). The Social Context of Interpersonal Attraction.In T.L. Huston (ed) *Foundations of interpersonal attraction.* New York and London: Academic Press.

Lewin, K.(1935). *A Dynamic Theory of Personality.* New York McGraw Hill.

Margolin, L. and White, L. (1987). The continuing role of physical attractiveness in marriage. *Journal of Marriage and the Family, 49*, 21–27.

Murstein, B.I. (1972). *Physical attractiveness and marital choice. Journal of Personality and Social Psychology, 22*, 8–12.

Newcombe, T.M. (1961). *The acquaintance process.* New York. Reinhart and Wilson.

Price, R.A. and Vandenberg, S.G (1979). Matching for physical attractiveness in married couples. *Personality and Social Psychology Bulletin, 5* (3), 398–400.

Shaw Taylor, L., Fiore, A.T., Mendelsohn, G.A. and Cheshire, C. (2011). 'Out of my league': A real-world test of the matching hypothesis. *Personality and Social Psychology Bulletin, 37* (7), 942–954.

Silverman, I. (1971). Physical attractiveness and courtship. *Sexual Behaviour, 1*, 22–25.

Sprecher, S. and Hatfield, E. (2009). Matching hypothesis. In H. Reis and S. Sprecher (eds.) *Encyclopedia of human relationships.* New York: SAGE.

Thornhill, R. and Gangestad, S.W. (1999). Facial attractiveness. *Trends in Cognitive Sciences, 3*, 452–460.

Walster, E., Aronson, V., Abrahams, D. and Rottman, L. (1966) The importance of physical attractiveness in dating behaviour, *Journal of Personality and Social Psychology, 4*, 508–516.

Walster, E.H. and Walster, G.W. (1969). The matching hypothesis. *Journal of Personality and Social Psychology, 6*, 248–253.

Appendix

Contained paired photographs for rating for attractiveness.

3500 words

This report is considerably shorter than it should be and this has been taken into account in the mark for AO3 as well as AO1. The material in the appendix is not included in the word count.

Overall moderator comments

All sources referred to have been cited using the Harvard method of referencing.

Phillippa carried out her project in a reasonably organised fashion, although there were some issues with meeting deadlines. She demonstrated independent working skills and responded well to supervisor's advice. A wide range of secondary sources have been selected and a high level of critical analysis is demonstrated in the introduction and the discussion.

Marks

AO1 = 7/10 The project plan was fully implemented and realised to a high standard. Philippa showed clear evidence of monitoring progress against her agreed objectives. There was some issue with time management.

AO2 = 10/10 There is detailed analysis of the collected data, demonstrated in the report, presentation and production log. A wide range of relevant sources was used. There is strong analysis throughout the report which links to the research question and to concepts and theories.

AO3 = 16/20 The report is a bit short. A little bit more content in all areas would have helped. Information is presented appropriately for a scientific report. Philippa has taken appropriate decisions to implement the project plan and made changes as necessary. There is some evidence of problem solving. The conclusion could be more robust.

AO4 = 6/10 Philippa supplied a rather brief reflection on her learning but she did suggest how her learned skills will help her in the future. However, her conclusion and summary statement are short. The presentation was well designed to illustrate and explain the journey travelled from original idea to product and to highlight the skills developed and their potential future uses.

Total = 39/50 Grade B (almost an A)

ACTIVITY APPENDIX
Improving Philippa's project

- What recommendations would you make to improve Philippa's project?

- Consider each assessment objective.

Suggested answers on page 124.

Page 7, Exercise 0.2 EPQ Consolidation activity

(1) False, this would be dual accreditation. (2) True. (3) True, your centre will provide 30 hours of taught skills and you will need to spend 90 hours on the product. (4) False, AO1 is worth 10 marks. (5) False, your reports and PRODUCTION LOGS must show your individual contribution to the product. If your reports and PRODUCTION LOGS are identical you could be disqualified. (6) False, if the moderator thinks that your supervisor's mark is too generous or too severe they can adjust the mark. (7) False, you can also select a topic of personal interest. (8) True.

Page 10, Exercise 1.1 Taught skills

(1) Communicating ideas within a group, working effectively to reach agreement, understanding group dynamics. (2) The format and content of rehearsal notes, production of initial sketches or other working documents required for a production. (3) Understanding ethical issues, carrying carry out risk assessment. (4) Safe laboratory practices or workshop techniques, risk assessment.

Page 23, Exercise 1.6 Arranging meeting with your supervisor

(1) She has taken responsibility for arranging the meeting. She could also send her supervisor an email immediately before the meeting with key points for discussion. (2) Place a reminder on her phone or use another suitable aide-memoire. Make sure that each meeting has a focus, e.g. deciding an initial title, learning how to perform a literature review. Identify any issues which she wishes to discuss. (3) This will depend on the stage of her project but could include: A research plan (if her project involves research); a summary of her progress to date (linked to her project plan); discussion of targets, results of data collection, any questions which she need to ask at this stage. (4) Helps to show evidence of planning and organisation. Helps to provide a focus for discussion. (5) Agree some action points to focus on before the next time they meet. Record any decisions taken. (6) Record the supervisor's advice and then show how she has acted on this advice including evidence that she has made her own decisions. (7) Listen to the advice but make her own decisions.

Page 30, Exercise 2.1 Time management

Lack of clarity about the topic, lack of objectives and deadlines, disorganisation, failing to anticipate problems, juggling multiple commitments, carelessness.

Page 33, Exercise 2.3 SMART or Not SMART

SMART 3, 6, 7, Not SMART 1, 2, 4, 5

(1) Proofread my project by Monday and make amendments by end of February. (2) Contact Professor Chivers by email and allow two weeks for a response. (3) Identify two relevant sources on the search engine Google Scholar by the end of the week. (4) Look at differences between super- and non-supervolcanoes, identify one to research.

Page 37, Exercise 2.4 Making changes

(1) I narrowed this down to look at two countries in Europe, France and Germany. Narrowing the focus enabled me to research the topic more easily. (2) I broadened the title, as the original one was too specific. (3) I narrowed the scope of my project to be more selective. (4) I looked at different newspaper reports, which represented the various political parties, I also looked at websites for various pressure groups such as the League against cruel sports.

Page 41, Exercise 2.5 Producing a Gantt chart

Work breakdown: Task to be completed	Week							
	1	2	3	4	5	6	7	8
1 Research and select various sources	X							
2 Gather research on the media		X						
3 Analyse relevant sources			X					
4 Write general notes on my findings				X				
5 Plan structure and main content of my essay				X	X			
6 Draft a conclusion						X		
7 First draft						X		
8 Second draft							X	
9 Final copy								X
10 Write references and bibliography								X
11. Plan and prepare presentation								X

Page 42, Exercise 2.6 Producing a PERT chart for a fashion show

Activity Answers
Arrange seating (J)
Print programmes (I)
Hire models (A)
Make costumes (E)
Book venue and date (B)
Advertise (G)
Sell tickets (D)
Rehearsal (C)
Make scenery and props (H)
Arrange refreshments (F)

Page 47 Exercise 3.1 Quantitative and qualitative

Blue/green colour, gold frame, texture shows brush strokes of oil paint, peaceful scene of the country, expensive-looking frame.

Page 49, Exercise 3.2 Identifying potential ethical issues

(1) Ethical, questions are unlikely to cause distress to respondents. (2) Ethical, people in the public domain expect to be observed. (3) Unethical, asking about illegal activities may cause distress and there are issues with invasion of privacy. (4) Ethical, although there will be safety issues such as the need to keep your fingers away from your eyes after handling iron filings. (5) Unethical, any research involving children requires parental consent and the nature of this study may also cause harm. (6) Unethical, this could cause harm by having various adverse effects. (7) Ethical, yeast do not need consent, no harm will be caused to the yeast! (8) Unethical, this will involve giving alcohol to people who may be under the legal age to drink.

Page 52 Exercise 3.4 Sampling methods

(1) Random (2) Opportunity (3) Volunteer/self-selected (4) Systematic (5) Stratified.

Page 55 Exercise 3.5 Questionnaire design

Possible problems: (1) Questionnaire is not anonymous and so participants may not be truthful. (2) There is an overlap with the ages 13–14 and 14–15 and so, if a student is 14, which one would they circle? (3) Response set may occur with the rating of the subjects. (4) There are 5 lines for students to write their subjects at the side of the rating scale but some students may study 8 or more GCSEs!

Positive points: (1) The questionnaire begins with factual questions, which will put the respondent at ease. (2) The rating scale is easy to fill in and they will not make the participant feel too anxious.

Page 61, Exercise 3.8 Experiments

(1) To see if one side of the face is perceived as more friendly/ conveys emotion better. (2) Side of face. (3) Rating face for friendliness. (4) Creating faces to represent all left or all right side. (5) Using test-retest, test same people twice to see how similar their answers. Time interval of a few weeks. (6) People rate the left side of the face as more friendly. (7) You might conclude that the right side of the face is better at displaying emotion. (8) This would ensure it wasn't just a fluke that the right side is better. Testing a number of faces would make the conclusion more certain.

Page 65, Exercise 3.10 Synthesising sources

(1) Passage 1 presents the religious arguments against euthanasia as being morally wrong. Passage 2 presents the arguments for euthanisa, considering the rights of the individual. (2) Both passages suggest that euthanasia affects other people's rights, not just those of the patient. (3) Passage 1 argues that God decides when life ends. Passage 2 argues that the person themselves should be able to determine at what time, in what way and by whose hand they will die.

Page 67, Exercise 3.11 Evaluation sheet

(1) Type of source: Unfamiliar website, tabloid newspaper has reported the study but it is likely to have been published in a peer-reviewed article. (2) Author's background: Expert in the field Dr Rafael de Cabo, has PhD, senior investigator (Google him). (3) Date published: Recently revised, Feb 2014. (4) Depth of reviews: Controversial reviews 'experts warn that research is in early stages'. (5) Sources cited: none. (6) Objectivity: Balanced, neutral.

Page 67, Exercise 3.12 Being analytical

(1) D, (2) A, (3) A, (4) A, (5) A, (6) D, (7) D, (8) A.

Suggested answers

Page 75 Exercise 4.1   Blank page syndrome

(1) Sorted notes into a pile, wrote down some possible subheadings for essay, created an essay plan. (2) Broke down planning process into visuals, functions and historical relations and giving each section a working title. (3) Set achievable goals. (4) Drew up a large flow chart to summarise reading, divided the information up into categories. (5) Went for a run, cleared mind and could write opening paragraph. (6) Think first about what to achieve.

Page 77, Exercise 4.3   Useful phrases

In 2010 there were 160,181 … alcohol dependency. Therefore, this is an increase of 6% on the 2009 figure in comparison of 150,445 and a 56% increase on the 2003 figure of 102,741. So we can see that alcohol misuse … British drinking culture. However, in the recent past the Government … serious violence, antisocial behaviour, crime and injury. One consequence of restrictive controls may result in an increase in the production of illicit liquor, difficulties of law enforcement, loss of tax revenues and a reduction of personal and social enjoyment.

Page 79, Exercise 4.4   Identifying the sections

AIM: The aim of this EPQ … fear of spiders (Costello 1982).

BACKGROUND RESEARCH: In studies conducted on adult populations … the US movie *Arachnophobia*.

HYPOTHESIS: It was hypothesised … biting (e.g. jumping, orb).

METHOD: Two groups … higher scores indicating greater fear.

RESULTS: The results … critical value of U = 138.

CONCLUSIONS: It was concluded that spider … in different cultures.

Page 79, Exercise 4.5   Abstracts

Missing results and conclusion.

Page 81, Exercise 4.6   Overview

Starting point + definition = Lads' mags … are defined.

Brief outline = There is a need for … sex and sexuality.

Research territory = It is important … debate for politicians.

Niche = The role of … sex and sexuality.

Background = Research has shown … gender stereotyping.

Statement of scope = The key question … a comprehensive school.

Page 83, Exercise 4.7   Writing a concise procedure

Suggested response example 1: An inoculating loop was used to transfer E coli culture to a petri dish. In order to spread the culture the inoculating loop was moved backwards and forwards several times. The next step was to incubate the culture for 24 hours at 37°C.

Suggested answer example 2: Two test tubes were used to test oxidation. Test tube 1 could have iron nails placed in it and a piece of cotton wool preventing calcium chloride crystals. Test tube 2 has some moistened iron nails placed in it, exposed to air. The test tubes were left for three weeks.

Page 85, Exercise 4.8   Interpreting data

Bar chart 1: Summary =The most common descriptions of feedback received were useful, clear and constructive. Feedback was least commonly described as useless and negative. Conclusion = This suggests that students overall found the feedback helpful.

Bar chart 2: Summary = In year 8, 7% of males and 7% of females reported getting drunk on one day per week and 1% of females and males more than once per week. By year 10 the number of females getting drunk once per week exceeded males 21% and 16% respectively. Conclusion = This suggests that pupils who reported getting drunk on more than one occasion increased with age.

Page 87, Exercise 4.9   Good discussion

Sentences 1–5 = Explanation of the results in relation to the hypothesis/previous research. Sentences 6 and 11 = implications. Sentences 7–10 = limitations.

Page 89, Exercise 4.10   Conclusions

Blue = conclusion words   Green = take-home message

Whether 'medical marijuana' (*Cannabis saliva* used to treat a wide variety of pathologic states) should be accorded the status of a legitimate pharmaceutical agent has long been a contentious issue. In effect the decision whether to legalise the medical use of marijuana should be based on a dispassionate scientific analysis. Indeed, a number of such investigations have recently been published in the peer-reviewed literature. Data from these studies suggest that medical marijuana has demonstrated safety and efficacy in treating several devastating human pathologies. Some individuals as a result may believe that this documentation now warrants marijuana's approval for use as a legitimate

therapeutic agent. Others may think that additional scientific scrutiny is necessary. So should marijuana be approved as a bona fide medication? In conclusion, this essay was not intended to provide an answer instead it has strongly argued in favour of the concept that scientific data and methodology, rather than political and ideological considerations, ultimately should lead to a rational decision. Whether the data derived from current and future scientific investigations will justify the approval or disapproval of medical marijuana remains a challenging issue for the future.

Page 91, Exercise 4.11   Referencing

Example 1: author and when accessed.

Example 2: the publisher.

Example 3: initials of the author, volume and page numbers.

Example 4: name of journal, issue number.

Page 92, Exercise 4.12   Checking academic style

Yellow = spelling   Green = informal style   Blue - colloquialisms

Over this project I have found many different reasons for both the initiation and the continuation today. Many of these factors cannot be singled out and it was part and parcel of the combination of several different internal and external reasons that created the war we see today. I feel that unknowingly it was the American aid in supporting the first military coup that started the ball rolling for the escalation; this is due to the beginnings of the political system the people were fighting against. There is no way we cannot conclude fully this was down to America as many other factors may have been involved in this political system, but it was the creating of a dictatorial system that created the need for reform.

Page 97, Exercise 5.1   A good presentation

Expresses points in graphical terms.

Has elements visible from 4 feet away.

Displays the essential content – the message – in the title, main headings and graphics. Would have been more effective to have the EPQ title in full for this poster.

Uses fonts that are easy on the eye such as Arial.

Shows only the main findings of the project.

Uses colour to emphasise, differentiate and to add interest.

Uses clip art to add interest to the display and complement the subject matter.

Page 105, Exercise 5.5   Annotate a summary statement

4, 2, 1, 5, 3

Page 107, Exercise 5.6   Reflection

'Advice you would give to others' is missing, such as: Manage your time more effectively, prioritise during busy times, and choose something you are interested in.

Page 110, Appendix, Improving Robert's project

General comments: Presentation needs to focus on the EPQ journey not just the final artefact. Conclusion and summary statement need to be more detailed.

AO1 – Use of management tools such as diary of progress would help Robert to manage his time more effectively. Production log was thin on detail.

AO2 – Robert needs a more systematic approach to his research. His questionnaire needs to be piloted and his research needs to inform his study. He should have evaluated his sources and justified why he had chosen the material he did. A source evaluation sheet would have been helpful.

AO3 – The meter of the poem needs to be consistent. The poem needs to be similar to the style of Dr Seuss. The report to accompany the poem is just all I know about Seuss and spider poems; it should relate more closely to the final product. There also needs to be more background information on what makes a good poem for children and why Robert's poem meets these criteria.

AO4 – Reflective statement needs to be more detailed.

Page 122, Appendix, Improving Philippa's project

AO1 – Time management could have been improved by the use of additional management tools or by setting SMART objectives.

AO2 – No improvement possible.

AO3 – The discussion could have been more fluent. The discussion of results was brief and the strengths and limitations section could have been more coherent and less like a list of points. She could have developed some of her points more effectively by providing examples and by supporting unsubstantiated comments with evidence. The conclusion could have been more detailed.

AO4 – The reflective statement and the summary should have been more detailed.

Acton, Q.A. (2013). *Schizophrenia: New insights for the Healthcare Professional*. Atlanta, Georgia: Scholarly Editions.

Ang, I. (2001). *On not speaking Chinese. living between Asia and the West*. London, Routledge.

Asselin, M.E. (2003). Insider research: Issues to consider when doing qualitative research in your own setting. *Journal for Nurses in Staff Development*, 19(2), 99–103.

Bachorowski, J.A. and Owren, M.J. (2001). Not all laughs are alike: voiced but not unvoiced laughter readily elicits positive affect. *Psychological Science*, 12, 252–257.

Bailey, J.M. and Pillard, R.C. (1991). A genetic study of male sexual orientation. *Archives of General Psychiatry*, 48 (12), 1089–1096.

Baldwin, F. cited in J. Adair (1987). *How to Manage your Time*. The Talbot Adair Press (page 87).

Bazelon, E. (2010). Was Phoebe Prince once a bully? Did her school in Ireland turn a blind eye to early warnings of her troubles. Available at: http://www.slate.com/articles/life/bulle/2010/08/was_phoebe_prince_once_a_bully.html [Accessed March 2014].

Beckles, H. (1994). *An arena of conquest: Popular democracy and West Indies cricket supremacy*. Jamaica: Ian Randle.

Benn, T.C., Dagkas, S. and Jawad, H. (2010). Embodied faith: Islam, religious freedom and educational practices in physical education. *Sport, Education and Society*, 16, (1), 17–34.

Bennett-Levy, J. and Marteau T. (1984). Fear of animals: What is prepared? *British Journal of Psychology*, 75, 37–42.

Bieber, I., Dain, H., Dince, P., Drellich, M., Grand, H., Gundlach, R., Kremer, M., Rifkin, A., Wilbur, C. and Bieber, T. (1962). *Homosexuality: A psychoanalytic study of male homosexuals*. New York: Basic Books.

Bordens, K.S. and Abbott, B.B. (2008). *Research design and methods: A process approach (7th ed.)*. Boston: McGraw Hill.

Bourne, P.E. (2007). Ten simple rules for making good oral presentations. PLoS Comput Biol 3: e77. doi:10.1371/journal.pcbi.0030077 [Accessed March 2014]

Brockbank, A. and McGill, I. (1998). *Facilitating Reflective Learning in Higher Education*. Buckingham: SRHE/Open University Press.

Brontë, C. (1847). *Jane Eyre*. London: Smith, Elder and Co.

Brown, J.R. (1994). *Laboratory of the mind: Thought experiments in the natural sciences, [2nd ed]*. London: Routledge.

Bryman, A. (2001). *Social research methods*. Oxford: Oxford University Press.

Cameron, C., Oskamp, S. and Sparks, W. (1977). Courtship American style: Newspaper ads. *Family Co-ordinator*, 26, 27–30.

Carroll, L (1871). *Through the looking glass and what Alice found there*. London: Macmillan.

Charlton, J. (1998). *Nothing about us without us: Disability, power, and oppression*. Berkeley, CA: University of California Press.

Chiffons (1963). *He's so fine*. Laurie Records.

Churchill, W. (1945). Speech at the House of Commons. Cited in Matthews, J.R. and Matthews, R. W. (2008). *Successful scientific writing: A step-by-step guide for the biological and medical sciences*. Cambridge University Press. Cambridge. (page 71).

Churchill, W. in J. Adair (1987). *How to manage your time*. Guildford, Surrey: The Talbot Adair Press. (page 87).

Coolican, H. (2014). *Research methods and statistics in psychology (6th edition)*. London: Hodder and Stoughton.

Communications Act (2003). Available: http://www.legislation.gov.uk/ukpga/2003/21/contents [Accessed March 2014].

Cooper, P. (1999a). Changing perceptions of EBD: maladjustment, EBD and beyond. *Emotional and Behavioural Difficulties*, 4(1), 3–11.

Cooper, P. (1999b). Emotional and behavioural difficulties and adolescence. In Cooper, P. (ed.) *Understanding and supporting children with emotional and behavioural difficulties*. London: Jessica Kingsley.

Cornelius, R.R. and Averill J.R. (1983). Sex differences in fear of spiders. *Journal of Personality and Social Psychology*, 45, 377–383.

Costello, C.G. (1982). Fears and phobias in women: A community study. *Journal of Abnormal Psychology*, 91, 280–286.

Crime in England and Wales 2009 to 2010: findings from the British crime survey and police recorded crime. Available at: https://www.gov.uk/government/publications/crime-in-england-and-wales-2009-to-2010-findings-from-the-british-crime-survey-and-police-recorded-crime [Accessed March 2014].

Cziko, G. (1989). Unpredictability and indeterminism in human behaviour: Arguments and implication for educational research. *Educational Researcher*, 18, 17–25.

Daily Mail, Prigg, M. (2014). *The pill that could slow aging: Researchers reveal groundbreaking study to extend lifespan and improve health of the elderly*. Available at: http://www.dailymail.co.uk/sciencetech/article-2570629/The-pill-slow-aging-Researchers-reveal-groundbreaking-study-boost-health-eldery.html [Accessed March 2014].

Danielson, C. (1996). *Enhancing Professional Practice. A framework for teaching*. Alexandria. VA: Association for Supervison and curriculum development.

Data Protection Act (1998). Available at: http://www.legislation.gov.uk/ukpga/1998/29/contents [Accessed March 2014].

Davey, C.L. (1994). *The 'disgusting' spider: The role of disease and Illlness in the perpetuation of fear of spiders*. The White Horse Press: Cambridge UK.

Doran, G.T. (1991). There's a SMART way to write management's goals and objectives. *Management Review*, 70 (11), 35–36.

Drucker, P.F (1955). *The practice of management*. Oxford: Butterworth Heinemann

Dunbar, R. (1995). Are you lonesome tonight? *New Scientist*, 11 February, 26–31.

Eagly, A.H. (1978). Sex differences in influenceability. *Psychological Bulletin*, 85, pp.86–116.

East, W.N. (1946). Sexual offenders. *Journal of Nervous and Mental Disease*, 103, 626–666.

Economic and Social Research Council (2006). *Research Ethics Framework Swindon, Economic and Social Research Council*.available at: http://www.esrc.ac.uk/_images/Delivery_Report_06_07_tcm8-13459.pdf. [Accessed March 2014].

Flanagan, C. (2012) *The research methods companion for A level Psychology*. Oxford: Oxford University Press.

Flintoff, A. (1993). One of the boys? Gender identities in physical education initial teacher education. In I. Siraj-Blatchford Race (ed), *Gender and the Education of Teachers*. Oxford: Oxford University Press (pages 74–91).

Franklin, B. (1770). Available at: http://www.brainyquote.com/quotes/quotes/b/benjaminfr151632.html [Accessed March 2014]..

Franklin, B. (1774). Available at http://www.brainyquote.com/quotes/quotes/b/benjaminfr133951.html. Item [Accessed March 2014]

Freud, S. (1905). Three essays on the theory of sexuality. In J. Strachey (Ed. and Trans.), *The standard edition of the complete psychological works of Sigmund Freud*. (Vol. 7, pp. 123–245). London: Hogarth Press. (Original work published 1905.)

Friedman, R.C. and Stern, L. (1980). Fathers, sons, and sexual orientation: Replication of a Bieber hypothesis. *Psychiatric Quarterly*, 52, 175–189.

Gagnon, J. and Simon, W. (1973). *Sexual conduct: The social sources of human sexuality*. Chicago: Aldine.

Gaugin, P. (1870). Available at: http://greatthoughtstreasury.com/taxonomy/term/800/all?page=310lf [Accessed March 2014].

Ghandi, I. (1981). Available at: http://www.goodreads.com/quotes/53583-the-power-to-question-is-the-basis-of-all-human [Accessed March 2014].

Gilbert, M. (2000). *Churchill a Life*. Pimlico. London.

Gilligan, C. (1982). *In a different voice*. Cambridge, MA: Harvard University Press.

Gleason, N. (1994). Preventing alcohol abuse by college women: A relational perspective: II. *Journal of American College Health*, 43, 15–24.

Gonsiorek, J.C. (1982). Results of psychological testing on homosexual populations. *American Behavioural Scientist*, 25 (4), 385–396.

Goodwin, L.J. (2007). *The Inclusion of children with physical disabilities in physical education. Rhetoric or reality?* Unpublished Ph.D. Thesis University of Surrey.

Gorski, R. (1978). Evidence for a morphological sex difference within the medial preoptic area of the rat brain. *Brain Research*, 148(2), 333–346.

Grinyer, A. (2002). The Anonymity of research participants: assumptions, ethics and practicalities. *Social Research Update*: Issue 36. University of Surrey. Available at: http://sru.soc.surrey.ac.uk/SRU36.html [Accessed March 2014].

Grunsfeld, J. (2013). How to build a Mars colony that lasts – forever. *New Scientist*, available at: http://www.newscientist.com/article/dn23542-how-to-build-a-mars-colony-that-lasts--forever.html [Accessed June 2014].

The Guardian, Chessum, M. (2010). *The privatisation of higher education is forcing out poorer students*. See http://www.theguardian.com/commentisfree/2012/jul/10/privatisation-higher-education-working-class-students. [Accessed March 2014].

Guédon, J. (2001). *In Oldenburg's long shadow: Librarians, research scientists, publishers, and the control of scientific publishing*. Presentation to the May 2001 meeting of the Association of Research Libraries (ARL), at http://www.arl.org/arl/proceedings/138/guedon.html. [Accessed March 2014].

Hacking, I. (2001). *An Introduction to Probability and Inductive Logic*. Cambridge: Cambridge University Press.

Harlow, H.F. (1959). Love in infant monkeys. *Scientific American*, 200 (6). 68–74.

Harrison, A.A. and Saeed, L. (1977). Let's make a deal: an analysis of revelations and stipulations in lonely hearts advertisements. *Journal of Personality and Social Psychology*, 35, 257–264.

Harrison, G. (1971). *My sweet lord*. Apple Records.

Heaney, S. (2001). *The spirit level*. London: Faber and Faber.

Herek, G.M. (2012). *Facts about Homosexuality*. Available at: http://culturecampaign.blogspot.co.uk/2011/08/normalization-of-pedophilia-urged-by.html [Accessed March 2014].

Hess, D.R. (2004). *How to write an effective dissertation*. Available at: http://www.cse.chalmers.se/~feldt/advice/hess_2004_how_to_write_an_effective_discussion.pdf [Accessed March 2014].

Hess, G.R., Tosney, K.W. and Liegel, L.H. (2009). Creating effective poster presentations: AMEE Guide no. 40. *Medical Teacher*, 31(4), 356–358.

Hocking, B.J. (2003). Reducing mental illness stigma and discrimination — everybody's business. *Medical Journal of Australia*, 178 (9), 47–48.

Howitt, M. (1829). *The spider and the fly*. Available at: http://www.goodreads.com/book/show/601598.Spider_and_the_Fly [Accessed March 2014].

Huffington Post (2012). *Yellowstone volcano: Will it erupt during our lives?* Available at: http://www.huffingtonpost.com/2012/06/04/yellowstone-supervolcano-eruption-unlikely_n_1569214.html [Accessed March 2014].

Humphreys, L. (1970) *The tearoom trade*. Chicago: Aldine.

Jackson, R. (2004). *Inclusion: A flawed Vision. GSSPL'*. Available at: http://www.gssp1.org.uk/html/inclusion_aflawed-vision [Accessed January 2014]

Jerome, J.K. (1889). *Three Men in a Boat*. London: Penguin classics.

Jordan, R.H. and Burghardt, G.M. (1986). Employing an ethogram to detect reactivity of black bears (*Ursus americanus*) to the presence of humans. *Ethology*, 73, 89–115.

Jose, S.K (2012). *Spiders of India. A glimpse into spider diversity of India*. Available at: http://indian-spiders.blogspot.co.uk/ [Accessed March 2014].

Kagan, J. (1964). Acquisition and significance of sex typing and sex role identity. In M. L. Hoffman and L. W. Hoffman (eds.), *Review of child development research* (pp. 137–167). New York: Sage.

Kardiner, A. (1963). The flight from masculinity. In H. M. Ruitenbeek (ed.), *The problem of homosexuality in modern society* (pp. 17–39). New York: Dutton.

Kass, L.R (1985). *Toward a more natural science: biology and human affairs*. New York City: Free Press.

Kass, L.R. (2001). '*Claim and its limits: Why not immortality?*' Available at: http://www.firstthings.com/article/2007/01/claim-and-its-limits-why-not-immortality-36. [Accessed March 2014].

Kehily, M.J. (1999). More sugar? Teenage magazines, gender displays and sexual learning *European Journal of Cultural Studies*, 2 (1), 65-89.

Khan, S. (2002). *Aversion and desire: negotiating Muslim female identity in the diaspora*. Ontario, Canada: Women's Press,

King, S. (2000). *On Writing: A memoir of the craft*. New York: Scribner.

Kittredge, G.L. (1912). Chaucer's discussion of marriage. *Modern Philology*, 9, 435–67.

Klorman, R., Hastings, J., Weerts, T., Melamed, B. and Lang, P. (1974). Psychometric Description of some specific fear questionnaires. *Behaviour Therapy*, 5, 401–409.

Labrie, J.W., Cail, J., Hummer, J.F., Lac, A. and Neighbors, C. (2009). What men want: the role of reflective opposite-sex normative preferences in alcohol use among college women. *Psychology of addictive behaviour*, 23(1), 157–162.

Levinger, C. and Clark, I. (1961). Emotional factors in the forgetting of word associations. *Journal of Abnormal and Social Psychology*, 62, 99–105.

Little Miss Muffett available at: http://en.wikipedia.org/wiki/Little_Miss_Muffet [Accessed March 2014].

MacDonald, D. (2002). Extending agendas: Physical culture research for the twenty-first century. In D. Penney (ed.) *Gender and physical education: contemporary issues and future directions*. London, Routledge, 208–222.

MacKay, G. (2002). The disappearance of disability? Thoughts on a changing culture. *British Journal of Special Education*, 29 (4), 159–163.

McAdam, D., Tarrow, S. and Tilly. C. (2001). *Dynamics of contention*. Cambridge: Cambridge University Press.

McAdams, D.P. and Bowman, P.J. (2001). Narrating life's turning points: Redemption and contamination. In D. P. McAdams, R. Josselson, and A. Lieblich (eds.) *Turns in the road: Narrative studies of lives in transition*. Washington, DC: American Psychological Association.

McCullough, D. cited in S.D. Stark (2012) *Writing to Win: The Legal Writer*. Crown Publishing Group, 23.

McHugh, M., Koeske, R. D. and Frieze, I. N. (1986). Issues to consider in conducting non-sexist psychological research. *American Psychologist*, 41, 879–890.

McMane, A.A. (2001). *Newspaper in education and building democratic citizens*. Available at: http://hrcak.srce.hr/file/41592. [Accessed March 2014].

McNamee, M., Olivier, S. and Wainwright, P. (2007). *Research ethics in exercise, health and sports sciences*, London: Routledge.

Martin, P. (1990). *Chaucer's women: Nuns, wives, and amazons*. Iowa City: University of Iowa Press.

Mennell, S. (1994). The Formation of we-images: A process theory. In C. Calhoun (ed.) *Social theory and the politics of identity*. Oxford, Blackwell Publications, 175–197.

Miéville, C. (2012). In *10 of the most powerful female characters in literature*. Available at: http://flavorwire.com/265847/10-of-the-most-powerful-female-characters-in-literature/ [Accessed March 2014].

Milner, D. (1970). Ethnic Identity and preference in minority-group children. In H. Tajfel (1981) *Human Groups and Social Categories*. Cambridge: Cambridge University Press (page 329).

Murstein (1972). Physical attractiveness and marital choice. *Journal of Personality and Social Psychology*, 22 (1), 8–12.

Njeze, M.E. (2013). *Use of newspapers and magazines in the academic pursuits of university students: Case study of Covenant University*. University of Nebraska. Lincoln:http://digitalcommons.unl.edu/cgi/viewcontent.cgi?article=2190andcontext=libphilpracandsei- [Accessed March 2014].

Nugent, P. and Faucette, N. (1995). Marginalised voices: constructions of and responses to physical education and grading practices by students categorised as gifted or learning disabled. *Journal of Teaching in Physical Education*, 14 (4), 418–430.

Offer, D., Ostrov, E. and Howard, K. (1981). *The Adolescent – A psychological self-portrait*. New York: Basic.

Orwell, G. (1945). *Animal Farm*. London: Penguin.

Payne, G. and Williams, M. (2005). *Generalisations in generalisation in Qualitative Research*. Sociology, 39, 295.

Peck, M.S. (1978). *The Road Less Travelled*. London: Random House.

Peter, J. and Valkenburg, P.M. (2007). 'Adolescents' exposure to a sexualized media environment and notions of women as sex objects. *Sex Roles*, 56, 381–395.

Peterson, C. (2010). Upspeak makes me cringe. *Psychology Today*. Available at: http://www.psychologytoday.com/blog/the-good-life/201012/upspeak [Accessed March 2014].

Pijenenberg, M.A. and Leget, C. (2007). Who wants to live forever? Three arguments against extending the human lifespan. J*ournal of Medical Ethics*, 33 (10), 585–587.

Popper, K.R. (1959). *The logic of scientific discovery*. London: Routledge.

Popper, K.R. (1979). *Of clouds and clocks. Objective knowledge, an evolutionary approach (revised edition)*. Oxford: Oxford University Press.

Rado, S. (1940). A critical examination of the concept of bisexuality. *Psychosomatic Medicine*, 2, 459–467.

Recinos, A.T. (1405). Female martyrs. In C. de Pizan (ed) *The Book of the City of Ladies*. London: Penguin classics.

Resnick, D. B. (2011). *What is research ethics and why is it important*. http://www.niehs.nih.gov/research/resources/bioethics/whatis/ [Accessed August 2014].

Rich, E. (2001). Gender positioning in teacher education in England: New rhetoric, old realities. *International Studies in Sociology of Education*, 11 (2), 131–155.

Ridley, D. (2008). *The literature review: A step-by-step guide for students. (SAGE Study Skills Series)*. London: Sage Publications.

The Rolling Stones (1965). '*The spider and the fly*' track from the album '*Out of our heads*'. London Records.

Rowling, J.K. (1998). *Harry Potter and the chamber of secrets*. London: Bloomsbury Publishing PLC.

Rudestam, K.E. and Newton, K.E. (1992). *Surviving your dissertation. A comprehensive guide to theory and process*. London: Sage Publications.

Rumbaut, R.G. (1994). The crucible within: Ethnic identity, self-esteem and segmented assimilation among children of immigrants. *International Migration Review*, 28 (4), Special Issue: The New Second Generation, 748-794.

Sagarin, E. (1975). *Deviants and deviance*. New York: Praeger.

Saks, E.R. (2008).*The centre cannot hold: A memoire of my schizophrenia*. London: Virago.

Schafner, A.C. (1994). The future of scientific journals: Lessons from the past. *Information Technology and Libraries* 13, 239-247.

Shaw, G.B. (1928). *The Intelligent woman's guide to socialism and capitalism*. New Brunswick, NJ: Transaction Publishers.

SHEU (2006) Self-reported drinking behaviour of school age children in Sunderland over a fourteen-year period. Available at: sheu.org.uk/x/eh312am.pdf Shipman, M. (1981). *The limitations of social research (2nd edition)*. New York: Longman Group Ltd.

Sieber, J.E. and Stanley, B. (1988). Ethical and professional dimensions of socially sensitive research. *American Psychologist*, 43, 49–55.

Silverman, I. (1971). Physical attractiveness and courtship. *Sexual Behaviour*, 1, 22–25.

Singer, P. (1975). *Animal Liberation*. New York: Avon.

Sneddon, L.U., Braithwaite, V.A. and Gentle, M.J. (2003). Trout trauma puts angles on the hook. *Proceedings from the Royal Society*, 270, 1115–1121.

Socarides, C. (1968). *The overt homosexual*. New York: Grune and Stratton.

Spider Phobia Questionnaire Available at: https://www.mun.ca/biology/bpromoters/spider_questionnaire.php [Accessed March 2014].

Storms, M.D. (1981). A theory of erotic orientation development. *Psychological Review*, 88. 340–353.

Stott, R. (2001). The essay writing process. In Stott R, Snaith A, and Rylance R. Harlow (eds.) *Making your case: a practical guide to essay writing*. Harrow: Pearson Education Limited (pages 36–58).

Swales, J.M. and Feak, C. (2004). Academic writing for graduate students, second edition: essential tasks and skills. *Michigan series in English for academic & professional purposes*, University of Michigan Press/ELT.

Tajfel, H. (1981). *Human groups and social categories*. Cambridge: Cambridge University Press.

Tinker, C. and Armstrong, N. (2008). From the outside looking in: How an awareness of difference can benefit the qualitative research process. *The Qualitative Report*, 13 (1), 53–60.

Tolkein, J.R.R. (1937).*The Hobbit*. London: Harper Collins.

Tolkein, J.R.R. (1954). *The Lord of the Rings*. London: Harper Collins.

Trainer, A. (2012). Performance Objectives just got smarta. *Silicon Beach Training*. Available at: http://www.managementtraining-uk.co.uk/smarta-objectives [Accessed March 2014].

Trzeciak, J. and MacKay (1994). *Study skills for academic writing: Students' book*. New York: Prentice Hall.

U.S Geological Survey (2012). *Questions about supervolcanoes*. Available at: http://volcanoes.usgs.gov/volcanoes/yellowstone/yellowstone_sub_page_49.html [Accessed March 2014].

Verkaik, R. and Laurance, J. (2002). *Miss B: Case is a warning to doctors not to act unlawfully*. Avaliable at: http://www.independent.co.uk/news/uk/crime/miss-b-case-is-a-warning-to-doctors-not-to-act-unlawfully-655081.html [Accessed June 2014].

Von Hoffman, N. Sociological Snoopers and Journalistic Moralizers, *The Washington Post*, January 30, 1970. Reprinted in *The Tearoom Trade*, 1970, Humphreys, L.., 215.

Walster, E.H., Aronson, E., Abrahams and Rottman, L. (1966). Importance of physical attractiveness in dating behaviour. *Journal of Personality and Social Psychology*, 4, 325–342.

Walster, E.H. and Walster, G.W. (1969). The matching hypothesis. *Journal of Personality and Social Psychology*, 6, 248–253.

Wasserman, E.B. and Storms, M.D. (1984). Factors influencing erotic orientation development in females and males. *Women and Therapy*, 3, 51–60.

Waynforth, D. and Dunbar, R.I.M. (1995). Conditional mate choice strategies in humans: Evidence from 'Lonely hearts' advertisements. *Behaviour*, 132, 755–779.

Weiner, B. (1992). *Human motivation: Metaphors, theories, and research*. Newbury Park, CA: Sage.

Werbner, P. (1997). Introduction: The dialectics of cultural hybridity. In P. Werbner and T. Modood (eds.) *Debating cultural hybridity. Multi-cultural identities and the politics of anti-racism*. London, Zed Books. (pages 1–26).

White, E.B. (1952). *Charlotte's Web*. London: Harper Collins.

Whitman, W. (1868). A noiseless patient spider. In P. Diehl (ed.) A noiseless patient spider: Whitman's beauty-blood and brain. *Walt Whitman Quarterly Review*. 6 (3), 117–132.

Wolchover, N. (2012). *Life's little mysteries. What if the Yellowstone supervolcano erupts?* Available at: http://www.lifeslittlemysteries.com/2518-yellowstone-supervolcano-eruption.html http://volcanoes.usgs.gov/volcanoes/yellowstone/yellowstone_sub_page_49.html [Accessed March 2014].

Working Party on Peer Review (2002). Peer review and the acceptance of new scientific ideas. Discussion paper from a Working Party on equipping the public with an understanding of peer review. *Sense About Science*, available at: http://www.senseaboutscience.org/data/files/resources/17/peerReview.pdf [Accessed March 2014].

Young, A.M., Morales, M., McCabe, S.E., Boyd, C.J. and D'Arcy, H. (2005). Drinking like a guy: Frequent binge drinking among undergraduate women. *Substance Use & Misuse*, 40, 241–267.

Young, R.J.C. (1995). *Colonial desire: Hybridity in theory, culture and race*. London, Routledge.

Zhang, Zuo-Feng, Morgenstern, H., Spitz, M.R., Tashkin, D.P., Yu, Guo-Pei, Marshall, J.R., Hsu, T. and Stimson, P. (1999). Marijuana use and increased risk of squamous cell carcinoma of the head and neck. *Cancer epidemiology, biomarkers & prevention*, 8 (12), 1071–1078.

Zoback, M.D. (2007). *Reservoir geomechanics: Earth stress and rock mechanics applied to exploration, production and wellbore stability*. Cambridge: Cambridge Press.

Index